To Free the Romanovs

To Free the Romanovs
Royal Kinship and Betrayal

Coryne Hall

AMBERLEY

To the memory of my parents Peggy and Ernie Bawcombe.
Always in my thoughts.

First published 2018

Amberley Publishing
The Hill, Stroud
Gloucestershire, GL5 4EP

www.amberley-books.com

Copyright © Coryne Hall, 2018

The right of Coryne Hall to be identified as the Author of this work has been asserted in accordance with the Copyrights, Designs and Patents Act 1988.

British Library Cataloguing in Publication Data.
A catalogue record for this book is available from the British Library.

ISBN 978 1 4456 8197 9 (hardback)
ISBN 978 1 4456 8198 6 (ebook)

Family trees by Thomas Bohm, User design.
Typesetting and Origination by Amberley Publishing.
Printed in the UK.

Contents

Family trees   6
List of illustrations   9
Author's Note and Acknowledgements   10
A Note on Names, Dates and Titles   12
Introduction: The Queen's Visit to Russia, 1994   14
1   Revolution and Abdication   17
2   Tsar for a Day   30
3   King George's Betrayal   44
4   The Scandinavian Connection   64
5   Prisoners of the Provisional Government   75
6   The Bolshevik Revolution   94
7   Germany's role   114
8   Towards the Urals   122
9   First Victims and First Escapes   137
10   Ekaterinburg   151
11   The Trust of Kings   168
12   Escape of a Tsar's Daughter   191
13   Romania, an Unlikely Saviour   200
14   The Doomed Grand Dukes   215
15   King George's Embarrassment   230
Postscript   247
Notes   262
Select Bibliography   275
Index   281

The relationship between Europe's monarchs (select family tree)

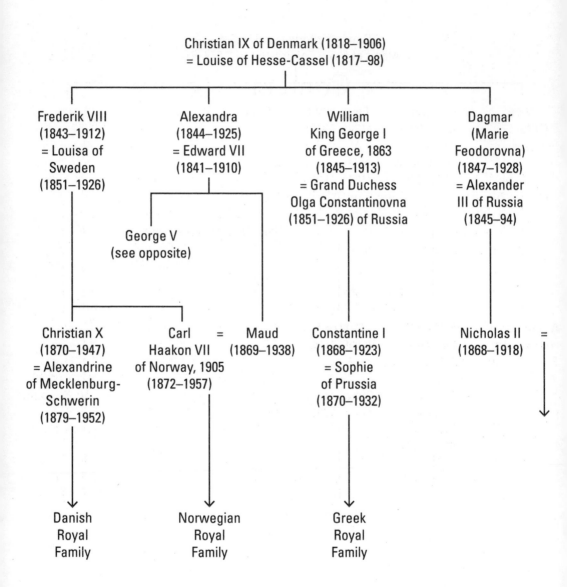

Christian IX of Denmark (1818–1906)
= Louise of Hesse-Cassel (1817–98)

Frederik VIII
(1843–1912)
= Louisa of
Sweden
(1851–1926)

Alexandra
(1844–1925)
= Edward VII
(1841–1910)

William
King George I
of Greece, 1863
(1845–1913)
= Grand Duchess
Olga Constantinovna
(1851–1926) of Russia

Dagmar
(Marie
Feodorovna)
(1847–1928)
= Alexander
III of Russia
(1845–94)

George V
(see opposite)

Christian X
(1870–1947)
= Alexandrine
of Mecklenburg-
Schwerin
(1879–1952)

Carl   =   Maud
Haakon VII   (1869–1938)
of Norway, 1905
(1872–1957)

Constantine I
(1868–1923)
= Sophie
of Prussia
(1870–1932)

Nicholas II   =
(1868–1918)

Danish
Royal
Family

Norwegian
Royal
Family

Greek
Royal
Family

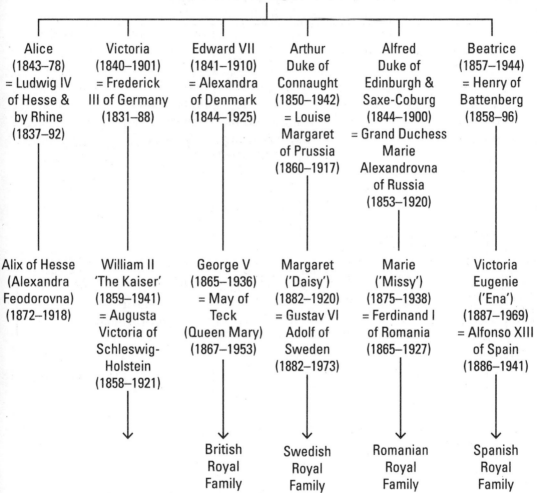

Queen Victoria (1819–1901)
= Albert of Saxe-Coburg-Gotha (1819–61)

| Alice (1843–78) = Ludwig IV of Hesse & by Rhine (1837–92) | Victoria (1840–1901) = Frederick III of Germany (1831–88) | Edward VII (1841–1910) = Alexandra of Denmark (1844–1925) | Arthur Duke of Connaught (1850–1942) = Louise Margaret of Prussia (1860–1917) | Alfred Duke of Edinburgh & Saxe-Coburg (1844–1900) = Grand Duchess Marie Alexandrovna of Russia (1853–1920) | Beatrice (1857–1944) = Henry of Battenberg (1858–96) |

| Alix of Hesse (Alexandra Feodorovna) (1872–1918) | William II 'The Kaiser' (1859–1941) = Augusta Victoria of Schleswig-Holstein (1858–1921) | George V (1865–1936) = May of Teck (Queen Mary) (1867–1953) | Margaret ('Daisy') (1882–1920) = Gustav VI Adolf of Sweden (1882–1973) | Marie ('Missy') (1875–1938) = Ferdinand I of Romania (1865–1927) | Victoria Eugenie ('Ena') (1887–1969) = Alfonso XIII of Spain (1886–1941) |

British Royal Family   Swedish Royal Family   Romanian Royal Family   Spanish Royal Family

Descendants of Nicholas I

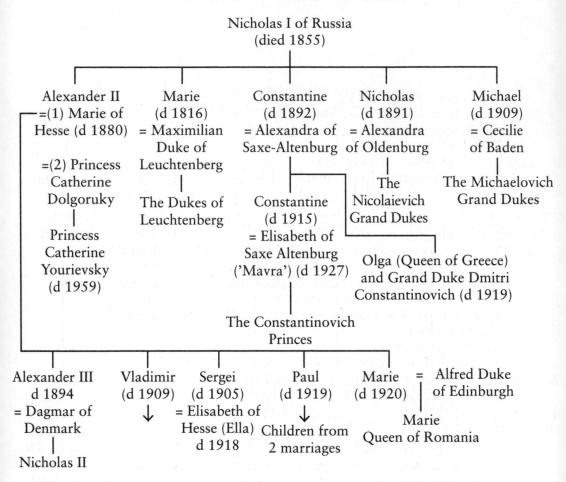

Nicholas I of Russia
(died 1855)

Alexander II
=(1) Marie of Hesse (d 1880)

=(2) Princess Catherine Dolgoruky

Princess Catherine Yourievsky (d 1959)

Marie (d 1816)
= Maximilian Duke of Leuchtenberg

The Dukes of Leuchtenberg

Constantine (d 1892)
= Alexandra of Saxe-Altenburg

Constantine (d 1915)
= Elisabeth of Saxe Altenburg ('Mavra') (d 1927)

The Constantinovich Princes

Nicholas (d 1891)
= Alexandra of Oldenburg

The Nicolaievich Grand Dukes

Olga (Queen of Greece) and Grand Duke Dmitri Constantinovich (d 1919)

Michael (d 1909)
= Cecilie of Baden

The Michaelovich Grand Dukes

Alexander III
d 1894
= Dagmar of Denmark

Nicholas II

Vladimir (d 1909)
↓

Sergei (d 1905)
= Elisabeth of Hesse (Ella) d 1918

Paul (d 1919)
↓
Children from 2 marriages

Marie (d 1920) = Alfred Duke of Edinburgh

Marie Queen of Romania

© Coryne Hall 2018

List of Illustrations

The Imperial family, 1913.
Grand Duke Michael Alexandrovich.
The Dowager Empress and Queen Alexandra.
Nicholas II and George V.
The Hesse family, 1903.
Nicholas and Alexandra in captivity, 1917.
The family of Grand Duchess Xenia and Grand Duke Alexander Michelovish ('Sandro'), 1909.
Ai-Todor, the Crimean home of Grand Duke Alexander Michaelovich and Grand Duchess Xenia.
The family of Grand Duke Constantine Constantinovich, 1909.
Prince Ioann and Princess Helen, 1911.
Nicholas II in captivity at Tsarskoe Selo, 1917.
The Tsar's children at Tsarskoe Selo, 1917.
King Christian X and Queen Alexandrine of Denmark.
Harald Scavenius.
Queen Olga of Greece.
King Haakon VII, Queen Maud & Crown Prince Olav of Norway.
King Gustav V and Queen Victoria of Sweden.
The semi-circular hall of the Alexander Palace.
Grand Duchess Elisabeth Feodorovna (Ella).
Grand Duke Sergei Michaelovich.
George Brasov, son of Grand Duke Michael.
'Georgie, 11 April 1919.'
King Alfonso XIII and Queen Victoria Eugenie (Ena) of Spain.
Nicholas II and the Kaiser.
The Impatiev House.
Grand Duke and Duchess George of Russia, 1900.
Grand Duke Paul Alexandrovich and family.
Grand Duke Dmitri Pavlovich, his sister Marie and Prince William of Sweden.
Princess Catherine Yourievsky.
Grand Duke Cyril Vladimirovich and his wife Victoria Melita ('Ducky').
Queen Marie of Romania ('Missy').
Grand Duke Nicholas Nicolaievich ('Nicholasha') on board HMS *Marlborough*.
Grand Duke Dmitri Pavlovich.
The British royals: King George V and Queen Mary and family.
Grand Duchess Olga Alexandrovna and her family.

Author's Note and Acknowledgements

Since I first began researching the various branches of the Romanov family thirty-seven years ago my few files have grown into a heap of books and a mountain of research notes. I originally had the idea for this book in 2001, but other projects intervened and I never went back to it. Now, in the centenary year of the murder of the tsar and other members of the imperial family, it seems an appropriate time to take up the project. Much of what follows is therefore based on material collected over a long period of time in many libraries and archives.

This is not a book just about Nicholas and Alexandra. So much has been written about them already that I decided to widen the focus to include other members of the family. Some escaped, others did not but they all have exciting or tragic stories to tell.

I would like to acknowledge the gracious permission of Her Majesty the Queen to publish extracts from Queen Mary's diary in the Royal Archives, Windsor, of which she owns the copyright.

For help with research material, photographs and general support I am immensely grateful to the following people: Prince Michael Romanovsky-Ilyinsky, the grandson of Grand Duke Dmitri Pavlovich, for permission to use unpublished extracts from his grandfather's diary; and Dr William Lee for his generous help with the diary entries and for permitting me to use his translations from the original Russian; Anthony Summers, for permission to quote from *The File on the Tsar* and for his enthusiasm, advice and encouragement over many years; *Kongernes Samling* (the Royal

Danish Collection) and Birgitte Momme at Amalienborg Palace for help in identifying the photographs of George Brasov.

A number of people have also lent me photographs, provided research material and translated text. To everyone listed below I therefore extend my grateful thanks. Without your help the book would have been all the poorer:

Mark Andersen; Arturo Beéche, for use of photographs from the vast Eurohistory photo archive; Julie Crocker at the Royal Archives, Windsor; Richard Davies, archivist at Leeds Russian Archive; Margaret Guyver; Professor Knud J V Jespersen of Syddansk Universitet, Odense; Marlene A. Eilers Koenig; Galina Korneva; Netty Leistra; Michael Lewis of Spink's; Anna von Lowzow of Nordisk Film Production A/S, Denmark; Ricardo Mateos Sainz de Medrano, for material on King Alfonso XIII of Spain, and Claudio who scanned it over to me; Alette Scavenius and Peter Scavenius, for help with Harald Scavenius; Ian Shapiro; Katrina Warne; Valerie Wright, for information on the Neame family and Charlotte Zeepvat.

My thanks also to everyone at Amberley, especially Shaun Barrington and my editors Cathy Stagg and Alex Bennett, for all their hard work in seeing the book through to completion.

Last but not least, grateful thanks to my husband Colin, who has lived with the Russian imperial family for nearly thirty years. Throughout all the problems encountered when I was writing this book he read all the drafts and offered support, criticism and encouragement. Once again he kept everything running smoothly while the Romanovs ran riot around the house. He never fails me.

My interest in imperial Russia began in childhood, when I discovered that my great-grandmother was born in St Petersburg and was an almost exact contemporary of Nicholas II. Although her parents were English, the story fired my interest. Consequently I am always delighted to hear about families who had connections with the Romanovs and I welcome people getting in touch. I can be contacted via my website, www.corynehall.com

A Note on Names, Dates and Titles

Russians used the Old Style Julian Calendar until 1 February 1918. This was twelve days behind the West in the nineteenth century and thirteen days behind in the twentieth century. I have used the OS Julian Calendar until 1 February 1918 for events inside Russia, and the NS Gregorian Calendar thereafter. Many members of the imperial family continued to use the OS dating system after February 1918 and this has been noted where necessary. Events in Europe are according to the NS Gregorian Calendar, although occasionally it has been necessary to use both sets of dates (for instance, in ambassadors' reports) to avoid further confusion.

The titles emperor, empress, tsar and tsarina are all correct and are used interchangeably. The eldest son of the tsar was the tsarevich, other sons were grand dukes. Daughters were grand duchesses. From 1886 the title of grand duke/duchess was limited by Alexander III to the sovereign's children and grandchildren in the male line only; great-grandchildren of the sovereign were prince or princess.

Russians have three names – their Christian name, patronymic (their father's name) and their surname. Alexander III's daughters were Xenia and Olga Alexandrovna; their brothers were Nicholas, George and Michael Alexandrovich. Nicholas II's eldest daughter was Olga Nicolaievna. The surname Romanov was hardly used at all.

The members of the Romanov family dealt with in this book were all descended from Tsar Nicholas I (1796–1855). Apart from the senior branch (represented by the reigning tsar) there were three other main branches, who all descended from Nicholas I's sons: the Constantinovichi (descendants of Grand Duke Constantine Nicolaievich, 1827–92); the Nicolaievichi (descendants of Grand Duke Nicholas Nicolaievich, 1831–91); and the Michaelovichi (descendants of Grand Duke Michael Nicolaievich, 1832–1909). The Dukes of Leuchtenberg were descendants of Nicholas I's eldest daughter Grand Duchess Marie Nicolaievna (1819–76).

Introduction

The Queen's Visit to Russia, 1994

In October 1994 Queen Elizabeth II and the Duke of Edinburgh paid a state visit to Russia. It was an historic occasion, the first time a reigning British monarch had set foot on Russian territory.

When the queen's great-grandparents King Edward VII and Queen Alexandra paid a state visit to Tsar Nicholas II and Empress Alexandra Feodorovna in 1908 things were very different. In the aftermath of the 1905 abortive Russian revolution there were very real security risks. The royal visitors and their hosts were therefore confined to entertaining on their respective yachts, which were anchored off Reval (now Tallinn) in the Baltic. The king and queen never set foot on Russian soil. At the request of the British government King Edward set out to counter the weight of Berlin, from where the kaiser exerted a notable influence on Nicholas. He was accompanied by several diplomats but, publicly, it was stressed both in England and abroad that the visit was a purely family affair. The king was visiting his Russian relatives. Tsar Nicholas's mother the Dowager Empress Marie Feodorovna was Queen Alexandra's sister; Empress Alexandra Feodorovna was King Edward's niece. To emphasise this family aspect the tsar and tsarina were accompanied by their five children, as well as the dowager empress and the tsar's sister Grand Duchess Olga Alexandrovna. The king and queen brought their unmarried daughter Princess Victoria. Over the next two days these links were reinforced as the Russian and British royal families exchanged visits, the tsar's young daughters wearing charming identical white *broderie anglaise* dresses and picture hats.

On the last evening there was a lively dance on board the imperial yacht *Standart*.

The visit of Queen Elizabeth II and the Duke of Edinburgh was far more poignant. On 20 October they visited the SS Peter and Paul Fortress in St Petersburg, burial place of the Russian tsars, arriving from the royal yacht *Britannia* on the royal barge. As the director Mrs Natalia Dementieva showed them around, the queen and duke moved among the rows of white sarcophagi, each with a golden cross on top, each the burial place of an emperor or his consort. The world's media published photographs of the queen standing in front of the imperial tombs – but the sarcophagi of the last tsar and tsarina were missing. Their remains were still awaiting burial.

It was noted earlier at the Hermitage Museum that the queen had sidestepped visiting the exhibition about Nicholas and Alexandra, where many of their letters and personal effects were on show. 'They said it would be too sad for her,' said one of the guides.[1] Reporters began to speculate whether she was thinking of her own family's links with the imperial family and their apparent failure to save them.

Nicholas II was not only the first cousin of the queen's grandfather King George V, as was Empress Alexandra, but the Duke of Edinburgh was one of the closest *living* relatives of the murdered imperial family. Alexandra was his great-aunt; the tsarevich and the young grand duchesses were cousins. The duke's great-aunt Grand Duchess Elisabeth Feodorovna was thrown alive down a Siberian mineshaft with other relatives. Another great-uncle, Grand Duke Dmitri Constantinovich, was executed by the Bolsheviks in the SS Peter and Paul Fortress, just a stone's throw from the cathedral where the queen and duke were standing. Many years earlier, when the subject of a Russian visit had been mooted to Prince Philip, he was quoted as saying 'he would like to go to Russia very much – although the bastards had murdered half his family.'[2]

In March 1917 there were fifty-three members of the Romanov family living in Russia. Less than three years later seventeen of them had been murdered by the Bolsheviks and one, Grand Duke Nicholas Constantinovich, had died from natural causes. The other thirty-five had fled for their lives, some with little more than the clothes they stood up in and a few trinkets.

For a family reared in an atmosphere of luxury and privilege, the revolution was a brutal shock. One grand duchess, visiting the Maryinsky Theatre for the first time after the fall of the monarchy, looked up from her unaccustomed seat in the stalls and fainted at the sight of dishevelled sailors and women with coloured woollen scarves on their heads sitting among the silk drapes and gilt chairs in the tsar's box. Worse was to come.

Almost overnight their pampered lifestyle vanished. Within months many of them were under arrest and they became 'Romanovs, enemies of the revolution and the Russian people'.[3] All of them showed great fortitude and courage during adversity. A few managed to smuggle their jewels or other valuables out of Russia, others became solely dependent on the charity of more fortunate relations as they faced life in exile.

Many of these relations were the grandchildren of Britain's Queen Victoria and had played together at Osborne and Balmoral. They included Kaiser William II of Germany, King George V and the Queens of Spain, Romania, Norway, Greece and the Crown Princess of Sweden – all first cousins of Tsarina Alexandra. Nicholas's cousins included King George V and the Kings of Denmark, Norway and Greece. He also had a more distant relationship to the Queen of the Netherlands.

As Queen Marie of Romania wrote to George V in 1916: 'I never imagined that it would be the lot of our generation, we who were children together, to see this Great War and in a way to have to remodel the face of Europe.'[4]

When revolution toppled the tsar most of them stepped up to the mark to help however they could, and many Romanovs were rescued – but for those who failed to escape, the questions remain. Why did they fail? What did their relatives do to help them? Were lives sacrificed to save other European thrones?

This book tells the stories of not only the tsar and his immediate family but also the no less tragic fate of the other Romanovs – his mother, siblings, aunts, uncles and cousins.

1

Revolution and Abdication

'All around me I see treachery, cowardice and deceit.'

In March 1913 the Romanov dynasty celebrated its tercentenary. In St Petersburg the red, white and blue Russian colours decked the streets, buildings and monuments were lavishly decorated and portraits of the Romanov rulers hung from façades. The press published special jubilee editions and the new one rouble coin showed Nicholas II with his ancestor Tsar Michael in profile behind him. A set of postage stamps showing all the Romanov monarchs was also printed but was withdrawn when postal officials refused to deface the tsar's portrait with a postmark.

Streets and windows were crammed with people anxious for a good view as the tsar's procession set off for the Kazan Cathedral in brilliant sunshine, accompanied by a Cossack escort. Troops lined the route and military bands struck up the national anthem as the tsar and his eight-year-old heir Tsarevich Alexei, both in uniform, acknowledged the crowds from their open carriage. The cheers rang out again for Nicholas's mother the Dowager Empress Marie Feodorovna, who followed in a state coach with her less popular daughter-in-law Empress Alexandra Feodorovna. The sight of the tsar's young daughters wearing white dresses and large flower-trimmed picture hats drew an especially warm response. Inside the cathedral the other members of the imperial family, the diplomatic corps, dignitaries from across the empire, as well as members of the nobility and the armed forces had taken their places for the thanksgiving service conducted by the Metropolitan.

Later, delegations from all over Russia, many wearing national dress, came to the Winter Palace to offer congratulations. That night the buildings were illuminated with double-headed eagles, chains of coloured lights along the tramlines lit up the words 'God Save the Tsar' and spectacular fireworks filled the sky.

The following evening crowds gathered to see the emperor and both empresses arrive at the Maryinsky Theatre, which was filled to capacity for a gala performance of Glinka's opera *A Life for the Tsar*. Among the audience were the Emir of Bokhara and the Khan of Khiva, wearing their national costumes, while the performance included the leading singers of the day, as well as the acclaimed ballerinas Mathilde Kschessinska, Anna Pavlova and Olga Preobrajenska.

The splendour of the ball at the Assembly Hall of the Nobility was worthy of old Russia. Empress Alexandra caused resentment by leaving early but the evening was notable for the first appearance in society of her eldest daughter seventeen-year-old Grand Duchess Olga Nicolaievna. After a glittering succession of balls and parties the celebrations in St Petersburg concluded with a lavish state banquet.

At the end of May, Nicholas and his family went on a dynastic pilgrimage to trace the path followed by Tsar Michael from his birth to the throne. In remote villages, peasants knelt to kiss his shadow as he passed and everywhere the cheers were deafening. As the tsar's steamer travelled down the River Volga peasants waded waist-high in the water to catch a glimpse of him.

In Kostroma the family received delegations and visited cathedrals, museums and the Ipatiev Monastery where Michael had been offered the crown. The city had recently been installed with electric lighting and impressive illuminations greeted the imperial visitors in the evening.

The climax came in Moscow in June, when Nicholas rode into the city on horseback through cheering crowds followed by a Cossack escort. Dismounting in Red Square, he walked behind a line of chanting priests, through the Spassky Gate into the Kremlin. Over the next few days the imperial family attended more church services, banquets and gala performances in Moscow.

For Easter the tsar presented his wife with the tercentenary egg created by Carl Fabergé the imperial court jeweller. The egg, with miniatures of the Romanov rulers set into its golden shell, was supported on an imperial double-headed eagle and when Alexandra lifted the lid, the surprise inside was a blue enamel globe showing Russia in 1613 and 1913. After three hundred years, the dynasty seemed secure.

'Nobody, seeing those huge enthusiastic crowds, could have imagined that in less than four years Nicky's very name would be spattered with mud and hatred,' recalled the tsar's sister Grand Duchess Olga Alexandrovna many years later.[1]

***

Nicholas had been on the Russian throne for eighteen years, succeeding after the unexpected death of his giant of a father Alexander III in 1894. Generally seen as mild and weak-willed, with impeccable manners and striking blue eyes, Nicholas had dared to defy his august father only once, when he insisted that the only bride he would take was Princess Alix of Hesse and By Rhine, a granddaughter of Queen Victoria.

Princess Alix, hastily summoned to her future father-in-law's deathbed in the Crimea, had made her first entry into St Petersburg riding in Alexander III's funeral procession. Superstitious peasants crossed themselves, murmuring, 'she has come to us behind a coffin,'[2] but nevertheless, twenty-six-year-old Nicholas and his twenty-two-year-old bride, now the Empress Alexandra Feodorovna, began their reign in an aura of expectancy. The new tsar, however, quickly dashed the hopes of those who wanted a more liberal regime by declaring in one of his first speeches that he would reign as an autocrat, just as his reactionary father had done.

Alexandra, ill at ease in the loose, immoral society of St Petersburg, drew Nicholas more and more into their own cosy little world at the Alexander Palace at Tsarskoe Selo, appearing in public only when absolutely necessary and gradually cutting herself off from the rest of the family. In her first ten years of marriage she bore Nicholas four daughters – Olga (1895), Tatiana (1897), Maria (1899) and Anastasia (1901) – before finally giving birth to the long-awaited Tsarevich Alexei in 1904. Daughters could not succeed to the throne, so the birth of this son was greeted with jubilation throughout the Russian empire. But unknown to

Nicholas and Alexandra, a fatal flaw in this precious child's genes would be partly responsible for the fall of the dynasty.

Although the sovereigns favoured simplicity in their private lives the gulf between rich and poor in Russia was nevertheless unbridgeable. The Romanov family's lifestyle was unsurpassed anywhere in Europe. They all had fantastic incomes and lavish lifestyles, enabling them to indulge every whim. Each of the grand dukes had an income of £20,000 per year; grand duchesses were given a dowry of £100,000. Their palaces were magnificent. The Winter Palace was decorated with malachite, jasper and other semi-precious stones from the Urals. Behind 40-foot-high doors huge chandeliers lit state rooms the size of which rivalled many cathedrals. The family travelled round Europe with large retinues and mountains of luggage and the eyes of many a *maitre d'hotel* lit up with expectation of a large tip when a grand duke entered his establishment.

Nicholas's resolve not to grant a more representative government was at the root of many of the evils which followed. The revolutionary movement, largely extinguished during the reign of Alexander III, became active again and in 1903 split into two groups – the Bolsheviks (majority), under Lenin; and the Mensheviks (minority).

The first warning notes were sounded in 1905, when the tsar's uncle Grand Duke Sergei Alexandrovich was blown to bits by a terrorist's bomb. This was followed by an abortive revolution, signalling that things could not remain unchanged forever. That October the tsar was forced to grant the country a constitution and a Duma (parliament). He was no longer an autocrat and the revolutionary movement remained active.

There were problems within the family too. In the early years of the century the strict moral code which had formerly bound the imperial family began to crumble.

The tsar's sister Grand Duchess Olga Alexandrovna was living in a *ménage à trois* with her husband Prince Peter of Oldenburg and his Aide-de-Camp (ADC) Nicolai Kulikovsky, a commoner with whom she was deeply in love.

The tsar's only surviving brother, Grand Duke Michael Alexandrovich, set up home with his twice divorced mistress Natasha Wulfert, by whom he had a son, George, in 1910. In 1912 they slipped away secretly to Vienna and were married. When Michael informed the tsar, he was banished from Russia.

The tsar's uncle, the widowed Grand Duke Paul Alexandrovich, was banished abroad in 1902 for contracting a second, morganatic marriage with Olga von Pistolkors, the divorced wife of his brother Vladimir's ADC. The two children from his first marriage to Princess Alexandra of Greece – Marie born in 1890, and Dmitri born in 1891 – were left behind in Russia under the guardianship of their uncle the childless Grand Duke Sergei. When he was killed in 1905 his widow Grand Duchess Elisabeth Feodorovna (Ella), the tsarina's sister, took over the children's guardianship.

The Tsar's cousin Grand Duke Cyril Vladimirovich defied an imperial decree by marrying the divorced Grand Duchess Victoria Melita of Hesse and By Rhine, despite first cousin marriages being forbidden by the Orthodox Church. Although she was a granddaughter of both Queen Victoria *and* Alexander II of Russia, Victoria Melita was also the former wife of the empress' brother Grand Duke Ernest Ludwig of Hesse. It was several years before Cyril was permitted to return to Russia and his wife was created an imperial grand duchess.

All this would not have been so important were it not for one vital fact. The tsar's only son and heir Alexei suffered from haemophilia, a disease that prevents the blood from clotting. Any bump or fall could be fatal. Alexei had already been near to death several times. Throughout the tercentenary celebrations the tsarevich, still unable to walk after his latest haemophiliac crisis, had to be carried in the arms of a burly Cossack.

After him the next heir was the unsuitably married Michael. Then came Cyril, whose wife had yet to produce a son, followed by his brothers Boris and Andrei, both of whom lived with their mistresses.

By 1913 most of the Romanovs had lost respect for the tsar and were blatantly going their own way as the empire lurched towards disaster. One of the reasons was the empress's reliance on Gregory Rasputin, 'Our Friend', on whose healing powers, she believed, her sickly son's life depended. Time and again when Alexei suffered a haemorrhage, the prayers of Rasputin almost inexplicably caused the bleeding to stop.

Yet, as the author Douglas Smith has shown, Rasputin never actually healed Alexei – the haemophilia remained. Nor did the tsarevich die from haemophilia after Rasputin's murder, as Smith has also noted. Alexandra *believed* that it was her faith, and also Rasputin's, that kept her son alive, 'and it was through the lens of faith that Rasputin's acts took on the aura of miracles.'[3] Alexandra was convinced that without him, her son would die.

Alexei's illness was kept a closely guarded secret and because few knew the nature of the disease, all sorts of rumours circulated. Rasputin's enemies were also at work circulating stories about him, stories that showed a different side of his character which Alexandra never saw. Many of these tales were invented, including a supposed incident when Rasputin revealed his sexual organs in the Yar Restaurant, saying he always behaved like that in female company. The imputation was obvious. The anecdote was invented in the hope of discrediting Rasputin in the eyes of the tsar, to whose attention the story was brought. When Alexandra found out that Deputy Minister Vladimir Dzhunkovsky had spread the story she was furious, calling him a 'liar' and a 'traitor.' 'The unintended consequence ... was to immunize Rasputin from all criticism in the eyes of the empress.'[4]

But the stories stuck and at each telling the details were embellished. The result was that the empress could not understand why the people objected to the appearance of a Holy Man in the palace; and the people could not understand why the tsar and tsarina received a drunken lecher.

Many members of the imperial family were concerned at the consequent discredit to the dynasty; in particular the tsar's mother the Dowager Empress Marie Feodorovna, and the tsarina's sister Grand Duchess Elisabeth Feodorovna (Ella). One by one, Alexandra's relationship with them cooled. Her dependence on Rasputin increased and she became prey to all sorts of psychosomatic illnesses as worry over her son took a toll on her health. Nicholas could not send Rasputin away because, if Alexei died, in her eyes he would have been the murderer of his own son.

* * *

The catalyst came in 1914 with the outbreak of the First World War. The tsar appointed his tall imposing cousin Grand Duke

Nicholas Nicolaievich (Nicholasha) as Commander-in-Chief of the army and contented himself with periodic visits to the front. Alexandra forgot her ills and, with her elder daughters Olga and Tatiana, trained as a nurse at the hospital at Tsarskoe Selo. Many other imperial ladies followed her example.

In the euphoria that followed the formal declaration of hostilities against Germany on 20 July/2 August many people failed to notice that Russia was in no state to wage a protracted war. The German-sounding St Petersburg was renamed Petrograd and the tsar took an oath never to make peace while a single enemy soldier remained on Russian soil.

The war went badly for Russia and in the spring of 1915, the army was forced to retreat. Later that year the tsar took the disastrous decision to dismiss Nicholasha and take command of the army. The dowager empress and many other members of the family tried to dissuade him, foreseeing the consequences, but Nicholas was firm. He departed for *Stavka* (military headquarters) at Mogilev, 500 miles from the capital.

Many blamed Alexandra for this decision as, slowly at first and then with more confidence, she took up the reins of government. Beside her stood Rasputin. In an almost hysterical stream of letters to the tsar she was soon proposing this or that protégé of Rasputin for a government post. 'Never forget that you are and must remain autocratic emperor,' she told him. 'We are not ready for constitutional government.'[5] Soon she began hectoring Nicholas to dismiss ministers who were opposed to Rasputin, the autocracy or both. People believed that they were replaced by Rasputin's incompetent nominees, but in fact Nicholas passed over many of 'Our Friend's' suggestions.

Nevertheless, in the space of just thirteen months, twelve ministers were replaced in what became known as Ministerial Leapfrog. Alexandra and Rasputin then turned their attention to the military situation. The empress faithfully transmitted Our Friend's instructions to Nicholas but, when the war went badly, the people believed that 'Dark Forces' were at work and that Alexandra was spying for the Germans.

The imperial family were united in their resolve that Rasputin must go but, despite repeated attempts, they failed to open Nicholas's eyes. Finally, in December 1916 Rasputin was murdered.

The plot was formed by a group of right-wing monarchists led by Prince Felix Youssoupov (husband of the tsar's niece Princess Irina), and the tsar's cousin Grand Duke Dmitri Pavlovich – but it now seems that the final bullet *may* have been fired by Oswald Rayner, a Special Intelligence Service officer attached to the British Embassy who had known Felix at Oxford. This theory is still being disputed, as 'there is no convincing evidence that places any British agents at the murder scene.'[6]

The family hoped that Alexandra would now withdraw from politics and perhaps retire to the imperial estate of Livadia in the Crimea. These hopes were soon dashed. When Nicholas returned to Petrograd, Grand Duke Dmitri was exiled to the Persian front and Felix was banished to one of his estates in Kursk province.

In the Imperial Yacht Club the grand dukes were discussing plots and counter plots. The dethronement of the tsar and the establishment of a regency for Alexei was very much on the minds of the imperial family. The only point they disagreed on was who should be regent.

Despite the pleas of the family, the tsar still refused to grant the country a more representative government. Yet he appeared briefly to waver. On 22 February he announced his intention of appearing at the Duma the next day to grant a responsible ministry. Later that night he changed his mind and decided to return to *Stavka*. Before leaving, Nicholas asked the Minister of Finance Peter Bark to provide him with 200,000 roubles (£20,000) from the Secret State Fund, which could be used personally by Nicholas or, with his and Bark's approval, by any of the ministries. The reason he wanted this money for his own personal use was never revealed.[7]

As his train moved further and further away from the capital, one by one his children went down with measles.

***

In February 1917 Princess Olga Putiatin was living in an apartment on Millionaya Street near the Winter Palace. All the men, including her husband Prince Paul, a former equerry to the tsar, were at the front. There remained only the servants and the princess's twelve-year-old daughter Natalie. Revolution was in the air and events were soon to involve Princess Putiatin in an unexpected way.

In Petrograd's bitter winter temperatures the railways froze to a standstill, factories closed through lack of fuel, and shortage of food pushed prices up to an exorbitant level. While food and fuel were in short supply, bread had all but disappeared from the shops and for several days there had been demonstrations and disturbances in the streets. Crowds sacked the bakeries and surged through the streets with red banners crying: 'Down with the government!' 'Down with the war!' Trucks drove up and down, full of soldiers firing indiscriminately. The snow was tinted with blood and the princess' cook refused to go out shopping for fear of being shot. Although people tried to carry on as usual, everyone sensed the tension as the government began to disintegrate and the troops sent to quell the disturbances sided with the rioters. Soon hatred of the empress reached fever pitch and the disorders turned into full-scale revolution.

On 25 February the premiere of Mikhail Lermantov's play *Masquerade* took place at the Alexandrinsky Theatre before an audience of 1,700 people. Petrograd society turned out in full for the occasion, which was held in honour of the actor Y.M. Yuriev's twenty-fifth anniversary performance. It was customary on these occasions for a gift to be sent by the dowager empress, who patronised the Alexandrinsky, and by the tsar, but the theatre director forgot to prompt both courts about Yuriev. Luckily, the leading actress Ekaterina Roshchina-Insarova had managed to ask two influential contacts to remind court officials about the occasion. The result was that as gunfire echoed in the distance outside, Yuriev was honoured with gifts of two gold cigarette cases with diamond eagles from the royal patrons. These were the last ever imperial presentation gifts.

* * *

It was Nero fiddling while Rome burned. As society enjoyed the gala performance, the tsar was being urged to return and appoint an acceptable ministry. Ignoring pleas for concessions and unaware of the seriousness of the situation, Nicholas sent General Ivanov to Petrograd with reinforcements to quash the uprising by force.

The decisive day was 27 February. The elite regiments of the Imperial Guard, although now comprising raw conscripts and factory workers, fraternised with the mob and the situation spiralled out of control. As the Petrograd soldiers defected to the revolution and the imperial government collapsed, Michael Rodzianko telephoned the tsar's brother Grand Duke Michael and asked him to come immediately to the Maryinsky Palace on St Isaac's Square in Petrograd.

Grand Duke Michael was a modest, not too intelligent man who had been pardoned by the tsar for his unsuitable marriage, mainly at the insistence of their mother the Dowager Empress Marie Feodorovna. On the outbreak of war the grand duke, his wife Natasha and their four-year-old son George returned to Russia where Michael commanded the Savage Division (the 'Wild Caucasians'). He was awarded the Cross of St George for bravery before ill-health forced him to relinquish his command. Since then he had lived quietly at his house in Gatchina, 30 miles from the capital. Michael was considered weak like the tsar. His sister Olga's rather telling nickname for him was 'dear, darling Floppy'.

The Duma had remained in session in defiance of the tsar's order that it be suspended. Michael Rodzianko, the burly president, had assumed chairmanship of the temporary executive committee formed by several members of the Duma to restore law and order – but it had no legal status. In another wing of the Tauride Palace, a Soviet of Soldiers' and Workers' Deputies was already meeting. Clutching at the last shreds of power, Rodzianko and leading members of the Duma were holding what was to be their last meeting at the Maryinsky Palace, where they were joined by Grand Duke Michael.

The grand duke was asked to have one last try to influence his brother by presenting some essential proposals to him that would stop the revolution. These included a regency under Michael, who would then appoint a competent new Prime Minister with the power to appoint his own cabinet. Rodzianko obviously had himself in mind. Michael left the meeting and went to the War Minister's residence by the Moika canal. From there he contacted *Stavka* via the Hughes apparatus (a kind of primitive telex machine) and urged the tsar to dismiss the Council of Ministers and appoint Prince Lvov as Prime Minister, with the power to select a cabinet which could command the people's confidence.

Half an hour later Nicholas replied through General Alexeyev. He was returning immediately to the capital and would deal with the situation from Tsarskoe Selo. At this point the ministers gave up and drifted away.

By nightfall more than 66,000 troops had mutinied and joined the revolution. Rodzianko's power was rapidly waning; the Duma and the Soviet reached a compromise and a Provisional Government was formed, with Prince George Lvov as Prime Minister and Minister of the Interior, Alexander Kerensky as Minister of Justice, Alexander Guchkov as War Minister, Paul Milyukov as Foreign Minister and Michael Tereschenko as Minister of Finance. The tsar's ministers gave themselves up to the protection of the Duma.

It was nearly 3.00am by the time Grand Duke Michael decided to return to Gatchina. Accompanied by an escort car, he and his secretary Nicholas Johnson drove down Morskaya Street in the direction of the railway station but soon found their car surrounded by a mob of revolutionary sailors. Keeping his presence of mind, Michael ordered his chauffeur to accelerate down a side street. Although the sailors started shooting no-one was hurt but the grand duke's escort car was stopped and the occupants arrested. When Michael's car reached the bank of the River Neva, he decided to pass the rest of the night at the Winter Palace. The huge palace was defended by one thousand troops under the command of General Beliaiev and General Khabaloff. Michael soon persuaded them to evacuate the building, thereby saving it from almost certain destruction by the revolutionaries. Nevertheless, he could not remain there unguarded and at the mercy of the mob. It was then he remembered that his friend Princess Putiatin had an apartment nearby. At five o'clock in the morning Michael and Johnson left the Winter Palace on foot.

* * *

At the Alexander Palace, Empress Alexandra was busy nursing Olga, Tatiana and Alexei, who had contracted measles. Rumours reached her that some of the elite Guards' regiments had mutinied. 'I can't understand it,' she told her friend Lili Dehn, who was staying with her. 'I'll never believe in the possibility of revolution – I'm sure the trouble is confined to Petrograd alone.'[8] She sent the tsar a wire, asking him to return to Petrograd immediately.

Although Alexandra said she did not believe that revolution was possible, there is a clue that she might have been thinking of evacuating her children in the weeks before the uprising occurred. It is alleged that towards the end of 1916 a man called Frank Best, who owned a timber company on the Baltic, was called to a meeting at the British Embassy in Petrograd, where among those present was the tsarina. He was asked whether he could let the imperial family use his sawmill to secretly house the tsarina's children until the Royal Navy could send a ship to take them to England. In gratitude at his willingness to help, Alexandra 'gave him an icon of St Nicholas, the patron saint of children.' There is sadly no contemporary evidence for this story, only a letter from the Rev'd G. V. Vaughan-James written in 1978 which briefly describes the plan.[9]

* * *

Early in the morning of 2 March Nicholas finally ordered his train to return to Tsarskoe Selo. *En route* he heard of the collapse of the imperial government and the passing of power to the Duma. A hundred miles south of Petrograd, revolutionaries were blocking the line at Malaya-Vichera. He could go no further. Instead his train doubled back to Pskov, headquarters of General Ruzsky's northern front. On arrival he learnt that General Ivanov's troops, sent to crush the uprising by force, had discreetly melted away. Meanwhile, Grand Duke Cyril, Nicholas's cousin, had marched to the Tauride Palace at the head of his regiment of Marine Guards to pledge allegiance to the Duma. He was the first Romanov to break his oath of allegiance to the tsar.

Nicholas finally agreed to make concessions and appoint an acceptable ministry. When General Ruzsky communicated this information to Rodzianko he was informed that it was too late. The Provisional Government had already decided that Nicholas must abdicate in favour of Alexei, with Grand Duke Michael as regent. General Alexeyev telegraphed the generals commanding the five Russian fronts to ask their opinion. They were unanimous; the tsar must abdicate. Even his cousin Nicholasha, now commanding the Caucasian front, begged him 'on my knees to save Russia and your heir. Pass your inheritance on to him. There is no other way out.'[10]

On 2 March Ruzsky boarded the imperial train to bring the answers to the tsar. There was a long, anguished silence. Isolated, unwilling to plunge his country into civil war, Nicholas took the course urged on him by the Provisional Government and the generals. The abdication document, signed at 3.00pm, bequeathed the throne to Alexei with Michael as regent.

Meanwhile, the Provisional Government had sent Alexander Guchkov and Vassili Shulgin to witness the tsar's signature and bring the abdication document back to Petrograd. They were expected to arrive in Pskov that evening.

While waiting for them, Nicholas summoned Dr Federov to ask his advice. He told Nicholas that Alexei's illness was incurable; he would probably be separated from his family and sent to live with Michael and his unsuitable wife. Furthermore, it was unlikely that the ex-tsar would be allowed to live in Russia. Consequently, when Guchkov and Shulgin arrived, Nicholas informed them that he had decided to abdicate for himself *and* Alexei, leaving the throne to Michael. 'I trust you will understand the feelings of a father,' he added.[11] He picked up a new draft of the document, left the room and returned with it signed and backdated to 3.00pm.

The next morning Nicholas's train left early for Mogilev, where he would say goodbye to the army and have a final heartbreaking meeting with his mother the Dowager Empress Marie. He poured out his feelings in his diary. 'At 1 in the morning left Pskov.... All around me I see treachery, cowardice and deceit.'[12]

2

Tsar for a Day

'I am in despair over everything.'

Soon after five o'clock in the morning of 28 February, Princess Olga Putiatin was woken by a violent banging on the bedroom door of her St Petersburg apartment. The princess was a light sleeper. Startled by the noise, she sat bolt upright in bed imagining armed men at the door. Number 12 Millionaya Street was situated just off Winter Palace Square and revolutionaries were roaming the area. From that moment, the thirty-seven-year-old princess found herself caught up in a series of dramatic events.

Two days earlier she had dined with a group of friends, including the tsar's thirty-eight-year-old brother Grand Duke Michael Alexandrovich and his morganatic wife Natasha. The grand duke had been watching events in the capital with some concern and his fears were justified. Now Princess Putiatin was relieved to hear the voice of Michael's secretary, Johnson, asking for shelter for his master. The hall porter had recognised the grand duke's voice and admitted them to the building. He then took them up the granite staircase with its wrought-iron banister and let them into the princess's apartment with her key.

The Putiatin family had a history of service to the crown. Princess Olga's father Admiral Paul Zelenoy had been Comptroller of the Department of the Institutions of the Empress Marie, which co-ordinated the activities of the charities and educational establishments headed by the dowager empress. Prince Sergei Putiatin, a distant relative, would later marry Michael's cousin Grand Duchess Marie Pavlovna the younger. Hearing that the grand duke needed assistance the princess quickly dressed and ordered coffee. Even as she was assuring Michael that she was not afraid of the consequences of harbouring him, a gang of drunken revolutionary soldiers was ransacking the apartment of the tsar's chamberlain immediately above.

Michael and Johnson snatched a few hours sleep on some couches. They were awakened by armoured cars racing past and the sound of shooting in the street. By now almost the whole of Petrograd was in the hands of the revolutionaries but the day passed uneventfully in Princess Putiatin's apartment. Michael did not venture out of doors and neither the telephone nor the telegraph was working. A message was sent by courier to Natasha, who had returned to Gatchina, to advise her of his whereabouts.

As the house searches by revolutionary bands continued Princess Putiatin lived in constant fear for the security of her guest. The next day the revolutionaries searched some of the other apartments in the house but, much to the princess's relief, she was left in peace due to the quick thinking of her hall porter who insisted that the only occupants were the princess and her young daughter.

Later that day Michael's ADC Nicholas Wrangel arrived. The grand duke was also visited by Nicholas Ivanov, a lawyer who acted as aide to Michael Rodzianko. He asked him to sign a manifesto announcing that the tsar was granting a full constitution. It had already been signed by Michael's uncle Grand Duke Paul and cousin Grand Duke Cyril. Michael added his signature and the paper was taken to the Duma, where one of the members merely remarked that it was 'an interesting document'.[1]

Once the telephone was working again, Michael contacted Rodzianko, who immediately provided a guard of eight officers and forty cadets from the Military School. The grand duke also managed to get in touch with the British Ambassador, Sir George Buchanan, who called later in the day to discuss the manifesto. Although the tsar was expected back from the front, he had not arrived in Petrograd and no-one knew his whereabouts.

* * *

The announcement of the tsar's abdication was an outcome nobody expected. The ministers, counting on a sympathetic outpouring of loyalty to Alexei, the legitimate heir, were aghast. Michael received the news in a telegram from Nicholas addressed to 'His Majesty the Emperor Michael'. It hit him like a thunderbolt.

He had been heir to the throne for five years before Alexei was born and, during the tsarevich's periods of illness, was aware that he could again become heir at any minute on the death of his nephew – hence his hasty marriage to Natasha, who was deemed unsuitable by his family. Michael had not expected to be more than regent if Nicholas died before Alexei came of age.

Another telegram followed, this time from Rodzianko, informing him that the members of the Provisional Government and the executive committee of the Duma would be coming to Millionaya to discuss his succession. Princess Putiatin recalled that he was overcome by the sudden responsibility and paced nervously up and down the room reading and re-reading the two telegrams.

At this point Michael's cousin, Grand Duke Nicholas Michaelovich ('Bimbo'), returned from his country estate, where he had been exiled by the tsar for speaking out against the empress's influence on affairs of state. His palace was opposite Princess Putiatin's apartment and as soon as he heard Michael was there, he hurried over to give support. He urged him to be brave and save both the dynasty and Russia. Unfortunately, this needed someone of greater calibre than Michael.

At six o'clock on the morning of 3 March Princess Putiatin was woken by the incessant ringing of the telephone. It was Alexander Kerensky, the thirty-six-year-old Minister of Justice in the new Provisional Government, asking to speak to the grand duke urgently. When Michael came to the telephone he was informed that all the members of the Provisional Government would be arriving at Princess Putiatin's apartment within the hour to discuss the situation.

It was 9.30am before the delegation arrived, to be greeted by Johnson and the grand duke's legal adviser Alexei Matveyev. They were joined by Rodzianko, who was not a member of the government as he was unacceptable to the Soviet. Most of those present had resolved to persuade Michael not to accept the crown. Shortly afterwards, Alexander Guchkov and Vassili Shulgin arrived from Pskov with the signed abdication document. The historic meeting in the princess's large, elegant drawing room lasted for several hours. Michael sat impassively in an armchair as the debate proceeded. Some urged him to accept, stressing that the monarchy would unify the country; but the majority favoured a Constituent Assembly elected by the people to choose an acceptable form of government. Kerensky, especially, was very eloquent in support of this view, adding that feeling against the Romanovs was running so high that if the grand duke accepted the throne he could not guarantee his safety. The Soviet was clamouring for a republic. With no decision made, and nothing signed, the meeting adjourned for lunch in the princess's dining-room.

When the meeting resumed, Michael sat pensively. Finally he stood up and asked for a few minutes in which to reflect. The ministers asked only for an assurance that he would not communicate with his wife, who they (and some members of the imperial family) considered a political intriguer. With a slight inclination of his head he left the room with Rodzianko. When he re-entered everyone rose. He had not needed much persuading. Faced with the prospect of uprisings and probable civil war, Michael, with tears in his eyes, declared his intention to refuse the crown unless it was offered to him by the Constituent Assembly. Two jurists drafted Michael's manifesto on the school desk of young Princess Natalie and it was copied out in one of her school notebooks.

For the good of the country, Michael's declaration said, '.... I have taken the firm decision to assume the Supreme Power only if such be the will of our great people, whose right it is to establish the form of government and the new basic laws of the Russian state by universal suffrage through its representatives in the Constituent Assembly...' Michael signed it, putting an end to 304 years of Romanov rule.

The pen and pen-holder of Caucasian oxidised silver that Michael used remained in the possession of Princess Putiatin's daughter as a silent witness of an historic occasion.

Princess Olga and her household were in tears when they heard the news but Michael retained his self-possession even after all the ministers had left, assuring the princess that his renunciation would calm the people and bring the revolutionaries to reason. While he was talking, his sister Grand Duchess Xenia arrived with Grand Duke Nicholas Michaelovich, her brother-in-law.

'What a meeting!' Xenia wrote in her diary. 'I was so happy to see him [Michael] at last. In these days he lost some weight, looks

older and ... says all the time "for what sins has he got all this."....
Unfortunately Nicky could not understand the danger.' Xenia felt
that if he had granted concessions sooner he could have saved his
throne. 'Those few hours made all the difference!'[2]

Princess Putiatin noticed that Xenia was unable to control her
emotions. She embraced her brother tearfully as he recounted the
day's events. It was probably the last time that brother and sister
met. Early the next morning Michael was informed that an escort
would be provided to enable him to return to Gatchina. He decided
to leave the following day.

On 5 March, as Princess Putiatin bade farewell to her guest at the
top of the main staircase, an unexpected sight met their eyes – on
both sides of the stairs the forty young military cadets were drawn
up as a guard of honour. As he passed between them they presented
arms and gave a military salute, which Michael returned, struggling
to control his feelings. Cries of 'long live Your Highness,' and 'long
live Russia' echoed through the hall. To those last military honours
Grand Duke Michael, the man who had been 'tsar for a day',
passed through the door and into his car.

* * *

Alone with her sick children at the Alexander Palace, Empress
Alexandra knew nothing of all this. As the situation in the capital
became more serious, mutinous soldiers looted the nearby town and
Count Benckendorff received a message from Rodzianko warning
that the empress and her children should leave immediately. He
also transmitted a command from the tsar that a train should be
prepared for the empress. Benckendorff begged her to leave while
there was still time but Alexandra refused and the children were
too ill to be moved anyway. It was her last real chance of escape.

In the early days of the revolution one Romanov relative did visit
the Alexander Palace and offer to help Empress Alexandra. This
was Princess Helen of Serbia.

Her father, King Peter, had ruled Serbia since the brutal murder
of his predecessor and rival in a palace coup in 1903. Helen's
mother Princess Zorka, who died in 1890, was a daughter
of Nicholas of Montenegro, that wily mountain ruler of an
operetta kingdom who once said that his most successful exports

were his daughters. Two more of these daughters, Militsa and Anastasia, were educated in St Petersburg and married the tsar's cousins Grand Dukes Nicholas and Peter Nicolaievich. They were also instrumental in introducing Rasputin to the tsar and tsarina. Their motherless niece Princess Helen, born in 1883, was educated at the Smolny Institute, the exclusive school for noble young ladies in St Petersburg. In 1911 she married Prince Ioann Constantinovich, eldest son of another of the tsar's cousins Grand Duke Constantine Constantinovich. They had two children, Prince Vsevolod born in 1914, and Princess Catherine who was born the following year.

Prince Ioann had returned home from the front having narrowly escaped death at the hands of his men. He and Helen were currently living at the beautiful summer palace of Pavlovsk, with Ioann's mother Grand Duchess Elisabeth Mavrikievna ('Mavra'). Also with them was Mavra's widowed sister-in-law Queen Olga of Greece.

The queen had been born Grand Duchess Olga Constantinovna in 1851, elder daughter of Grand Duke Constantine Nicolaievich. In 1867 she married twenty-one-year-old King George I of the Hellenes, second son of Christian IX of Denmark, who had been elected to the Greek throne in 1863 and was looking for an Orthodox bride. When George called at Pavlovsk it is said he was enchanted when he saw fifteen-year-old Olga peeping over the banisters. The couple's only common language was German. She later said that she had fallen in love with the man, not his position of king. Queen Olga visited her homeland regularly, always arriving in Russia with a stack of beautiful Greek embroideries in her luggage, which she then proceeded to try and sell in aid of her many charities.

After King George's assassination in 1913 Olga and Mme Baltazzi, her devoted lady-in-waiting, returned to live in Russia, where her brother Constantine (who died in 1915) and his wife Elisabeth Mavrikievna were only too pleased to welcome her back to the Marble Palace in St Petersburg and Pavlovsk. Olga was one of the few members of the family who still had sympathy for Alexandra, living alone with her sick children in the Alexander Palace, 'and she continued to send little gifts and messages of affection.'[3]

Princess Helen, who had been working as a nurse, went in her uniform to the Alexander Palace so that the guards would let her through without any problem. Inside the palace the beleaguered tsarina was still awaiting the tsar's return. Although her offer of help was refused, Helen was not one to give up easily. Despite the chaos in Petrograd, Helen and Mme Baltazzi caught a troop train into the city. There was no transport, so they walked to the Serbian Legation through streets 'littered with corpses' and echoing with gunfire to see if they could find out when the tsar was returning. The Serbian Minister Miroslav Spalaikovich was horrified at the appalling risks the princess had taken. He immediately telephoned the Duma to see what news he could glean and was informed that they were expecting the tsar's return 'within hours'.[4] Helen telephoned this information to a relieved tsarina the next morning. Shortly afterwards, the telephone lines to the palace were cut.

* * *

News of the abdication had hit no-one harder than the tsar's mother, the sixty-nine-year-old Dowager Empress Marie Feodorovna. Marie had spent the last twelve months living at the Maryinsky Palace in Kiev, away from the poisonous atmosphere of the capital and the ministerial leapfrog of Alexandra and Rasputin. Relations between the tsar's mother and wife had long been cool and Marie blamed her daughter-in-law for all the recent misfortunes of the dynasty.

Also in Kiev were Marie's younger daughter Grand Duchess Olga Alexandrovna, who had recently married her long-time love Nicolai Kulikovsky; and Grand Duke Alexander Michaelovich ('Sandro'), head of the Air Force and estranged husband of Marie's elder daughter Xenia.

By 27 February there had been no newspapers or telegraph communication for three days and Empress Marie had no idea what was happening in the capital. 'Where is my eldest son?' she telegraphed to the Ministry of Foreign Affairs in desperation.[5] In her diary she gave full vent to her worry and distress. 'No news at all from Petersburg [*sic*], very distressing,' she wrote the following day. The Governor of Kiev, Count Ignatiev, lunched with her at the palace but he had heard nothing either. 'The Duma closed, why?' her diary continued. 'People say that it is definitely her [Alexandra's] work again, a terrible error at a moment like this! She must be mad, it is unbelievable to assume such a responsibility.'[6]

As the revolution spread to the Baltic Fleet, Kronstadt and Moscow, the worried and despairing dowager empress heard rumours of the street disturbances in Petrograd from trusted friends. However, any news she did receive was usually out of date and she had no way of gauging the gravity of the situation. It was understood that the tsar was on his way back to Tsarskoe Selo but Marie still had no idea of his whereabouts. 'The empress, [Grand Duchess] Olga and myself ran out of words,' wrote Sandro. 'We glared at each other in silence.'[7]

By 1 March there was still no news. 'Horrible situation,' Marie wrote.

Captain Nicholas Fogel, Sandro's ADC, came to the Maryinsky Palace and told her that after the Duma was closed, rioting had broken out in the streets. Once again Marie laid the blame at Alexandra's door. 'For this we can thank her stupidity and hunger to rule in Nicky's absence; it is incomprehensible to assume such a responsibility.' She heard that the troops refused to shoot at the people, 'so the police shot at them; many killed!' Rodzianko had put himself at the head of a new government. 'All the previous ministers were dismissed and arrested...,' Marie continued.[8]

On 2 March Marie heard from her son Michael, who was with Xenia in the capital. There was a mutiny at the Kronstadt naval base and many people had been killed. 'They say that my poor Nicky is in Pskov,' she recorded. 'I can only speak and think about this horror. Got a telegram from Xenia, who says no-one knows where Nicky is; dreadful what they are going through! God help us!'[9] That night, restless and agitated, the dowager empress was unable to sleep.

She was totally unprepared for what happened next.

At nine o'clock in the morning of 3 March Sandro brought the news that Nicholas had abdicated in favour of Michael. 'It hit her like a thunderbolt,' recalled Grand Duchess Olga, who was nursing at the hospital in Kiev. She was 'in a terrible state and I stayed the night at her house.' Although Marie quickly recovered her composure, she still could not understand Nicholas's reasons for abdicating. She repeatedly called it 'the greatest humiliation of her life.'[10] 'Am completely disconsolate!!' Marie wrote in her diary. 'To think that I should live to witness such horror ... I am in despair over everything.'[11] At that point Marie had no idea that Michael had refused to accept the throne.

Meanwhile, Sandro had suggested that they travel to military headquarters at Mogilev to meet Nicholas, who had returned there to say goodbye to the army. Marie agreed, although she was unable to use her own personal train which was in Petrograd. She left Kiev with all the customary honours. A Cossack escort accompanied her to the station and Count Ignatiev came to see her off on the imperial platform. She was accompanied by her chamberlain Prince Schervashidze, her secretary Prince Dolgoruky and her lady-in-waiting Countess Zina Mengden.

They arrived at Mogilev at mid-day on 4 March in a snowstorm. Nicholas's train arrived shortly afterwards. He strode across the platform, greeted his mother's two Cossack bodyguards and entered her carriage. Zina Mengden recalled that he was quiet and dignified but looked deathly pale. Zina had brought her camera intending to photograph the historic moment but when the time came she was unable to bring herself to do it and left her camera on the train. The only picture she took of that significant event was a photograph of the train standing by a snow-covered platform.

At some stage during this momentous day, the dowager empress received the further shock that Michael had refused the throne. Her diary made no mention of this fact, merely giving Nicholas's explanation of why he had abdicated for himself and Alexei. She still could not believe the news. 'It was as if I had been hit on the head and do not comprehend it!'[12]

What passed between mother and son during the next two hours was never disclosed, although Marie later telegraphed to Xenia that the weather was as desperate as her mood. When Sandro was summoned he found the empress 'sobbing aloud, all trace of her habitual self-control gone'. Nicholas 'stood motionless, looking at his feet and, of course, smoking.' He was calm but pale and 'criticised ....Misha for refusing to accept the throne and for leaving Russia without a ruler.'[13]

Dinner that evening was a gloomy affair. Marie could not forget that her daughter-in-law's influence was responsible for the circumstances of this reunion. 'If only he had remained there with the army instead of going to Tsarskoe after [receiving] her telegram that asked him to come immediately and in that way *ruined* all,' she lamented years later in a letter to her sister Queen Alexandra in England. 'She has what they call not a lucky touch...'[14]

It also seems likely that they discussed with Sandro and his brother Grand Duke Sergei Michaelovich, who was also at *Stavka*, where Nicholas was to live in future. During the evening Prince Lvov contacted military headquarters to find out where the tsar wanted to go. Nicholas also discussed the matter with Sir John Hanbury-Williams, the head of the British Military Mission, who contacted London to endorse the idea of the tsar going to England with the assistance of the British Royal Navy.

Marie's visit was extremely painful. Red flags mingled with the bunting when they drove through the streets of Mogilev and, for the first time in 304 years, the names of the imperial family were omitted from the prayers on Sunday.

On 8 March members of the Provisional Government arrived to escort Nicholas back to Tsarskoe Selo. As he kissed his mother and boarded the train neither of them knew that they would never meet again. 'One of the most awful days in my life! When I was separated from my beloved Nicky!' she wrote that night. In a telegram to her sister, Marie described their final parting as 'heartcrushing'.[15]

When Marie returned to Kiev the outward change in her circumstances immediately became apparent. Civilians wearing red armbands stood on the platform, there was no reception committee, no Cossack escort and the train did not stop near the imperial waiting room. Approaching the Maryinsky Palace in a carriage with the imperial arms removed from its doors, Zina Mengden noticed that the imperial standard was no longer flying from the flagpole. Nevertheless, Marie at first refused to accept reality, insisting that she wanted to remain in Kiev to be closer to her son. She persisted in paying her usual visits to the hospitals, until one day she was turned away by the head surgeon. Shaken, Marie submitted to Sandro's pleas to find safety in the Crimea.

* * *

The Crimean peninsula had always been the favourite holiday retreat of the aristocracy and the imperial family. Every year it became fashionable to leave the cold of St Petersburg and travel south to the milder climate with 'its dark pine-topped mountains sloping down to the sapphire sea.'[16] The scenery was spectacular. 'After climbing up and up for the last time we went through an old archway, then suddenly the whole of the Black Sea spread before our eyes,' recalled Baroness de Stoeckl after making the trip south for the first time. 'It is the most beautiful and startling sight one can imagine.'[17]

All along the coast between Yalta and Sevastopol members of the imperial family owned estates with ornate villas. In 1911 the tsar demolished the larger palace on his estate of Livadia and built a new white Italianate style villa nearby. It became Alexandra's favourite home.

In the spring of 1917, as revolution overwhelmed Petrograd, it was natural that many members of the imperial family should gravitate to this earthly paradise. The tsar's distant cousin Grand Duke Nicholas Nicolaievich ('Nicholasha') and his wife Anastasia of Montenegro ('Stana') were among them. Reappointed commander-in-chief of the army as one of the tsar's last acts before he abdicated, Nicholasha had obligingly resigned his command when he learnt that the Provisional Government did not want the unpopular Romanovs occupying public positions. After taking the Oath of Allegiance to the new government Nicholasha, Stana and the grown-up children of her first marriage, Sergei and Elena of Leuchtenberg, retired to Tchair, Stana's Crimean estate. (Shortly afterwards, Elena married Count Stefan Tyshkevich and went to live in Yalta.) The original small villa had been enlarged and gardens had been laid out running down to the seashore. Tchair was previously the setting for military events, sometimes attended by the emperor and empress and ending with a banquet on the lawn overlooking the Black Sea. These carefree days had ended with the revolution.

Nearby at Djulber were Nicholasha's brother Grand Duke Peter Nicolaievich, his wife Militsa of Montenegro (sister of Stana) and their children Princess Marina, Prince Roman and Princess Nadejda.

At Koreiz were Princess Felix and Princess Zenaide Youssoupov, their son Felix (who had been involved in the murder of Rasputin), his wife Irina, the daughter of Grand Duchess Xenia, and their little daughter, also called Irina but known as Bébé.

The largest congregation of Romanovs was at Sandro's estate of Ai-Todor, where the dowager empress, Xenia and Sandro, their sons Andrew, Feodor, Nikita, Dmitri, Rostislav and Vassili were joined by Grand Duchess Olga Alexandrovna and her husband Nicolai Kulikovsky. Xenia had delayed her departure from Petrograd in the hope of being allowed to see the tsar. Only when this request was refused by the Provisional Government did she join the rest of her family. Ai-Todor was built by Sandro's parents Grand Duke Michael Nicolaievich and Grand Duchess Olga Feodorovna. Sandro inherited the estate on his mother's death in 1891. He would not permit any alterations to the Old House and, as his family grew, more buildings were constructed to accommodate them. By 1917 there were three buildings, which housed the Romanovs and their retainers.

The revolution had not yet reached the Crimea and at first it was difficult to believe what had happened in the north. The family were able to go on excursions to Yalta and the surrounding countryside and pay regular visits to other estates.

***

At Pavlovsk, Queen Olga of Greece continued to send messages and gifts to the Alexander Palace. Soon all cars were requisitioned but her widowed sister-in-law Elisabeth Mavrikievna sent some spare horses. On the night of 7 March Pavlovsk was searched. 'I slept soundly... but the soldiers would come into my bedroom' Olga wrote afterwards. '...I sprang out of bed and stood in my nightdress before the soldiers... The door was already open and the corridor full of soldiers with guns and bayonets. [The valet] asked the soldiers not to go into me... They were kind enough to go their way but went around the whole house from bottom to top and remained from one o'clock in the night until five o'clock in the morning'.[18] Princess Helen had some valuables stolen and the whole palace was illuminated by searchlights.

'I pray that... we shall see better times in our beloved Motherland and that some happy experiences should blot the disgrace of recent days from our minds...' Olga wrote to her niece Grand Duchess Xenia. 'All kinds of vile acts are being committed in the name of liberty, national self-determination and justice and they are being substantiated by using pompous, meaningless words. Comrade Xenia, I hope that you have become self-determined and that you stand on a firm platform without any annexations and reparations for the good of the people and international love of your enemies and the world proletariat,' she finished, tongue in cheek.[19]

* * *

But the Tsar failed to arrive at the Alexander Palace. The troops began deserting, electricity and water were cut off and on 3 March servants returning on foot from Petrograd said they had seen leaflets announcing the tsar's abdication. Alexandra refused to believe it. Later that day Grand Duke Paul was announced.

The tsar's uncle Grand Duke Paul Alexandrovich had been pardoned in 1912 for his unsuitable marriage. He returned to Russia in May 1914 with his wife Olga (created Princess Paley by the tsar in 1915) and their children Vladimir, Irene and Natalie Paley. In March 1917 the family were living in their new palace at Tsarskoe Selo, which the grand duke had begun building soon after news of his pardon reached him. It had been furnished by Princess Paley with infinite care.

Paul now had the difficult task of breaking the news of the tsar's abdication to Alexandra. When the empress emerged from the interview she was in tears. Tottering towards Lili Dehn she uttered one word – 'Abdiqué!'[20]

* * *

Late in the evening of 5 March Grand Duke Paul received a summons to the Alexander Palace. His health was not strong and he had already retired for the night but he immediately hurried from his bed.

Alexandra needed some male support. She was expecting a visit from the new Minister of War Alexander Guchkov, and General Lavr Kornilov, Commander of the Petrograd Garrison. As it turned out there was no cause for alarm but Alexandra spent the following days burning many of her diaries and letters. Her thoughts now turned to the safety of her children and she asked Doctor Botkin, her personal physician, whether they were physically in a good enough condition to be taken abroad through Finland. 'Under normal circumstances it would be undesirable,' Botkin replied, 'but at the moment I would be less afraid of measles than of the revolutionaries.'[21] In the meantime the executive committee had voted to detain the imperial family at Tsarskoe Selo, confiscate their property and deprive them of citizenship. They would not be allowed to leave the country without permission.

Three days later General Kornilov arrived to deprive the ex-empress of her liberty. Although this measure was taken at the insistence of the executive committee it also had the advantage of protecting Alexandra and her sick children from the excesses of the revolutionaries. He told the assembled staff that anyone who wished to leave could do so; those who remained would also be placed under arrest.

At four o'clock that afternoon the Alexander Palace was sealed. 'From now on, we are to be considered prisoners: shut up – may see nobody from outside,' Alexandra wrote in her diary.[22] She had rejected General Kornilov's suggestion that she go to England.

The following day the former tsar returned to the Alexander Palace under guard. Nicholas, Alexandra and their five children were now captives. Their one hope was that they would be allowed to go to Livadia, or perhaps be allowed to seek sanctuary abroad.

Of course this latter option would depend to a great extent on the attitude of their many European relatives.

King George's Betrayal

'I shall always remain your true and devoted friend...'

'Bad news from Russia,' King George V wrote in his diary on 13 March [NS] 1917, 'practically a revolution has broken out in Petrograd and some of the Guards regiments have mutinied and killed their officers. This rising is against the government not against the tsar. Nicky is at headquarters.'[1]

George V and Nicholas II were first cousins but the physical resemblance between them was so striking that they could easily have been mistaken for brothers. 'Exactly like a skinny Duke of York [George's title at this time] – the image of him,' was how one of Queen Victoria's ladies described the tsar when he visited Balmoral in 1896.[2]

George, born in 1865, was the second son of Albert Edward, Prince of Wales, and Princess Alexandra of Denmark (later King Edward VII and Queen Alexandra). Alexandra's sister Dagmar, the future Empress Marie Feodorovna, was the mother of Nicholas. The sisters were close, often meeting in Denmark at the home of their parents King Christian IX and Queen Louise, so George and Nicholas knew each other from childhood. They had last met at the Berlin wedding of the kaiser's daughter Princess Victoria Louise in 1913, where George was delighted to note that Nicholas 'was just the same as always.'[3]

On his father's side George was also a first cousin of Empress Alexandra. Her mother the late Princess Alice, Grand Duchess of Hesse and By Rhine, had been the sister of Albert Edward,

Prince of Wales. These intricate family relationships would cause King George a lot of problems.

On 16 March the king's cousin the former Princes Marie of Greece, wife of Grand Duke George Michaelovich of Russia, arrived for tea at Buckingham Palace. She had learnt the news through making enquiries at the Russian Embassy.

In 1914 Marie had planned a holiday in Harrogate, ostensibly for three weeks to improve the health of her younger daughter. When war was declared shortly afterwards Grand Duchess George (as she was known in England), and her daughters Nina and Xenia, were allegedly unable to go back home. The grand duke was in Russia, unable to understand why his wife was seemingly unable to return when British and Russian officers made the journey frequently, carrying his letters.

At the palace she found King George and Queen Mary 'very anxious and depressed' as they discussed what the queen described as 'the surprising events in Russia.'[4] The previous afternoon the grand duchess had visited her aunt Queen Alexandra, who she found terribly worried over the safety of her sister the dowager empress. King George poured out his feelings in his diary. 'I fear Alicky [Empress Alexandra] is the cause of it all and Nicky has been weak. Heard from Buchanan [the British Ambassador] that the Duma had forced Nicky to sign his abdication and Misha [Nicholas's brother] had been appointed regent, and after he has been twenty-three years emperor. I am in despair.'[5]

On 19 March King George sent a telegram to Nicholas. 'Events of last week have deeply distressed me. My thoughts are constantly with you and I shall always remain your true and devoted friend as you know I have been in the past.'[6] The Provisional Government did not forward the message. Paul Milyukov, the new Minister of Foreign Affairs, later said that the telegram was addressed to the tsar and that there was now no such person. Also, he was afraid that the message might be used by the extremists as an excuse to detain the ex-emperor.

Meanwhile, the king was respectfully requested to reveal its contents to the Prime Minister David Lloyd George. The king replied that it was a private message and that since it had not been delivered he felt it should be cancelled anyway. Sir George Buchanan was then instructed to notify the Provisional Government that 'any violence done to the emperor or his family would have a most deplorable effect and would deeply shock public opinion in this country.'[7] Nicholas merely received a message via the Minister of Justice, Alexander Kerensky, 'that the king and queen of England were asking for news of their Russian relatives.'[8]

The king and queen were not the only relatives in Britain who were concerned. The tsarina's sister Princess Victoria was living in the Isle of Wight with her husband Prince Louis of Battenberg, who had been forced to resign as First Sea Lord in 1914 because of his German birth. Like many royals, Victoria had relatives on both sides of the conflict. Her brother Ernest Ludwig, the Grand Duke of Hesse, and her sister Irene, married to Prince Henry of Prussia the kaiser's brother, were in Germany and she had no direct communication with them. Her widowed sister Grand Duchess Elisabeth Feodorovna (Ella) was in Russia, although there seemed to be no need for alarm where she was concerned.

In 1884 the beautiful Ella had married Nicholas's uncle Grand Duke Sergei Alexandrovich, who in 1891 was appointed Governor General of Moscow. An unpopular reactionary, Sergei resigned in 1905 but was blown to pieces by a terrorist's bomb a few days later as he was leaving the Kremlin in his carriage. After her husband's murder Ella divested herself of all her worldly goods in order to fund the building of a convent in Moscow of which she became abbess. The Martha and Mary Convent of Mercy began its activities in 1909. In a last gesture of worldly flair Ella had her pearl-grey robe and white veil designed by the religious painter Michael Nesterov, who also painted the interior frescoes of the convent church. The sisters were Deaconesses, 'not ordained but distinguished by their dress...[and] employed in works of mercy.'[9] Besides their spiritual duties they took food to the poor and, having attended a short course in first aid, could give immediate medical attention when necessary. They worked in the clinic giving massages and injections, taught in the orphanage school, or worked in the kitchen. Ella was loved by the people of Moscow and after the revolution had quickly recognised the Provisional Government, asking to be allowed to continue with her sisterhood.

The empress, however, was another matter and Prince Louis of Battenberg had no doubt about where blame for the revolution lay. 'No news from Russia from our dear ones. It's terrible and really all Aunt Alexandra's [the empress'] fault,' he told his daughter Princess Louise.[10]

Victoria was pleased that Nicholas had abdicated for himself *and* Alexei, 'for no-one can tell how far the revolution may go and whether the socialists & anarchists may not get the upper hand before long and then had Alix still been empress they might have fallen on her – this danger I hope is now averted. I hope the rumour that they will be sent to the Crimea is true & that later on they can leave Russia,' she wrote to a friend.[11]

* * *

The thoughts of many European sovereigns now turned to the question of how best to help the fallen Romanovs. After all, monarchs were an exclusive club and the fall of one monarchy could lead to the fall of others. There were only two powers strong enough to exert any influence over Nicholas's fate. These were Britain and Germany. It was unthinkable to approach the kaiser, an enemy for the last three bitter years, but the tsar could surely expect help from his devoted cousin George in England. Yet things were not that simple. George was obviously concerned about Nicholas's safety but as a constitutional monarch he had to act on the advice of his government. There was unrest in Britain, where republican rallies were being held in London's Albert Hall to celebrate the fall of the tsarist regime and there were calls to abolish the British monarchy. Industrial centres like Glasgow and Liverpool were witnessing socialist demonstrations and even the army was not immune. Before the end of the war, trouble fermenting in the armed services would lead to 3,000 soldiers marching on Whitehall.

Lloyd George had already sent a message to the Russian Provisional Government calling the revolution 'the greatest service which the Russian people have yet made to the cause for which the Allies are fighting.' The king protested that the message was 'a little strong.'[12] It is against this background of rising socialism and discontent that King George and his government had to deal with the plight of the tsar.

The British Government at first seems to have considered the suggestion of General Wallscourt Waters, former military attaché in Russia, who suggested sending 'a fast torpedo boat and a few bags of British sovereigns' to the Gulf of Finland to rescue the imperial family before they fell into the hands of extremists.[13]

Meanwhile, on 4/17 March Prince Lvov, head of the Provisional Government, had received a telegram from General Alexeyev, who was with Nicholas at *Stavka*: 'The emperor, having abdicated, requests that I communicate with you concerning the following issues. First. That he be allowed unrestricted passage with his attendants to Tsarskoe Selo, where his large family are located. Second. That his safety and that of his family with the same attendants be guaranteed in Tsarskoe Selo until the children are well. Third. That he and his family with the same attendants be granted and guaranteed unrestricted passage to [Port] Romanov.' He also wanted an assurance that at the end of the war he could return with his family to live at Livadia. This section of the memo was not forwarded to the Provisional Government.[14]

During the winter, roughly from October until the beginning of May, the River Neva in Petrograd was frozen. Port Romanov (soon to be renamed Murmansk) was Russia's ice free port in the Arctic. If the family could be sent there by special train, a cruiser could be despatched to take them to safety abroad. The Provisional Government would be responsible for transporting the family safely to the port but they would have to pass through Petrograd, where the Soviet was threatening to tear up the railway lines so that the tsar could not pass. The Provisional Government had no intention of harming the family and were discussing the merits of exile abroad versus internal exile, where it would be more difficult to guarantee their safety. Their main concern was the tsar and his brother Michael, who could form the focus of counter-revolutionary activity if they were left too close to Petrograd. They were not worried about the wider members of the imperial family.

Buchanan, a moustachioed old-school diplomat who was now acting as the go-between, reported to London that Milyukov had indicated that permission would be granted for the family to travel. He 'asked me whether I knew if arrangements were being made for H.M. to go to England.'[15] Buchanan replied that no arrangements had been made. A cautious reply was then sent by the Foreign Office in London, who pointed out that they had not yet sent an invitation and that perhaps Denmark or Switzerland might be a more suitable destination. The response was a formal request from a very anxious Milyukov. He urged 'the earliest possible departure of the emperor from Russia, and suggested that the king and British government should offer His Imperial Majesty asylum' in Britain. He seemed to take it for granted that the British would send a ship to pick up the Romanovs and he pointed out the danger from extremists, 'who were exciting opinion against His Majesty.' His appeal was endorsed by Buchanan in a cable to the Foreign Office.[16] The British government now had to make a decision.

The following day Lord Stamfordham, the king's private secretary, attended a cabinet meeting at 10 Downing Street. Present were the Prime Minister David Lloyd George; the Chancellor of the Exchequer Mr Bonar Law; and the permanent Under-Secretary of the Foreign Office Lord Hardinge. Stamfordham pointed out that before any reply was made to Milyukov's formal request to grant the tsar asylum the king would of course wish his opinion to be taken into account. They then discussed the possibility of Nicholas going to Denmark or Switzerland. Lloyd George was against this because it was too close to Germany and, through the empress's influence, might cause the tsar to become the focus for German intrigue or a counter-revolution by disaffected Russian generals. The risk of this, which would play right into Germany's hands, must be avoided at all costs. Finally, the government decided that as Britain was endeavouring to support the new Russian Provisional Government their proposal that the tsar should come to England could not be refused. However, there was concern as to what financial means would be provided for the imperial family so that they could live with appropriate dignity. Lloyd George suggested that perhaps the British government might give the tsar an allowance. Stamfordham, probably worried that at some future date the king might have to take over the payments, quickly vetoed that suggestion. Lloyd George then suggested that the king might be able to place one of his houses at the tsar's disposal. Stamfordham reminded him that Buckingham Palace and Windsor were not the king's private property; the only houses he actually owned were Balmoral (where the castle had been closed for the duration of the war) and Sandringham, which was still being used by Queen Alexandra under the terms of King Edward VII's will. Nearby Wood Farm was the home of the king's youngest son Prince John, York Cottage was occupied by the king and queen, and the other houses on the Norfolk estate were also in use. Balmoral, he said, was a summer home and would be unsuitable at this time of the year – as if that would matter to people used to the harsh Russian winters.

Finally, a reply was sent to Sir George Buchanan: 'In order to meet the request made by the Russian government, the king and His Majesty's Government readily offer asylum to the emperor and empress in England, which it is hoped they will take advantage of during the war ... In order to avoid any possible doubt in the future as to the reason for asylum being given ... you should emphasise the fact that the offer made has been entirely due to the initiative of the Russian government.' Then came the main worry: 'Can you possibly ascertain what are the private resources of the emperor? It is very desirable that His Majesty and his family should have sufficient means to live in a manner befitting their rank as members of an imperial family.'[17] In other words, the Russian government should allow the tsar sufficient means to enable him to live in England with suitable dignity by paying his expenses. The wealthy British royal family would not be footing the bill.

Buchanan informed Milyukov that 'King George, with the consent of his ministers, offers the tsar and tsarina hospitality in British territory, confining himself only to the certainty that Nicholas II will remain in England until the end of the war.'[18] He was given a confidential assurance by Milyukov that suitable financial provision would be made, adding for good measure that he believed the tsar 'had a large private fortune of his own.'[19]

While the government was quibbling over money, Kerensky had stated that the tsar would be taken to the harbour under his own supervision and from there he could leave by ship for England. News of this plan caused a storm of protest from the Petrograd Soviet.

In accordance with instructions, Buchanan officially recognised the Provisional Government on 9/22 March. This was vital, as it was imperative to keep Russia in the war. On the following day Buchanan received a cable from the Foreign Office, increasingly concerned at the growing hostility towards the tsar from left-wing extremists. 'You should immediately and urgently press Russian government to give absolute safe conduct to whole imperial family to Port Romanov as soon as possible ... we rely on Russian government ensuring the personal safety of His Majesty and the imperial family.'[20]

Through the Danish Minister in Petrograd, who acted as mediator, the kaiser had promised that German forces would not hinder any ship bringing the imperial family to safety and he even offered to supply a guard of honour. There could of course be no co-operation between Britain and Germany over what was obviously a family matter while the war was still raging. If such co-operation became public knowledge the outcome could be alarming.

Nicholas clearly expected to be allowed to go abroad and the obvious place was the country ruled by his cousin. Before he left *Stavka* he had told the British military attaché that if he could not go to Livadia, his preferred destination would be England. At the Alexander Palace, Nicholas 'sorted my belongings and books, and sorted the things I want to take with me in case I go to England.' The Provisional Government had given a verbal assurance that the contents of Nicholas's request to Prince Lvov of 4/17 March would be adhered to but, as the children's tutor Pierre Gilliard recorded, 'the days passed and our departure was always being postponed.'[21]

The Provisional Government now hesitated, fearing the anger of the extremists if they tried to move the tsar to safety. The delay proved fatal. Feeling in Petrograd was mounting and the press, released from censorship, had a field day with lurid tales of the empress's relationship with Rasputin and accounts of the luxurious lifestyle of the autocratic tsar. The Petrograd Soviet were worried that, once in England, Nicholas would have access to funds that would enable him to mount a counter revolution. With public opinion further roused, the Soviet began demanding that Nicholas be incarcerated in the SS Peter and Paul Fortress.

While the Provisional Government wavered, King George had time to change his mind.

* * *

On 30 March [NS] King George sent a message to Arthur Balfour, the Foreign Secretary. He was now deeply concerned about the proposal that the imperial family should come to England. 'As you are doubtless aware,' Stamfordham wrote on the king's behalf, 'the king has a strong personal friendship for the emperor, and therefore would be glad to do anything to help him in this crisis. But His Majesty cannot help doubting, not only on account of the dangers of the voyage, but on general grounds of expediency, whether it is advisable that the imperial family should take up residence in this country. The king would be glad if you could consult the Prime Minister, as His Majesty understands no definite decision has yet been come to on the subject by the Russian government.'[22]

This message caused consternation. Balfour replied a few days later: 'His Majesty's ministers quite realise the difficulties to which you refer in your letter, but they do not think, unless the position changes, that it is now possible to withdraw the invitation which has been sent, and they therefore trust that the king will consent to adhere to the original invitation, which was sent on the advice of His Majesty's ministers.'[23]

King George rather grudgingly accepted this answer but within forty-eight hours he instructed Stamfordham to write to Balfour again: 'Every day, the king is becoming more concerned about the question of the emperor and the empress coming to this country. His Majesty receives letters from people in all classes of life, known or unknown to him, saying how much the matter is being discussed, not only in clubs, but by working men, and the Labour members in the House of Commons are expressing adverse opinions to the proposal. As you know, from the first the king has thought the presence of the imperial family (especially of the empress) in this country would raise all sorts of difficulties, and I feel sure that you appreciate how awkward it will be for our royal family who are closely connected both with the emperor and the empress.' Many members of the public, he continued, assumed that the asylum offer had originated with the king; others felt if the tsar came to England King George would be placed in a 'very unfair position'. Not only was the tsar regarded as a bloodthirsty tyrant, but the unpopular empress was German born. Perhaps the Russian government could be asked to find some other country of residence for the imperial family?[24]

The reports the king had been receiving had in fact been deliberately exaggerated by the head of Special Branch, Basil Thomson, who wanted to centralise control of domestic intelligence. They certainly rattled the king, who was by now so worried that he instructed Stamfordham to write a second letter to Balfour later that day. 'The king wishes me to write again on the subject of my letter of this morning. He must beg you to represent to the Prime Minister that from all he hears and reads in the press, the residence in this country of the ex-emperor and ex-empress would be strongly resented by the public, and would undoubtedly compromise the position of the king and queen...' Opposition was so strong, he continued, that Britain should be allowed to withdraw agreement to the proposal.[25]

On reading this Balfour faltered. Later that evening he sent a memo to the Prime Minister: 'I think the king *is* placed in an awkward position. If the tsar comes here we are bound publicly to state that *we* (the government) have invited him – and to add (for our own protection) that we did so on the initiative of the Russian government (who will not like it).' Balfour thought that perhaps they should suggest that the tsar go to the South of France or Spain.[26]

* * *

The Spanish monarch was thirty-one-year-old Alfonso XIII. In 1906 he married Princess Victoria Eugenie (Ena) of Battenberg who, as a granddaughter of Queen Victoria, was a cousin of both George V and Empress Alexandra. Her late father Prince Henry of Battenberg had been the brother of Prince Louis, whose wife Victoria was the tsarina's sister.

Few people have had such a dramatic start to married life as Ena and Alfonso. As they returned to the palace in Madrid after their marriage ceremony (which was attended by the future King George V and Queen Mary) a bouquet was thrown from a balcony towards their carriage. Among the flowers was a concealed bomb, which exploded near the carriage's front wheels killing the horses and leaving dead and wounded everywhere. Even Ena's wedding dress was spattered with blood. Alfonso was therefore no stranger to the threat of assassination and was more sensitive to danger than many of his European counterparts. Although Spain was officially neutral during the First World War, the king's Austrian mother, Queen Maria Cristina, made no secret of her support for Germany, while Ena's brothers, Alexander and Maurice, were serving with the British army. King Alfonso now began a huge humanitarian effort. He set up an office in the royal palace where the fifty employees traced missing prisoners and other victims of war. More that 136,000 prisoners of war and more than 70,000 civilians were repatriated due to Alfonso's initiative. They also forwarded letters between prisoners of war and their countries of origin. As part of this humanitarian effort, when Neklioudov, the new Russian Ambassador, presented his credentials at the royal palace King Alfonso took the opportunity to raise the matter of the imperial family's freedom, asking that his urgent request that they be freed be passed to the Provisional Government. Not content with that, Alfonso then approached Britain, the country ruled by his wife's cousin. He asked King George's ambassador what his government were doing about the situation of the tsar.

A few days later the Ambassador Sir Arthur Hardinge, who came from a distinguished family of courtiers and had previously served in St Petersburg, told Alfonso that King George had offered asylum to the tsar. Ironically, this message was given to him on 1 April, which in Britain is April Fool's Day. Alfonso asked him to speak to King George and the British government and request that they protect the imperial family. He also asked his own government to approach the British and work alongside them in order to bring the imperial family to safety. As negotiations with the Provisional Government stalled, Alfonso wrote personally to King George asking him to intervene with the British government. Unfortunately, Alfonso's appeal was made at the very time that Britain was suggesting France or another destination as a suitable residence for the tsar. The Foreign Office had voiced concerns that the tsar's residence in Spain would provoke constant intrigues. During a cabinet meeting on 13 April, Lloyd George said that Spain would only be suitable if that country joined the Allies – yet it was Spain's neutrality that made the idea so attractive both to the Provisional Government and to the other European powers.

***

'Had a talk with Motherdear about Russia and Nicky, she is very much upset about it, all,' King George recorded in his diary on 10 March.[27]

'Motherdear' was Queen Alexandra. The king's mother had been pressing for news of her sister the Dowager Empress Marie Feodorovna, who had now left Kiev and reached the relative safety of the Crimea. The queen expected to be able to maintain contact but her letters to the empress, although received and read by the Provisional Government, were not being delivered. Alexandra wanted to know why. In fact some of the queen's language about events in Russia was so vehement that an official at the Foreign Office in London finally sent a memorandum to her equerry Sir Arthur Davidson explaining the position. 'The government are very apprehensive lest it should be thought that influence is being exerted from England in order to restore the imperial regime. If the revolutionary committee were able to produce any evidence that such was the case the government would be greatly weakened and the whole question of the alliance and of the continuation of the war by Russia might be endangered. The safety of the whole imperial family depends in a great measure on the strictest and most careful avoidance of any form of interference or expression of opinion from England, especially from the king, queen and Queen Alexandra. Even the simplest messages of sympathy may easily be distorted into political views or actions.'[28] This was not easily explained to seventy-two-year-old Queen Alexandra.

On 10 April Stamfordham had another meeting with Lloyd George at 10 Downing Street to emphasise the points made previously. He also reminded him of the abuse to which King George had been exposed after he received his Greek relatives, the brothers of the allegedly pro-German King Constantine of Greece. The tsarina was distrusted in England because of her German background and Stamfordham feared a similar outcry when the king received the tsar and tsarina, which he would be obliged to do as they were his cousins. Stamfordham then reinforced some of the comments which had been made about the inevitable disastrous results of such a meeting.

An article was published in the radical paper *Justice* which condemned both the tsar and his regime and maintained that the invitation had been sent at the behest of the royal family. In London a rally had been held to celebrate the downfall of the Russian autocracy. The British people, wearied by the war, were turning more and more towards the socialists. In response Lloyd George agreed to approach the French government, admitting that he had not realised the asylum question was so serious.

Stamfordham then went to see Balfour, concerned that Buchanan had rather taken it for granted that the imperial family were coming to England and that it was only the need to clear up a few matters that was causing the delay. He expressed surprise that the ambassador had obviously not been informed that the matter was being reconsidered and that the previous offer had not been binding. Balfour meekly promised to draft a telegram to Buchanan immediately.

Suspicion of Russia's intentions in the Middle East and Asia, which threatened British India, as well as her ambitions for access to the Dardanelles, all fuelled the deeply held feelings against the tsar. In April 1917 the *Daily Telegraph* weighed in: 'We sincerely hope that the British government has no intention of giving the tsar and his wife asylum in England. In any case, such an intention, should it actually emerge, will be frustrated. This must be stated quite frankly.'

The king and his government were now against Nicholas coming to England, but for different reasons. King George was afraid that his throne could be in danger, while from the government's point of view it was vital to keep national unity intact; the cost to the country could be the loss of the war. They also needed a closer understanding with the Provisional Government and it was essential to keep Russia as a wartime ally.

On 13 April the doubts were discussed in the War Cabinet, without mentioning the king's involvement in the withdrawal. Spain or the South of France were mentioned as possible places of residence. Balfour urged the Cabinet Secretary to 'try and keep an eye on anything that may be put into the War Cabinet minutes likely to hurt the king's feelings.'[29] King George's role in the affair was not to be made public.

Meanwhile the Provisional Government had decided to examine the correspondence of the tsar and tsarina and they therefore hoped that the family's immediate departure would not be insisted upon. This delay suited both King George and his government. A message was sent to Buchanan marked 'personal and most confidential', asking him to henceforth avoid the subject. Perhaps, the message continued, it would be better if France was the tsar's destination.

Buchanan agreed. He had just received a visit from William Thorne, a British radical socialist politician, who was insistent that 'we must not allow him [Nicholas] to stop in England under any circumstances, so long as the war lasted.' The Provisional Government wanted to get the tsar out of Russia as soon as possible, 'without exciting suspicions of the extremists,' but if the tsar came to England, Buchanan continued, 'the consequences might be very serious ... Perhaps it would be well to sound them [the French] on the subject and, in the event of their consenting, I might tell the Minister for Foreign Affairs that the revolution, which had been welcomed with such enthusiasm in England, had so indisposed the British public against the old regime that the presence of the emperor in England might provoke demonstrations that would cause serious embarrassment.'[30]

On 17 April Lord Hardinge wrote a private letter to Lord Bertie, the British Ambassador in Paris, asking if he thought France would be willing to give asylum to the tsar. 'It is a situation of grave embarrassment here,' he continued, 'for naturally the king, who is devoted to the emperor, would not like to show him the cold shoulder.'[31] It was surely a little late for that sentiment. Stamfordham asked Bertie the same question, adding that the king had been against the asylum offer from the beginning. Bertie's reply was negative; he did not think France would welcome the couple. 'The empress is not only a Boche by birth but in sentiment. She did all she could to bring about an understanding with Germany. She is regarded as a criminal or a criminal lunatic and the ex-emperor as a criminal from his weakness and submission to her promptings.'[32]

Britain now effectively abandoned the Romanovs. From the Foreign Office, Lord Hardinge explained the change of heart to Buchanan – stressing that the radicals and socialists were against giving asylum to the tsar and would attribute the decision to do so to the king. This was especially true as 'owing to his relationship and affection for the emperor he will, as the king told me himself, go out of his way to be civil to him.' By May Buchanan was telling Milyukov that '... we should probably refuse permission to any members of the imperial family to reside in England during the war.'[33] In fact, this had already been done.

* * *

In Russia, the grand dukes were unaware of this.

In the spring of 1917 Grand Duke George Michaelovich was staying with his cousin Grand Duke Michael Alexandrovich, the

Tsar's brother, at Gatchina, south of Petrograd. George was now anxious to join his wife Marie and their daughters in London and, having resigned from the army, wrote to Prince Lvov to ask the Provisional Government's permission to do so. George told his wife that he and Michael 'have decided to leave our poor country never to return.' The request was refused, as the Provisional Government considered the absence of any member of the family from Russia 'undesirable.'[34] He then went to see Sir George Buchanan, hoping that the embassy might take charge of forwarding letters to his wife. This request was refused, ostensibly on the orders of the Foreign Office. He also raised the prospect of joining Marie but was informed that the grand dukes would not be permitted to go to England.

On receipt of her husband's letter breaking this news the grand duchess went to see Lord Hardinge at the Foreign Office. He proved 'as hard as nails,' and maintained that the grand dukes were not in any danger.[35] With the British Embassy refusing to take letters, George went to see the Norwegian Minister Prebensen, who proved most helpful. George also said he would write to his wife's cousin Queen Maud of Norway and 'beg her to forward my correspondence through the Norwegian Legation in London.'[36] Then an order went out from the Provisional Government forbidding the embassies and legations from forwarding any letters and parcels on behalf of the Romanovs.

On 4 April Buchanan cabled the Foreign Office to report that Grand Duke Michael had called at the embassy the previous day 'and asked me to enquire whether His Majesty's Government have any objections to him and the Grand Duke George [Michaelovich] coming to England should the Russian government consent to them doing so.' Until he knew London's views he would not approach the Russian government on the subject. Michael 'also asked whether I could help him transfer money from Petrograd to London.'

On his return to Russia in 1914 Michael had telephoned his cousin Princess Victoria, the king's sister, and asked if he could pay the rent and expenses incurred on his rented property in Sussex by transferring money to her. Since then, he had 'been in the habit of sending Princess Victoria from time to time certain sums ... but he wanted now to send over a lump sum of which he did not, however, name the amount. I told him I was afraid this would be difficult ....,' Buchanan added.[37]

It seems that Princess Victoria disliked the whole arrangement but in the present circumstances did not want to appear to be acting unkindly towards her cousin.

During his pre-war exile in England Michael had rented Paddockhurst, a property near Crawley in West Sussex belonging to Lord Cowdray. By 1916 the grand duke was finding that the cost was becoming excessive, so instead he rented Ely Grange at Frant, also in Sussex, and the arrangement with Princess Victoria continued. When the money reached England it was sent on to Madame Johnson-Missievitch, the mother of Michael's secretary Nicholas Johnson, who was living in the rented property. Michael had been generous before he left England. He had placed his expensive sports car, an Opel, at the disposal of the War Office and offered them Paddockhurst as well. In fact only the stables and outhouses were used, as the War Office was worried about damage clauses in Michael's lease – but it does not negate the fact that the grand duke had made the offer. Yet however generous Michael had been, the prospect of a whole host of Russian grand dukes coming to England sent a shiver of fear through the palace. '...I *do* trust that the whole question of the Emperor and Empress of Russia's coming to England and also that of the proposal now made that the Grand Dukes George and Michael should do the same will be reconsidered,' Stamfordham wrote to Balfour's private secretary on 5 April. 'It will be very hard on the king and arouse much public comment if not resentment.'[38]

On 16 April Buchanan wrote again. Grand Duke Michael wanted to transfer 100,000 roubles to England and had also requested an answer regarding the projected visit. Grand Duke George was so eager to rejoin his family that he even suggested coming incognito under the name Mikaeloff. It made no difference. The reply sent to Buchanan was unequivocal. Visits of the grand dukes were to be deprecated, unless they were in personal danger, in which case 'they would receive the asylum that has always been open to victims of political disturbance.' Surely Grand Duke Michael could arrange to pay 100,000 roubles into Barings' office in Petrograd for transfer to whoever he wanted in England? It was 'unnecessary and undesirable' to use Princess Victoria as an intermediary at the present time, he continued.[39]

On 28 April a remittance was sent to Princess Victoria from the grand duke through the Ministry of Finance and Baring Brothers. 'Bearing in mind the extremely delicate position of the imperial family and the suspicions entertained by the Provisional Government towards correspondence with the English royal family,' Lord Robert Cecil of the Foreign Office told Buchanan, 'I think that, unless there is some special reason which is recognised and approved by the Provisional Government, it is not advisable that he [Michael] should send further remittances' to the princess.[40] It could only give rise to misconceptions and further difficulties.

* * *

Meanwhile, Buchanan had been informed that the government was 'sounding out the French' with regard to the tsar and tsarina receiving asylum there, but he was warned that he 'should not hold out any hopes that they could be received in England during the war.'[41] If the Russians were informed about this they did not take the hint. Some weeks later, when the situation in Petrograd had eased slightly, the Provisional Government again asked 'at what date a cruiser could be sent to fetch the former tsar and his family.' Alexander Kerensky, now Prime Minister of the Provisional Government, recalled that Buchanan then informed him of 'the British government's final refusal to give refuge to the former Emperor of Russia.' According to the historian Alexander Bokhanov, the wording used to the new Russian Foreign Minister was that 'the government of Britain cannot advise His Majesty to extend hospitality to people whose sympathy with Germany is more than well known.'[42]

In his memoirs Lloyd George blamed the failure of the asylum offer on the Provisional Government. Buchanan maintained that 'our offer remained open and was never withdrawn,'[43] falsifying his memoirs, according to his daughter, under the threat of his pension being stopped.

To protect the monarch further, in 1931 Stamfordham added a postscript in his own hand to his letter to Balfour of 6 April 1917: 'Most people appear to think that the [asylum] invitation was initiated by the king, whereas it was *his government* who did so.'[44]

For many years the fiction was maintained that it was Lloyd George and the British government who had denied asylum to the tsar. 'I understand … that Mr Lloyd George was not responsible for the decision, but that it is not expedient to say who was….,' a Foreign Office official minuted dryly.[45]

* * *

Although the British government had refused entry to the Romanov men, there was in fact a grand duke already living in England. Grand Duke Michael Michaelovich was a cousin of the tsar. Born in 1861, he was one of seven children of Grand Duke Michael Nicolaievich (a son of Tsar Nicholas I) and Grand Duchess Olga Feodorovna. His brothers Grand Dukes George, Nicholas, Sergei and Alexander (Sandro) Michaelovich, the husband of Grand Duchess Xenia, were all in Russia. In 1891 Michael was banished by Alexander III for contracting a morganatic marriage with Sophie von Merenberg, a granddaughter of Pushkin. Although a commoner she had an impressive list of relatives, being a niece of Queen Sophie of Sweden and a cousin of the Queen Mother Emma of the Netherlands. Sophie was created Countess de Torby by her uncle the Grand Duke of Luxembourg and she and Michael eventually settled at Kenwood House in Hampstead. In 1912 Michael asked the tsar to allow Sophie to be given a title by King George V, a request that the king said it was not in his power to grant.

In 1916 Michael had written to warn the tsar about the deteriorating situation in Russia. He was now devastated by news of the revolution. On 11 March 1917 he went to see King George and, the monarch recorded, 'we discussed the idea of poor Nicky coming to England.'[46]

The revolution also meant the loss of Michael's Russian income. The grand duke wrote to Balfour that he was now left 'entirely without means for his living requirements'. He asked him to arrange with Sir George Buchanan to 'have all his securities placed in the name of Drummond's Bank so that a temporary loan could be negotiated.' The request was refused with regret. Michael and Sophie had to sublet Kenwood and move to a smaller house at 3 Cambridge Gate, Regent's Park.

Meanwhile, King George and Queen Mary agreed to advance a loan of £10,000 without securities.[47] This kindness did not extend to Michael's Russian relatives.

* * *

King George's apparent change of mind about the asylum question is seen in a different context by what he did for the tsar's elder sister Xenia, the king's favourite cousin. Learning via Sir George Buchanan that Xenia was still in Petrograd, King George sent a young officer from the Highland Light Infantry out to Russia on a secret mission to help her.

Xenia and her elder sons Andrew and Feodor were in her Petrograd palace by the Moika Canal and all her cars had been requisitioned. The officer took Xenia, her sons and two attendants through the snowy streets by sledge to the station. She left Petrograd on 25 March [OS], her forty-second birthday. From there she went by train to join her younger children, mother, husband and sister Olga in the Crimea. With the family all together at Sandro's estate of Ai-Todor it would surely be possible for the British to eventually rescue them all.

When the officer came back to London, Lloyd George apparently was livid because he was afraid England would be over-run by Romanovs. The king later presented the officer with a dirk – a ceremonial dagger – in recognition of his help to Xenia. The officer's grandson later made contact with Xenia's granddaughter and told her the story. He also said that, according to his grandfather, King George was persuaded to write the letter to Lloyd George rescinding permission for Nicholas to come to England because 'there was also a suspicion at the time that MI5 had been penetrated by a mole sympathetic to the Bolshevik cause. Anything written had to be in code to preserve total secrecy.' The threat posed by this suspected mole put the royal family in a very difficult position, he said.[48]

* * *

The king's decision to deny Nicholas asylum has usually been explained by fear for his own throne. Family ties were no reason to risk the future of the monarchy. 'He did not hesitate to make a decision as a head of state,' Prince Nicholas Romanov said in an interview. 'He acted not as "cousin Georgie" but as King George V... His duty was to his country and his people...,' although Prince Nicholas did not think that the presence of the imperial family would have caused the 'phlegmtic British people' to revolt. There was certainly not the surge of republican feeling which had been so in evidence in England in the 1870s.[49]

Dominic Lieven explained that 'the British royal family was most anxious not to be associated with an autocratic regime which had collapsed.' Both Prince Nicholas and Professor Lieven agreed though, that had the situations been reversed, the tsar would have acted with his heart and welcomed George and his family to Russia.[50]

The Duke of Edinburgh also defended King George's role. 'George V's involvement was in March 1917 just after the tsar had abdicated,' he told Robert Hardman in an interview in the *Daily Telegraph* in 1994. 'At that time there was no threat to his life. There was a very strong revolutionary movement throughout Europe. The king effectively said don't let's stir it up by bringing him here. After that, things deteriorated. Then I think the window of opportunity had gone. At the time of the window, it did not seem to be necessary.' George was in 'an impossible situation....' the duke continued. All monarchs had to 'compromise between their family interests and their national interests.' King George had his empire to think about.

There is also that nagging question about the tsar's private wealth. Was George afraid that he would be obliged to support the imperial family in the manner to which they had become accustomed?

King George's fault lies not only in his *volte-face* but in his attempt to cover it up and deceive posterity. To this day it remains his most controversial act. It is to be hoped that Nicholas never learnt about his cousin's apparent betrayal.

In the spring of 1917 there was no immediate danger to the imperial family and King George could not have foreseen the Bolshevik takeover later that year. Only after Lenin's takeover of power may he finally have realised the extreme danger in which Nicholas had been placed and, perhaps, try to do something about it.

4

The Scandinavian Connection

'The queen's family has pushed my family from the throne.'

'Heard about the revolution in Russia,' King Haakon of Norway recorded briefly in his diary on 15 March [NS] during a skiing trip with the explorer Fridtjof Nansen.[1] The next day he was informed by Prebensen, the Norwegian Minister in Petrograd, that Nicholas had abdicated and that it was believed that Alexei would now be tsar.

Haakon was closely related to the Russian imperial family. Born Prince Carl of Denmark in 1872, he was the second son of the dowager empress's eldest brother King Frederik VIII of Denmark, making him the tsar's first cousin. Charles, as Carl preferred to be called, was an officer in the Danish navy when in 1896 he married his cousin Princess Maud, youngest daughter of the future King Edward VII and Queen Alexandra. In 1905 Norway dissolved the union with the Swedish crown and Prince Charles of Denmark was elected to the Norwegian throne. He took the name Haakon VII and the couple relocated to Kristiania, Norway's capital. Maud, the sister of the future King George V and first cousin of both Nicholas and Alexandra, was now Queen of Norway.

When war broke out in 1914 Norway remained neutral. In December King Haakon and his brother King Christian X of Denmark held a meeting in Malmø with King Gustav V of Sweden to affirm solidarity and neutrality. This did not allay Haakon's fears that the pro-German King Gustav would be drawn into the fighting on Germany's side. As the conflict dragged on, Haakon was concerned that either the Allies or the Central Powers would exert pressure on his kingdom. He feared that Britain or Germany would demand use of the strategic naval bases along the Norwegian coast.

Haakon was fond of his cousin the tsar, with whom he had stayed in touch during the war. 'I see the kaiser has become very angry with you allies [*sic*] because you didn't accept his peace offer,' he wrote to Nicholas on 29 January 1917. 'I fear the brutal way he will fight the war in this year will look like the other cruelties he has already introduced in modern warfare...'[2]

The tsar replied on 12/25 February: 'I often think about you and your country too, because we all know what difficult times you've had and still undergo. Nothing is worse than trying to satisfy two ... different opinions...' The winter in Russia was harsh and snow storms were preventing regular railway deliveries. 'You can imagine what it means when the most necessary supplies ... remain standing somewhere instead of being used in the big cities and factories,' Nicholas continued. 'Of course, it makes people uncertain and nervous.' It was Nicholas's last letter to Haakon and he ended with the traditional greeting: 'With our fondest love to you both I remain, dearest Charles, your devoted cousin and friend Nicky.'[3]

Meanwhile, in London Lloyd George was enquiring whether Bergen, on Norway's west coast, would be a suitable alternative to exile in Denmark for the imperial family. The empress had told Baroness Buxhoeveden that, if they had to go abroad at all, she would prefer to go there as she felt that the climate would suit Alexei. The Norwegian Social Democrats were already reported to be saying that Alexei should be sent to Norway 'for the sake of his health'. Lord Hardinge thought that the Provisional Government would prefer that the tsar be sent to Murmansk. He would then be under their control until he boarded a British ship, whereas 'if he travelled to Bergen he would be free as soon as he crossed the Russian frontier.'[4]

This solution would also place King Haakon in a difficult position. In 1913, the Norwegians had elected a government who favoured a republic rather than a monarchy. Having the ex-autocrat of Russia in Norway would not go down well with the people. Christian Lange, the Secretary of the Interparliamentary Union, had just returned to Kristiania from Russia. He told Haakon that the chances of *any* member of the Romanov family taking the Russian throne were slim. There were also rumours that the empress had been a German spy. Haakon and Maud's only son, Crown Prince Olav, who was fourteen at the time, recalled this period in his memoirs: 'I also remember that at home, by the end of the war, they talked about how the Russian relatives fared, because we didn't know much. With the family in England there was contact throughout the war, through a courier. But regarding the situation in Russia, one didn't know more than what the newspapers could say about how the revolution went, and there were many rumours. I don't think there had been any warm connection at all really. Our Russian relatives did live very isolated.'[5]

In May Baron Nicholas Wrangel, who had had been ADC to Grand Duke Michael Alexandrovich for many years, arrived in Kristiania and announced himself at the royal palace. 'General [*sic*] Wrangel from Russia [came] in order to ask me from Misha [Michael] if his son can get permission to come here to this country,' Haakon recorded in his diary. Michael also wanted to send a jewel box to Kristiania through the Norwegian Legation in Petrograd.[6]

When Grand Duke Michael was allowed to return to Russia on the outbreak of war in 1914 he had travelled via Norway, Sweden and Finland with his morganatic wife Natasha and their son George. On his way through Norway he had lunch with Haakon and Maud at the royal family's summer estate at Bygdøy, while Natasha and George remained in the Grand Hotel in Kristiania. Natasha was never received at the Russian court so presumably it was not thought appropriate for Haakon and Maud to receive her either.

Although George was the son of a grand duke and a grandson of Tsar Alexander III, he was a commoner. When he was born on 6 August 1910 Natasha was still married to her second husband Vladimir Wulfert – so although Michael was the father, by law the child was George Vladimirovich Wulfert. That November Natasha was divorced, the decree was backdated and Wulfert relinquished paternity for a payment of 200,000 roubles (about £20,000 in 1910). George's birth certificate was doctored and the Tsar gave him the name of George Michaelovich Brasov, but he was not granted a title.

Now, faced with Michael's request to give sanctuary to his son, King Haakon promised Wrangel that little George could come to Norway – but nothing happened. Nor is it known if the jewel box Michael referred to was ever sent. At that time, with the moderate Provisional Government in charge, there seemed no cause for alarm over little George's safety. It was only later, when things became more serious, that Michael decided that something had to be done.

* * *

The Russian revolution sent shockwaves throughout the courts of Europe but, of all the neutral countries, Denmark had the strongest family reasons to assist the Romanovs.

King Christian X, who succeeded his father Frederik VIII in 1912, was King Haakon's elder brother. More at home in the army than on the throne, Christian has been described as a 'stiff, stubborn and intractable' man, infused with 'strict military discipline.'[7] He had a hot temper, was said to treat his home as a barracks and was hard and uncompromising with his sons Frederik and Knud. This was not the complete picture. In private Christian was a different person and, in the company of friends, could be an entertaining companion. His daughter-in-law Queen Ingrid of Denmark later recalled a man who could be moved to tears by organ music.

His wife also exercised a beneficial influence on him. The German-born Queen Alexandrine was the daughter of Grand Duke Frederick Franz III of Mecklenburg-Schwerin and Grand Duchess Anastasia Michaelovna of Russia, a cousin of Tsar Alexander III. Alexandrine was a very private person, whose main interest was music (a passion inherited by her elder son). Although she occupied herself most with the children's upbringing, Christian was not above crawling on the floor and playing games with his sons. There are 'countless photographs' of him skating or walking with younger members of the family, showing the more human side of a man 'who definitely did not fit any stereotypes. He could be extremely warm and sensitive when he was in secure surroundings.'[8]

At 6 feet 4 inches, Christian X was probably the tallest monarch in Denmark's history. In his youth his grandfather often joked that he needed to stand on a chair to talk to him. At a reception he overheard a lady remark to her friend that the king was 'not very good looking'. 'No,' he exclaimed loudly, 'but his hearing's good!'[9]

He felt more at home among his former comrades from the regiment and in keeping with these military preferences the court became more formal. Sir Frederick Ponsonby considered him 'a much cleverer and stronger character' than his father.[10] Christian had known the tsar since childhood, when their grandparents King Christian IX and Queen Louise held family gatherings every summer at Fredensborg Slot, 25 miles north of Copenhagen. Here light-hearted amusements, games and practical jokes filled their days.

Christian was close to his brother and, like Haakon, remained pro-British – but with a German-born wife he was in a difficult position when war broke out. Queen Alexandrine helped relatives on both sides to keep in touch, copying letters in her own hand before sending them on.

In July 1915 King Christian sent Hans Niels Andersen, founder of the East-Asiatic Company, Denmark's largest trading empire, to Tsarskoe Selo with an offer to act as mediator. Andersen made several trips between London, Paris and Berlin but the tsar turned down the king's offer of mediation.

The queen had four uncles living in Russia – her mother's brothers Grand Dukes Alexander, Sergei, Nicholas and George Michaelovich. Her other uncle, Grand Duke Michael Michaelovich, lived in England. To complicate matters further, Queen Alexandrine's sister Cecilie was married to the kaiser's eldest son Crown Prince William of Germany. News of the tsar's abdication reputedly prompted King Christian to tell his Prime Minister Carl Theodore Zahle that 'the queen's family has pushed my family from the throne.'[11]

***

On 24 March [NS] 1917 the British Ambassador in Copenhagen, Sir Ralph Paget, told the Foreign Office that the King of Denmark and his uncle, Prince Valdemar (brother of the dowager empress) 'are much disquieted by reports they have received from Russia which go to show that the stability of the present government is very dubious. It might be upset by the Socialist party who it is to be feared may be influenced to conclude a separate peace.

German agents and money are working desperately to this end.' They were hoping for the best but knew they must be prepared for the worst, he added. Three days later Sir Ralph was still reporting that King Christian was 'seriously perturbed' about the revolutionary events.[12] Little Denmark seemed an unlikely saviour for the Romanovs but the king was very fortunate to have a remarkable man in a key position at this critical time.

Harald Scavenius, the forty-five-year-old Danish Minister in Petrograd, was from a famous family of diplomats, ministers and entrepreneurs. His cousin Erik Scavenius was the Danish Foreign Minister. Harald, who was fluent in Russian, French and English, had been at his post since he took over from his cousin Otto Scavenius in 1912. He and his wife Anna Sophie Steensen, whom he married in 1909, lived in an apartment at 11 Millionaya Street near the Winter Palace and Harald brought the cook and several other servants from his Danish estate of Gjorslev to run the household. He was a fiery man with rare courage and a strong sense of duty, who once went into the street to prevent a man from being lynched by the soldiers. His typist, 26-year-old Esther Aksel-Hansen, described him as 'a funny little stammering man, but terribly nice.'[13]

Soon after the February revolution Harald Scavenius was instructed by his Foreign Ministry to report on the situation in Russia and the possibility of the departure of the tsar and his family abroad. The matter would naturally have been discussed with King Christian, who received many of Scavenius's reports about the political situation in Russia during 1917 and 1918. The result was an approach to the German Chancellor Theobold von Bethmann-Hollweg to see if Germany could rescue the tsar. The kaiser was doubtful. 'There are two fighting lines of German and Russian troops facing each other between him and me,' he said. Nevertheless, a message was conveyed via neutral Denmark to Kerensky and the Provisional Government that 'if a hair of the Russian imperial family's head should be injured, I would hold him personally responsible...'[14]

On 22 March (the very day the British government decided to receive the imperial family) the Danish Prime Minister Carl Theodore Zahle mentioned the subject in his diary. The government wanted the tsar, tsarina, their children and the dowager empress to take up residence in Denmark. The question had been raised either by him or the Foreign Minister Erik Scavenius during an audience with the king.

It is not known whether the initial approach was made by the Russian Provisional Government but the possibility of asylum in Denmark was also being raised in London. The matter then seems to have been quietly dropped in Copenhagen, as it was felt that Nicholas II's fate was an internal issue for Russia. The Danes therefore concentrated on helping the only Danish-born princess living in Russian territory. This was the king's aunt, the Dowager Empress Marie Feodorovna, born Princess Dagmar of Denmark, a daughter of King Christian IX.

***

Immediately after the tsar's abdication, Harald Scavenius telegraphed Kiev, where the dowager empress was currently living, asking for news of her welfare. On 4 March [OS] he heard that she was well and not in any danger. A few days later the tsar and tsarina were arrested and Harald received assurances from the Provisional Government that the same fate would not befall the Empress Marie. He asked permission to maintain contact with the dowager empress and requested that any letters from the Danish royal family would be delivered to her promptly and unread. This request, although approved by the Provisional Government, was refused by the Petrograd Soviet. Scavenius therefore had to pass on this news to Copenhagen.

By late March the Empress Marie was at Ai-Todor, the Crimean estate owned by Grand Duchess Xenia's husband Grand Duke Alexander Michaelovich ('Sandro') the uncle of the Danish Queen. The dowager empress was now cut off from her relatives in Denmark, as well as from her sister Queen Alexandra in England. Her only contact with Scavenius was through official, censored channels and to get round this all telegrams to or on behalf of the empress were sent via Prince and Princess Youssoupov at their nearby estate of Koreiz, which had a telegraph office in the vicinity.

Letters sent by the Danish Foreign Ministry or the Embassy were returned, including five from Empress Marie's brother Prince Valdemar. The Provisional Government asked Scavenius not to send correspondence out of Russia for the Romanovs.

Scavenius tried to obtain Kerensky's permission to visit the dowager empress but the Foreign Office in Copenhagen told him that he must not leave his post. His request for a Red Cross delegate to visit her also came to nothing.

By April the revolution had reached the Crimea. Soviets were established in Yalta and Sevastopol to take control of the area and these rival Soviets both claimed jurisdiction over the Romanovs.

* * *

In Sweden there was another close relative of the imperial family, the tsarina's cousin Princess Margaret, known as 'Daisy'. Thirty-five-year-old Daisy was the elder daughter of Prince Arthur, Duke of Connaught (third son of Queen Victoria) and Princess Louise Margaret of Prussia; in 1905 at St George's Chapel, Windsor, she had married Prince Gustav Adolf of Sweden, grandson and eventual heir of King Oscar II. Daisy feared that the pro-German Swedish royal family might resent a British princess, especially as her cousin Maud was Queen of Norway, a country newly independent from the Swedish crown. She need not have worried, receiving a warm welcome in her new home.

Another link with Russia was formed in 1908 when Gustav Adolf's brother William married the tsar's cousin, eighteen-year old Grand Duchess Marie Pavlovna. 'I like her a lot, she is so intelligent, quick and talkative,' Daisy said after the newlyweds visited their summer home, Sofiero.[15] When Marie's son Lennart was born the following year, Daisy supported her young sister-in-law through the hours of labour and held the chloroform-soaked mask as she gave birth.

In 1914 Marie divorced Prince William and returned to Russia, leaving Lennart to be raised by his relatives in Sweden. Her status as a former member of the Swedish royal family would be a great help after the Russian revolution.

Sweden remained neutral during the First World War although the government maintained their right to trade with both sides in the conflict, a situation that was particularly favourable to Germany.

The war caused problems for British-born Daisy. She was now the crown princess, as her father-in-law had succeeded as

King Gustav V in 1907. His well-known pro-German feelings were accentuated by those of his wife Victoria, born a princess of Baden, who was a cousin of the kaiser (through her mother) and also a cousin of Prince Max of Baden, who in 1918 would be the last Chancellor of Imperial Germany. Victoria made no secret of her German sympathies. Daisy, who through her father the Duke of Connaught was also the kaiser's cousin, was staunchly pro-British.

There was no fear of Sweden being dragged into the war, although Daisy found the situation difficult. As crown princess of a neutral country she kept relatives on both sides in touch with one another by copying letters in her own handwriting for despatch to a relation on the opposing side. In addition she took on a more active role, organising parcels of clothing and tobacco to be sent to prisoners of war and setting up an organisation to trace and send messages to them, and founding a sewing society to knit socks and roll bandages for the troops. She also published two books about her gardens, which were sold in aid of war charities. Then in 1917 came two bitter blows. On 14 March her mother the Duchess of Connaught, whom Daisy had not seen since before the war, died suddenly and she was unable to return home for the funeral. This was quickly followed by news of the Russian revolution.

Despite grief over her mother, Daisy was concerned for the fate of her cousins the tsar and tsarina. She had known Nicholas since her childhood and had been at Balmoral when he and Alexandra visited Queen Victoria in 1896, bringing their baby daughter Olga. Now she heard rumours that they were imprisoned in the SS Peter and Paul Fortress in Petrograd. Daisy immediately went to see King Gustav but the news was not reassuring. 'I have spoken with my father-in-law,' she wrote to Queen Mary on 3 April, 'but he believes he cannot do anything.'[16] Later the crown princess told Queen Mary about unrest in Sweden, which she said was partly owing to the shortage of food, after America's entry into the war placed restrictions on international trade, 'and partly owing to the Russian revolution. The Socialist party mean to have several more or less fundamental laws changed and I fear that my father-in-law will have anything but a pleasant time! My mother-in-law too has contrived to make herself more and more unpopular and that falls back on him, people even go as far as comparing her to Alicky [the tsarina] and say she is just as reactionary!...'[17]

It was clear that warm-hearted Daisy would not be able to do anything for her unfortunate Russian relatives.

* * *

At the end of May, Harald Scavenius telegraphed Prince Valdemar to update him on the situation regarding the dowager empress. 'Her Majesty is in good health and maintains a surprising calm,' he reported. 'However, it would be foolish to deny that events have made a severe impression on her and, in particular, that the lack of knowledge as to the tsar's fate has heavily affected Her Majesty's frame of mind. To be completely without news from Denmark or England is also depressing. The empress often talks about Your Royal Highness and about Denmark and I believe that Her Majesty is longing to be at home again and surrounded by a sympathetic atmosphere.'[18]

One of the events that had so upset the empress was an early morning house search of Ai-Todor by rough and ready sailors from the Sevastopol Soviet. One late April morning the Romanovs were woken by Soviet sailors and forced to watch while they searched for anti-revolutionary propaganda. Clothes were strewn across the floor, curtains torn down, carpets ripped up and furniture scattered about. Forced to get out of bed, with barely time to throw on a dressing gown, the empress sat behind a screen for hours while sailors ransacked drawers and cupboards looking for what they described as compromising documents. Finally her letters, diaries and even her Danish Bible were taken away – but they missed her jewel box standing on the table.

Sandro sent a formal complaint to the Provisional Government but, although an inquiry was held, none of the letters and diaries were returned. However, the empress' old Danish Bible, seized as a 'revolutionary book', was returned a few weeks later.

A Special Commissar from the Provisional Government now moved in to Ai-Todor with twenty heavily-armed Soviet sailors. The entrance was patrolled by sentries and if the family wanted to go out they had to make an application in advance. Letters arrived with their imperial titles crossed out. Xenia received one addressed to the 'former Grand Duchess Xenia.'[19]

The family now became extremely worried about the valuables left in their Petrograd palaces. Prince Felix Youssoupov, who was married to Xenia's daughter Princess Irina, was not under arrest and made several trips to the capital during this period to save whatever he could. He had mixed success. He was too late to save the dowager empress's major jewels, which had already been sent to Moscow, but Felix managed to cut her favourite portrait of her late husband Alexander III out of its frame. In the Youssoupov palaces in Petrograd and Moscow many of the family's treasures were concealed under Felix's supervision, in the hope they would be able to retrieve them in better times. Much of this haul was later discovered by the Bolsheviks, but many people believe there are still hidden caches waiting to be found. However, Felix did manage to bring back two Rembrandts, which he cut from their frames.

Meanwhile Irina, who accompanied him on one of these trips, went to see Kerensky in the Winter Palace, where he was living in the rooms of Alexander III. Bravely, she asked him to ensure better treatment for her grandmother the dowager empress.

Felix informed Buchanan that the dowager empress was under arrest and he protested to the Minister of Foreign Affairs about this treatment of the British King's aunt. The result was that by the end of June the empress was permitted to send letters through the British and Danish Embassies. The Danish Foreign Ministry also forwarded letters from the empress to her sister Queen Alexandra in England.

In the spring Prince Valdemar wrote to the Provisional Government. Although the contents of the letter are unknown, it was probably a request to allow the dowager empress to leave Russia. The communication was sent via the Danish Foreign Service for forwarding and, as Professor Bent Jensen states, the request was probably refused.[20]

In June Scavenius was recalled to Copenhagen for urgent discussions.

Prisoners of the Provisional Government

'Bundled off in the middle of the night...'

It is inconceivable that King George V was not kept informed about the conditions under which his relatives were imprisoned during the final year of their lives – but after the withdrawal of the offer of asylum there is a long, unexplained gap in the files in the Royal Archives and also in the National Archives. Yet the monarch did show some concern. On 4 June George wrote to his former private secretary, the now retired Lord Knollys. 'I own that I feel very anxious for the safety of the emperor,' he told him. '...If he once gets inside the walls of the prison of St Peter and St Paul, I doubt he will ever come out alive.'[1]

Then there is silence.

* * *

King George was also battling with his own problems. In the wake of the Russian revolution, he was nervous. Whispers were circulating about the king's patriotism because of his German name and ancestry. The House of Saxe-Coburg-Gotha had been on the British throne since Queen Victoria's marriage to her cousin Prince Albert in 1840, and Victoria once said that the German connection was the one she would most like to cultivate. Before that, Britain had been ruled by the House of Hanover, which had been imported from Germany in 1714 because of a lack of Protestant heirs to the throne. The royal family were therefore undisputedly Teutonic. 'I wonder what my little German friend has to say to me,'

Lloyd George remarked, on being summoned to see George V at Buckingham Palace in 1915.[2]

Queen Mary, born Princess Victoria Mary of Teck, was a German princess. Her grandfather Duke Alexander of Württemberg had contracted a morganatic marriage with a Hungarian countess, meaning that their son Francis, Queen Mary's father, had no succession rights in Württemberg. In 1866 Francis married the rather large thirty-two-year-old Princess Mary Adelaide of Cambridge, a granddaughter of George III, whose family were desperate to find 'Fat Mary' a husband. Francis was created Prince, and later Duke, of Teck by the King of Württemberg. So although Queen Mary was born in Kensington Palace and raised in England, her father's family was undeniably German.

There were also the king and queen's relatives, who had names such as Battenberg, Teck and Schleswig-Holstein. By 1917, with anti-German feeling at its height, all these connections were embarrassing and inconvenient to say the least. The writer H. G. Wells referred to George's 'alien and uninspiring court', which prompted the king to respond 'I may be uninspiring, but I'll be damned if I'm an alien.'[3] Things came to a head in May 1917, when at a small Buckingham Palace dinner party Lady Maud Warrender, a lady of impeccable aristocratic connections who sometimes acted as Queen Mary's lady-in-waiting, told one of the guests that there were rumours about the king's patriotism. The remark was overheard by King George, who was mortified.

With the German origins of the king and his relatives being attacked, something had to be done to publicly show George's patriotism. Letters had already been arriving from concerned countrymen, worried about anti-monarchist feeling. Stamfordham put them all in a file marked 'Unrest in the Country'.

Then on 13 June 1917 fourteen German Gotha bombers scored a direct hit on a school in Poplar, East London; 162 people were killed, eighteen of them children. The connection between the name of these bombers and the British royal family could not be ignored.

What was needed was a rebranding of the royal house by giving it an unassailably English name. In fact, since that Buckingham Palace dinner Stamfordham had already been giving the matter a great deal of thought and had suggested various new names. Guelph was discarded as too Germanic; Fitzroy sounded like an illegitimate line of the royal family; Plantagenet, Tudor and Tudor-Stuart were also deemed inappropriate. With the King pressing urgently for a solution, by now Stamfordham was at his wits' end. Then on 13 June, the very day the Gotha's bombs landed on the school, he sent a memorandum to the Prime Minister suggesting 'The Royal House of Windsor'. This met with immediate approval. Windsor was not only the name of the royal family's oldest home, but it suggested stability and continuity. It was an inspired choice.

King George had already directed all his relatives with German titles to assume English surnames. On 6 June Prince Louis of Battenberg wrote to tell his daughter Princess Louise that they would have to give up their German titles. 'It has been suggested that we should turn our name into English, viz: Battenhill or Mountbatten,' he wrote. 'We incline to the latter as a better sound... Of course we are at his [King George's] mercy. We are only allowed to use our German title as the sovereign has always recognised it, but he can refuse this recognition any moment. If so we are plain Mister, which would be impossible... For you, my dear children we feel deeply.' Whatever he may have said in public, Prince Louis made it clear to his daughter that he was not at all happy about this turn of events. 'You know the rules of the peerage,' he continued, 'the eldest son bears the 2nd title... but the sons and daughters are Lord – and Lady – surname. I fear this will trouble you.'[4]

Prince Louis and Princess Victoria now became the Marquess and Marchioness of Milford Haven and their children were Lord [Christian name] and Lady [Christian name] Mountbatten. Victoria, a Princess of Hesse in her own right, could have kept her title of princess but decided to drop it in favour of her husband's new name. 'It was suggested that I should continue to be Princess Victoria something or other of nothing,' she wrote to her friend Nona Crighton, 'but what is good enough for my husband is good enough for me....'[5]

The various branches of the Teck family became British peers as Cambridge, Athlone and Carisbrooke. The two Schleswig-Holstein princesses, King George's cousins, dropped the Schleswig-Holstein and simply became known as Princesses Helena Victoria and Marie Louise.

On 17 July 1917 the change of name was publicly announced in the *London Gazette*.

... as from the date of this Our Royal Proclamation our House and Family shall be styled and known as the House and Family of Windsor, and that all the descendants in the male line of Our said Grandmother Queen Victoria other than female descendants who may marry or may have married, shall bear the said Name of Windsor...

In Germany, the kaiser responded by announcing that he was looking forward to attending the next operatic performance of *The Merry Wives of Saxe-Coburg-Gotha*.

* * *

In Petrograd the Minister of Justice Alexander Kerensky was given responsibility for the tsar's family. He paid his first visit to the Alexander Palace on 21 March [OS]. Confronted by an understandably nervous family group, he told Nicholas to have complete confidence in the new regime and assured them that they were safe. A few days later Alexandra was separated from the rest of the family while an investigation was conducted into her suspected treasonable, pro-German activities. After an enquiry lasting eighteen days, Kerensky announced that he had found nothing incriminating.

Nicholas spent his time reading and walking in the small section of the park which he was allowed to use so that he could have some physical exercise. Even this proved problematical and the outings had to be arranged in advance. When the tsar left the palace armed soldiers blocked his path with their rifle butts, prodding him in the direction they wanted him to walk. One evening a band of revolutionary soldiers from the Petrograd Soviet burst through the palace gates in armoured cars and demanded the tsar be handed over to them for incarceration in the SS Peter and Paul Fortress. Rebuffed by officers guarding the palace, they agreed Nicholas could remain there providing they were allowed to see him. A hasty 'inspection' was arranged.

Alexandra, bitter at the overthrow of the monarchy, spent most of her time lying on a couch in her daughters' rooms. When she moved around the palace she did so in a wheelchair, pushed by Nicholas. Her devoted friends Anna Vyrubova and Lili Dehn were arrested but many other retainers were allowed to remain. These included Alexei's two sailor attendants, twenty-nine-year old Klementy Nagorny and Andrei Derevenko.

Also with the family were Count and Countess Benckendorff, Baroness Sophie ('Isa') Buxhoeveden, Countess Anastasia Hendrikova, Elizaveta Naryshkin (Alexandra's Mistress of the Robes, who remained until she was taken ill in May), the tutor Pierre Gilliard, Catherine Schneider, Dr Eugene Botkin and Dr Vladimir Derevenko (no relation of the sailor).

The four grand duchesses, Olga, Tatiana, Maria and Anastasia were now fully recovered from measles, although their heads had been shaved after the illness as was customary in those days. The tsar and tsarina had dismissed earlier suggestions from members of their entourage that they should take any opportunity offered to go abroad, leaving the children with Count Benckendorff (the Grand Marshall of the Imperial Court) and Elizaveta Naryshkin who would bring them to join their parents when they were well.

Olga was twenty-one when the family began their captivity. She loved her father more than her mother, with whom she had a strained relationship. She was a serious young woman who read widely but was described by people at court as capable of flashes of temper. Her chestnut hair and blue eyes gave her an air of innocence that belied the strength of her private feelings. While nursing at the Tsarskoe Selo hospital during the war, Olga had fallen in love with a 3rd Lieutenant from the 13th Erivan Grenadier Regiment, Ensign Dmitri Shakh-Bagov, a dark-eyed twenty-two-year-old Caucasian she called 'Mitya'. Olga's great wish was to live a normal life in a village without any formality but Mitya returned to the front at the end of 1916 and she never saw him again.

Nineteen-year-old Tatiana was the organiser, called 'the governess' by her sisters. Tall, slender and elegant, she was close to her mother and inherited Alexandra's sense of authority. Many people said that they could feel that she was an emperor's daughter. Tatiana had also formed an attachment during the war. Her favourite was Sub-Lieutenant Vladimir Ivanovich Kiknadze, a Georgian from the 3rd Guards' Rifle Regiment, but her romance fared no better. Kiknadze was sent to the Crimea in the autumn of 1916.

Maria, aged seventeen, was the most beautiful of the girls. She also loved her father more than her difficult mother. Physically strong like her grandfather Alexander III, Maria was unassuming, generous and flirtatious. What she wanted most in the world was a husband and children.

Fifteen-year-old Anastasia was the family tomboy who liked to climb trees and play practical jokes. Witty and vivacious, she rarely cried. She was a brilliant mimic but could often be nasty when playing with her cousins.

The household had always centred on the frail Alexei, whose illness was kept a closely guarded secret. Few members of the imperial family were even told. 'When he was well,' wrote Pierre Gilliard, 'the palace was transformed. Everyone and everything seemed bathed in sunshine,'[6] but during his frequent attacks of haemophilia everyone was shrouded in gloom. The empress spent hours, sometimes days, by his bedside and afterwards collapsed completely from nervous exhaustion. Aged twelve when the revolution occurred, his illness had precluded the normal life of a boy his age. Derevenko and Nagorny watched over his every move. When the inevitable accidents happened the devoted Derevenko spent hours massaging the boy's stricken limbs. Sometimes selected boys from the military academy were allowed to come and play with him, but most of the time Alexei played with his sisters. The six sons of his aunt Grand Duchess Xenia were deemed too boisterous to be companions for the sick heir.

Secluded for most of their young lives in the Alexander Palace, the tsar's children were soon to learn the realities of a life for which they were totally unprepared.

* * *

Outside the walls of the Alexander Palace others were planning how to free them. There was at least one monarchist plot to rescue the imperial family. Sergei Markov, a former officer in the Empress's Own Crimean Regiment, collected a group of officers with the idea of attacking the palace, freeing the Romanovs and taking them through Finland to neutral Sweden. The plan was dismissed as too risky.

Oliver Locker Lampson, a British officer who had met the tsar at *Stavka* after his Armoured Car Division was sent to assist the Russian army, had a plan to bribe the guards with 'cigarettes, vodka and British bully beef'. Then he would smuggle a clean-shaven Nicholas out of the palace in a British uniform, leaving one of the servants in a cloak and false beard in his place. Nicholas would be taken to Archangel in a field ambulance and put on board a British ship. The scheme foundered because the tsarina and her children would have to be left behind at Tsarskoe Selo.[7]

When it became clear that nothing would come of the British offer of asylum, King Alfonso realised that the imperial family were now increasingly in danger. He approached the three Scandinavian monarchs with a plan to send a Spanish warship to a northern port to pick up the family. The offer was transmitted to the Provisional Government.

In June a report from a British army general landed on the desk of the British Under Secretary for Foreign Affairs. Returning home via Stockholm, he had spoken to the Russian Minister who said that if the British brought the tsar and his family out of Russia in a submarine, King Gustav would send a submarine to pick them up and take them to Sweden, where they would be offered asylum. The plan was dismissed as impractical by the Foreign Office and the Under Secretary noted rather laconically on the bottom 'The Trust of Kings.'

* * *

As spring turned to summer, the imperial children walked in the park with their father, always surrounded by guards with fixed bayonets. The commander of these guards was thirty-year-old Colonel Eugene Kobylinsky, formerly of the Petrograd Life Guards. In September 1916 he had been lying wounded in the hospital at Tsarskoe Selo where he was visited by the empress and her daughters. He was loyal to the imperial family and helped them adjust to their new circumstances. Nicholas called him his last friend.

Life had settled into a monotonous routine, with the family subjected to petty humiliations inflicted by the guards. A toy rifle was removed from Alexei when one of the soldiers spotted it and told his comrades that the Romanovs were armed. Later it was quietly returned, piece by piece, by Colonel Kobylinsky and Alexei continued to play with it behind the closed doors of his room. Alexei found relief from boredom by giving performances with a cine projector and some films given to him by the Pathé company. Lessons also resumed, given by the French tutor Pierre Gilliard, members of the household and even the tsar and tsarina.

Physical exercise was a necessity to Nicholas. He shovelled snow, felled old trees and as the weather improved, helped by his daughters he laid out a kitchen garden in the Alexander Palace park where they could grow produce to feed the occupants of the palace. They were never able to reap the rewards. For their own safety, the Provisional Government decided in July that the family were to be moved.

* * *

The Tsar's cousin Grand Duke Boris Vladimirovich had also been arrested. Boris, born in 1877, was the second surviving son of Grand Duke Vladimir (who died in 1909) and Grand Duchess Marie Pavlovna the elder. Known as 'Miechen' to the family, she was usually called Grand Duchess Vladimir to distinguish her from her niece, the daughter of Grand Duke Paul.

Grand Duchess Vladimir had been banished to Kidslovodsk in the Caucasus by the tsar early in 1917 for speaking out against the imperial regime. She was soon joined by her youngest son Grand Duke Andrei. Boris was at Mogilev when the tsar returned to say goodbye to the army. He remained at *Stavka* until Nicholas was taken under arrest to the Alexander Palace.

On 15 March Grand Duke Boris was detained under house arrest at his English style dacha at Tsarskoe Selo. An indiscreet letter from his mother in which she said that Nicholasha, the former commander-in-chief of the army, was the country's only hope, had been intercepted and read by the Provisional Government.

By July his arrest had been lifted and that month the Bolsheviks nearly pulled off a successful coup. Worried about the future and realising that the Bolsheviks were gaining in strength, Boris conceived an audacious scheme. One of Boris's friends was the Honourable 'Bertie' Stopford, a rather shadowy figure who had some high powered connections. Although he had no official status as a King's Messenger or as a member of staff of the British Embassy or the Foreign Office, he travelled regularly between London and the continent during the war and on one occasion is thought to have acted as a personal messenger for Queen Mary. He also delivered personal correspondence from George V to the tsar in 1916 and is rumoured, although it has never been proved, to have worked for the Secret Intelligence Service.

Stopford dined with Boris two or three times a week and together they hatched a plan to save Grand Duchess Vladimir's jewels from her Petrograd palace on Palace Embankment. Stopford knew the layout of the rooms in the official part of the building very well, but to get to the grand duchess' safe in her private apartments would not be so easy.

Boris told Stopford that there was a secret passage from a side entrance, which led directly up to his mother's first floor boudoir. In this Moorish-style room was a concealed door leading to several such passages. From her boudoir it would be easy to reach her dressing room and, nearby, the locked metal safe containing her jewels. Instrumental in helping Stopford to gain access was the palace's loyal caretaker, who ensured that entry to the building would be possible during the night.

Stopford disguised himself as a workman and made his way into the palace unseen, through the suite of rooms to the safe. Carefully taking the jewellery apart, he wrapped it in newspaper and stuffed it into two rather shabby old Gladstone bags, with any money he found in the safe. Some of the tiaras, however, were left intact, including the one of linked diamond circles which is often worn by Queen Elizabeth II today.

Now he had to get out of the palace and through streets teeming with soldiers and police. The risk of being stopped and searched was great and he could not implicate the grand duchess or her son if he was caught red handed. He could even be shot for looting or theft. It is not known exactly what Stopford did with the jewels that night but, as his hotel room had already been searched at least once, it is more likely that he used his contacts at the British Embassy to place them temporarily in the chancellery. Then, as the grand duchess had been president of the Imperial Academy of Arts, they were lodged with the director. Stopford took the cash to Kislovodsk, concealed in his boots and in September, having obtained permission to travel, Boris joined his mother and brother Andrei in the Caucasus.

The jewels were taken out of Russia. Oliver Locker Lampson's Armoured Car Division was withdrawing and, by a strange coincidence, one of the men was called John Stopford. John's route took him eastwards via Vladivostok, Japan and America to London; Bertie Stopford left in the opposite direction by ship via Sweden. One of these men took the jewels and deposited them in a London bank vault.

In 2008 two pillow cases were found by the Swedish Foreign Ministry in Stockholm when they were tidying their archives. It transpired that after the Bolsheviks seized power the director of the Imperial Academy of Arts deposited them at the Swedish Legation. They then sent them by courier to Stockholm, where they were soon forgotten. Inside the pillowcases were more than 100 exceptional cigarette boxes and cufflinks made by Fabergé and Bolin, Russia's leading jewellers. The treasure had belonged to Grand Duchess Vladimir. Did Stopford sweep these up as he left one of the rooms of the Vladimir Palace?

***

On 8/21 July Prince Lvov resigned and Alexander Kerensky became Prime Minister and Minister of War. Paul Milyukov had resigned as Foreign Minister in May, so it was his replacement Michael Tereschenko who informed Sir George Buchanan in confidence about the transfer of the imperial family from Tsarskoe Selo.

Tereschenko had considered the idea of sending the family to Finland, from where they could reach a Scandinavian port and cross the North Sea. This idea was rejected because the Soviet would never permit them to cross the Russian rail network, although the Finnish border was only 25 miles from Petrograd. Instead the family's destination was Siberia, the place of exile of many political prisoners under the Romanovs' rule.

The minister informed Buchanan that in Tobolsk the imperial family would enjoy complete freedom. Furthermore, he said the tsar 'was content with the proposal to change his place of residence,' which was prompted by 'the growing fear of a counterrevolution among the socialists.' Buchanan reported to Balfour that he had told the Foreign Minister that 'such a fear is groundless, because the point is the dynasty.'[8]

The news that the tsar and his family were to be moved prompted another enquiry from Buckingham Palace, from where Lord Stamfordham was instructed to ask Buchanan whether the tsar and tsarina had yet been removed to Siberia. Three days later Buchanan replied that he was uncertain but would advise. 'The removal has been kept such a profound secret that even the Minister of Foreign Affairs … could not give me a positive answer,' he reported.[9]

By 31 July/13 August he was still uncertain about the tsar's whereabouts but the following day was able to confirm the transfer. They were '… bundled off in the middle of the night to some unknown destination,' as the tsar's aunt, the former Grand Duchess Marie Alexandrovna, now the Duchess of Coburg, expressed it. 'May God have mercy on them!'[10]

Nicholas had been given news of the transfer by Kerensky. He was told that the British had refused to give the family asylum and that they should pack quietly in preparation for a move. He was not informed of the destination, but Kerensky had hinted to others that they would be back in Petrograd in November.

The tsar had been quite willing to go to England if Livadia proved impossible. Kerensky later wrote of the unfeasibility of transporting the family to the Crimea by rail through central Russia, where there were peasant riots, big industrial towns and a large population. Other destinations were considered – Brasovo, Grand Duke Michael's estate near Orel, and Grushevka in Ukraine, the estate of Grand Duke Nicholas Michaelovich. Both options were rejected as impractical.

On 31 July/13 August the Tsarevich's diary recorded the last day at Tsarskoe Selo. 'During the day I bathed. The water was 18 degrees C [centigrade]. I threw Olga fully clothed into the lake from the gangplank. We said goodbye to people who are not coming with us. We showed Isa [Baroness Buxhoeveden], Nastinka [Countess Anastasia Hendrikova] and Trina [Catherine Schneider] Papa's room. We have not slept all night and watched how the fusiliers loaded the baggage. We drank some tea with Mama at midnight. Kerensky came and said we must leave at 6.10 in the morning. Have left Tsarskoe Selo by train...'[11]

Forty-two people, plus the family's personal possessions, cameras, photograph albums, letters, china, linen and a fortune in jewels accompanied them into exile. Alexei's sailor attendant Andrei Derevenko was refused permission to follow them and his subsequent fate is unknown.

* * *

One incident Alexei's diary did not record was an emotional meeting between his father and his uncle Michael the evening before they left the palace. The brothers had not met for five months, but now all they could manage was small talk – 'How is Alix? How is mother?' while Kerensky sat in the corner pretending to read a book. After ten minutes they were informed the meeting was over. Michael's request to see the children was refused. 'I found that Nicky looked rather well,' he recorded later in his diary.[12]

Michael returned to his house in Nikolaevskaya Street, Gatchina. He had earlier been spotted waiting to ask a favour from Kerensky. After waiting outside his office for two hours he was finally announced as Mr Romanoff. This visit may have been in connection with an application to go to his country estate, but to his chagrin all requests to go to Brasovo were refused. The Provisional Government would not grant him a travel permit. Nor could he go to England. Arthur Balfour had sent a 'private and secret' telegram to Sir George Buchanan confirming that no grand dukes would be admitted to the country.

By this time Michael had other problems. A so-called plot had been discovered. Margarita Khitrovo, a friend of Grand Duchess Olga Nicolaievna, had travelled to Tobolsk carrying a pile of innocent letters to the imperial family contained in a pillow. When the letters were found she was arrested and sent back to Petrograd.

Kerensky now feared a monarchist counter-revolution. The result was that on 21 August armed troops arrived to place Michael under house arrest on Kerensky's orders, as it was felt that he posed a threat to the defence of Russia. When Natasha and Johnson returned home they were also arrested. A week later, they were taken to Petrograd under guard, along with the children Tata Mamontov (Natasha's daughter from her first marriage) and George with their governess Margaret Neame.

Their prison was to be a small apartment on Morskaya Street but, when they arrived they protested that it was not in a fit state for them to live in. Johnson then discovered that Natasha's brother-in-law Alexei Matveyev was at his apartment on the Fontanka Canal, so they were permitted to stay there under guard. Michael's stomach ulcers were now exacerbated and, at Natasha's insistence, three specialists were permitted to examine him.

Meanwhile, Johnson made his way to the British Embassy to see Sir George Buchanan. Michael, after all, was the British king's cousin. The ambassador immediately complained to Tereschenko about the grand duke's treatment. Three days later he was informed that 'a secret meeting of the cabinet' had decided that 'certain members' of the imperial family would be allowed to leave Russia. Among them was Grand Duke Michael.[13]

Buchanan then tried a bid for sympathy, reporting to Lord Stamfordham at Buckingham Palace that, 'the poor Grand Duke Michael has, I am afraid, had rather a bad time of it lately...'[14] His bid failed – but Buchanan's hope that Michael would soon be released was not long in coming. On 6 September the family were taken back to Gatchina. Although they were still under guard they were at least at home.

On 13 September Michael's guard was removed. Two days later, he received a travel permit to go the Crimea. Back in June he had also obtained a permit to travel to Finland with two cars. By October he was writing to the dowager empress that his ulcer was again giving him trouble. He desperately wanted to go abroad but felt the chances were slipping away from him.

Still, he had the travel permits. The question was, which would the grand duke make use of and when would he use it?

***

By 1917 Tobolsk was a backwater. Situated at the junction of the Tobol and Irtysh rivers it had once been an important trading station but now it was isolated. There was no railway; the nearest station was Tyumen, 200 miles south. Due to its remote location, even as late as February 1918 Tobolsk had 'no Communist Party cell and its Soviet remained under the control of the S.R.s [Socialist Revolutionaries] and Mensheviks.'[15] Although it was distant, it boasted good telegraph links.

Nicholas had been there before. In 1890 his father Tsar Alexander III sent him on a tour of the Far East and on 10 July 1891, while returning overland across Siberia, he stopped for a few hours in Tobolsk. He had recorded the visit in his diary. 'On the wharf, as always, I was met by the mayor with bread and salt, the citizens of the town of Tyumen, with platters with the craft guild, and an honour guard ... Took a carriage and rode up the hill to the cathedral – through the original wooden streets of the town. From the cathedral we went to view the vestry, where they keep most of the objects relating to the subdal of Siberia. Went to the museum...'[16] Now he was returning as a captive.

The Romanovs arrived at Tyumen on a train bearing a sign showing that it was ostensibly part of the Japanese Red Cross Mission. Nicholas and his family then faced a two-day journey by steamer along the Tura and Tobol rivers. Then there was a further eight-day wait, during which time they lived on board the steamer while their accommodation was made ready. The fact that no suitable residence was prepared for them (despite the fact that Kerensky had despatched representatives to evaluate Tobolsk as a suitable place of exile) has led some historians to debate whether Kerensky intended their stay to be brief, preparatory perhaps to a transfer further east and safety abroad.[17]

The imperial family moved into the former Governor's House, now renamed Freedom House, a large white two-storey building on the corner of the street with a balcony over the entrance. Its thirteen rooms plus five attics for the servants proved inadequate to accommodate the family and all their retainers. A large villa across the road was therefore requisitioned from the merchant Kornilov for the remainder of the household. Their large suite included maids, valets, tutors, Dr Eugene Botkin and Dr Vladimir Derevenko. Botkin even opened a small medical practice in the town.

Kerensky had detailed the Socialist Revolutionary Pavel Makarov to accompany the party and keep an eye on Kobylinsky. At first conditions were not too bad. Colonel Kobylinsky, who remained in nominal charge, allowed the family to walk across to the Kornilov House to see their retainers and they were permitted to cross the public garden to the local church. As they walked through a line of guards some of the inhabitants crossed themselves or fell to their knees. But soon the guards objected that the Romanovs were being given too much freedom. A high fence was put up around the house and the side street and they were confined to the limits of this space. It at least provided room for the family to take exercise and for Nicholas to saw up logs for the winter helped by Gilliard, Tatishchev, Dolgoruky or one of his daughters. There were hens, ducks, chickens and piglets for the family to look after and when the sun shone the tsar and his daughters sat on the roof of the greenhouse, where they were often spotted by passers-by.

Alexei was overjoyed when the doctor's son Nicholas ('Kolia') Derevenko was allowed to come and play with him. The children's lessons continued with the tsar teaching his son Russian history, and to while away the evenings Pierre Gilliard produced one-act plays for them to act.

But Freedom House was not sufficiently secure. The ground floor windows facing the street, only 6 feet from the ground, were unprotected and it would have been relatively easy for someone to gain access. (Later during the family's captivity a schoolboy was arrested for trying to climb the fence at the side to see the tsar's children.) During the first few months Colonel Kobylinsky would have turned a blind eye to any attempt to rescue the family. He also considered taking an escort of around thirty soldiers and fleeing north with the family towards the Arctic Ocean. At Obsorsk (now Salekhard) they could escape on one of the Norwegian schooners that regularly called there. To carry out this plan he needed money. The imperial family could easily have paid for their freedom with the jewels they had brought from Petrograd. Yet they did not do so, because Nicholas felt that he could not abandon his country.

* * *

On 1 September Kobylinsky's sole authority over the family ended when two civilian commissars arrived to replace Commissar Makarov. Vassili Pankratov, a small bespectacled man, was another member of the Socialist Revolutionary Party. Although he had spent years as a political prisoner, first in the notorious Schlusselburg Prison and then in Siberia, he did his best for the family and became fond of the imperial children.

His deputy Alexander Nikolsky, also a Socialist Revolutionary, was a bitter man who blamed the tsar for his years of exile in Siberia. He insisted that the imperial family be photographed full face and in profile, just like the police had once photographed him. When the tsarevich tried to watch, Nikolsky yelled at him in rage. Alexei, who had never been shouted at before, quickly retreated in amazement.

In October King Alfonso of Spain instructed his ministers to reach an agreement with Britain and the Provisional Government so that plans could be made to evacuate the tsar and his family via Finland, Sweden and England. An appeal to King George V, King Gustav of Sweden and King Haakon of Norway failed to bring any result. One of the letters of response to King Alfonso's initiative was sent by Balfour to the Spanish Ambassador in London, Alfonso Merry de Val, on 17 October 1917. It is possible that the Spanish king had failed to realise that, with winter closing in, Tobolsk would soon be cut off from the outside world until the spring thaw around the end of April. As the long, cold Siberian winter began and the temperatures dropped to -29 degrees centigrade (-20 degrees fahrenheit) the family's chief enemy was boredom.

* * *

At Pavlovsk that autumn there was an imperial wedding. The bride was the tsar's cousin Grand Duchess Marie Pavlovna, who had returned to live in Russia after her divorce from Prince William of Sweden. On 6 September she married Prince Sergei Putiatin in a ceremony overshadowed by anxiety and sadness. The bride's father Grand Duke Paul was under house arrest, despite pleas to allow him to attend, and the local Soviet forbade her grandmother, Queen Olga of Greece, to allow her staff to wear livery, 'in the name of liberty.'[18] In these uncertain times both Marie and her father thought that as Princess Putiatin she would be safer than as a Romanov grand duchess. Paul and his wife Princess Paley were hoping they would be banished abroad so that they could go back to their house in Boulogne-sur-Seine in France.

There were also fears for the future of Pavlovsk. As the property of a younger branch of the Romanov family, it was not considered an imperial residence and now stood in danger of expropriation. Shortly after the wedding the head of the family, Prince Ioann Constantinovich, was advised to leave.

In September Prince Ioann and his wife Princess Helen of Serbia reluctantly moved to another family property, the Marble Palace in Petrograd, with their children Vsevolod and Catherine. Ioann's mother Grand Duchess Elisabeth Mavrikievna (Mavra), widowed two years earlier, was also living there with her younger children Prince George and Princess Vera. When the Serbian Legation left Russia in 1918 the Minister, Spalaikovich, offered to take Ioann and his family to Finland under Serbian protection. They refused. It was their last chance to get away together.

Although Queen Olga spent her days nursing at the local hospital, when she returned to Pavlovsk at night she was now alone with the servants.

* * *

In the Crimea confirmation that the tsar and his family had been moved to Siberia had given the dowager empress a dreadful shock. She had turned down an earlier offer from the Danish government to leave for Denmark, despite pleas from her son Michael to consider it, because her younger daughter, thirty-five-year-old Olga, was pregnant and unable to travel. Now, after the brutal house scarch and all the restrictions, the only good piece of news had been the birth of a son, Tihon, in August to Olga and her husband Nicolai Kulikovsky.

News of the harsh treatment to which his aunt was being subjected reached King George V, who expressed his shock to Buchanan. 'I beg you to protest on my behalf against this attitude towards my mother's sister who has lived for over fifty years in Russia and done everything in her power for the good of the country,' he wrote. '...I cannot exaggerate my feelings in this painful matter.'[19] Buchanan had already been exerting pressure on the Provisional Government but the situation was about to change again.

In September Kerensky declared Russia a republic. The Provisional Government's hold was becoming increasingly insecure. After the Bolsheviks' nearly successful coup in July, the following month General Kornilov attempted to rout the Soviet and replace it with a military dictatorship. Kerensky turned to the Soviet for help. The attempt failed when Kornilov's men fraternised with the Bolsheviks, who then refused to return the weapons issued to them by Kerensky.

In the wake of this the dowager empress and her family were placed under arrest at Ai-Todor, with nobody allowed in or out for almost a month. There was no money and little food. This news soon reached other members of the family.

Later, Xenia heard how her cousin Grand Duchess Cyril (who by then had reached safety in Finland) had tried to get help for them from England and failed. 'Nobody cares for us abroad, nasty selfish brutes!' Grand Duchess Cyril wrote in despair '... [they] said perhaps Romania could help. It fills my heart with boiling wrath. The Danes have all through been the kindest and the best.'[20]

* * *

The Danish Foreign Ministry now received some disturbing bulletins from Petrograd. The dowager empress was seriously ill, suffering from influenza and virulent bronchitis. Her health had been suffering since the house search in April, when she had been forced to sit in her nightgown for several hours. King Christian was immediately informed. On 5 September the Foreign Minister Erik Scavenius contacted his cousin Harald in Petrograd (with whom he had a strained relationship) to ask if it would be possible for the dowager empress to come to Denmark.

Several times Scavenius had intervened strenuously to protest about the treatment being given to the dowager empress but communication was a problem. In October *kammerjunker* Castenskiold Benzon arrived in the Crimea bringing letters for the empress from Prince Valdemar. This was probably Ludwig Helmuth Frederik Holger Castenskiold-Benzon a Red Cross delegate working with prisoners-of-war in Germany.

Various people had offered to smuggle letters to the dowager empress but Scavenius did not think it right to use the servants. Prince Valdemar was also in contact by telegraph with other members of the family in the Crimea via the telegraph centre at Koreiz, the village near the Youssoupovs' home.

The legation in Petrograd had been informed that the conditions of captivity endured by the empress were unseemly for a member of a royal family. This had prompted Harald to explore another idea to free the empress. He reasoned that although she no longer remained a member of the Russian imperial family, she remained a *Danish* princess. There had been no formal accusations against the dowager empress by the Russian authorities, so the Danish government could therefore request the return of a member of their own royal family. He telegraphed Erik in Copenhagen to ask if he should make an official request to the Russian government.

The matter had to be kept secret. The Danish government were reluctant to act, afraid that any official move would be seen as interference in Russian internal affairs and compromise government ministers. They wanted the empress to approach the Provisional Government herself and request permission to leave – but she was too proud to do so, as she considered it an illegal regime. It would be humiliating to ask the very people who were responsible for her family's misfortunes.

The Danish government immediately saw the difficulty. Harald Scavenius was instructed to find a way that the Russian government could be asked to suggest to the dowager empress that she return to Denmark.

On 10 September Scavenius received a coded telegram from the Danish Foreign Ministry. The Danish government had agreed that the dowager empress could come to Denmark and they asked that a date be determined for her arrival. The arrangements should be prepared in strict secrecy 'to avoid compromising high officials.'[21] Scavenius then approached Kerensky and the Russian Foreign Minister Tereschenko to obtain permission for her to leave. Permission was granted *in principle*. The Provisional Government would decide the date. Scavenius asked that this news be communicated immediately to King Christian and Prince Valdemar. Everything now depended on the Petrograd Soviet, in which the Bolsheviks had gained a majority, and no date could be set. In the strictest confidence, an official application on behalf of the Danish government was made for the tsar, the dowager empress and the whole of the imperial family to go to Denmark, as they were close relatives of the Danish royal family. The Danish government would promise to give all the political guarantees demanded by the Provisional Government. According to the Russian Foreign Ministry, Scavenius was the only foreign representative who made an *official* approach to the Provisional Government on behalf of the tsar and the dowager empress.[22]

Scavenius saw Kerensky again but he was unsympathetic. 'Political considerations' (Scavenius could not imagine what these were) prevented Kerensky from raising the matter with the government. They were not satisfied that comprehensive safeguards were in place both in the case of the tsar and of the dowager empress. Scavenius found him 'cold and haughty'. It appears that Tereschenko turned the scheme down and no concrete permission was ever given.[23]

* * *

In September a French diplomat stood contemplating the view of Petrograd, with 'its background the splendid scenery of the Neva, all blurred in the cold autumn light ... the gold spire of the Fortress, the red ochre of the palaces, and the rostral columns of the Stock Exchange.'[24] He was witnessing the calm before the storm. The following month Lenin and the Bolsheviks took power.

6

The Bolshevik Revolution

'I am in despair to find myself in such a sorrowful situation...'

'We older men may not live to see the decisive battles of the approaching revolution,' the Bolshevik leader Vladimir Ulyanov, known to his followers as Lenin, had written despondently from exile in Switzerland in January 1917. Then in February the unthinkable happened and the tsar abdicated. Yet the new Provisional Government had vowed to continue the war and Lenin was desperate to return to Petrograd. He did so with the help of the Germans, who saw in Lenin and his Bolsheviks a regime who would end the war with Germany, thus freeing up German troops who could then fight the Allies on the western front.

The German Minister in Berne now arranged for Lenin and his followers to travel on the so called 'sealed train' through Germany, Sweden and Finland to Petrograd, where they arrived to a rapturous welcome on 3 April [OS]. After the abortive coup in July, which saw Lenin forced to flee to Finland in disguise, by the autumn they were ready to seize power. In Petrograd, the Bolshevik Central Committee voted for an immediate insurrection.

* * *

The Bolsheviks seized power on 25 October 1917. Stealthily, and with few casualties, Lenin became master of Petrograd. The former ministers of the Provisional Government were arrested, banks were nationalised, private bank accounts frozen and army ranks abolished, along with private ownership of land and the rights of inheritance. The only titles were 'citizen' and 'comrade'. In the Red Terror that followed, a man's class would seal his fate more than his political sympathies.

On 25 December/7 January Sir George Buchanan left Russia, ostensibly for a holiday for the sake of his health. The British government did not recognise the new regime in Russia and no successor was appointed. The British Embassy was left in the charge of the Counsellor, Sir Francis Lindley, who now became the *Chargé d'Affaires*.

* * *

Gatchina was 30 miles south-west of Petrograd and by the end of October the situation there was critical. Although it was still in the hands of troops loyal to the Provisional Government, Alexander Kerensky had fled to Gatchina Palace hoping to rally support. Meanwhile, the Third Cavalry Corps under General Peter Krasnov was marching towards the capital in anticipation of an armed uprising in their favour, but when the battle between the Bolsheviks and Krasnov's army took place, Krasnov was outnumbered and forced to retire. Kerensky fled into exile.

With the Bolsheviks now in the ascendant, Grand Duke Michael Alexandrovich decided it was time to make use of his Finnish travel permit. It was now or never. Natasha began packing their valuables.

Early on 1 November Michael's Packard motorcar left Gatchina. Inside were the governess Miss Neame with Tata and George, and Natasha's friend Nadine Vonlyarlarskaya with her daughter Sophie. Their destination was the Batovo estate about 15 miles south, owned by Nadine's brother Vladimir Nabokov. After dropping the party off at the house, the car returned to Gatchina to collect the luggage and some provisions. The children would remain at Batovo until the second car arrived with Michael and Natasha.

Unfortunately, their arrival had been seen and mistaken for ministers of the Provisional Government trying to escape. As they were having breakfast the estate's manageress burst in and informed them that the local commissars were on their way to arrest everyone and that the telephone lines to the house had already been cut. It was now imperative that Michael be warned. Nadine therefore set off on horseback to the local hospital and used the telephone there to call the grand duke, speaking in English so that the conversation would not be understood. Michael said he would send the car back with a message.

He was too late. Shortly afterwards the Bolsheviks arrived at Nikolaevskaya Street and confiscated his cars. Assured by Michael that the children had merely gone on a day trip with their governess, the Bolshevik Commandant Semen Roshal allowed the Packard to pick them up from Batovo later that evening – with an armed guard sitting beside Michael's chauffeur.

A few days later, Michael was informed that he was to be taken to Petrograd under arrest. As long as he did not leave the city he would be free to go out and could even select somewhere to stay. He immediately telephoned Princess Olga Putiatin at Millionaya Street to ask for use of her apartment.

The princess was in Odessa but her husband and brother-in-law welcomed Michael warmly on his arrival. 'The grand duke put a finger to his lips, warning them that he was not alone, and that they must be careful,' the Princess later wrote.[1] After a few minutes' conversation with Michael, Roshal departed, leaving sailors from Helsingfors (Helsinki) to oversee his movements. Natasha remained with Michael, while Miss Neame took the children to stay with Alexei Matveyev.

After ten days, during which time he was able to walk around the capital untroubled by his sailor guards, Michael was informed he could return to his home at Gatchina, where he would remain under guard. Michael and the children returned home but Natasha delayed her departure until she had visited the State Bank. There she asked to see some papers in her strongbox and managed to smuggle out some of her jewellery concealed in her muff.

Apart from petty annoyances, such as confiscation of wine and provisions, for the next three months Michael was left in peace.

* * *

When the Bolsheviks took power a *frisson* of shock ran through the European courts.

In November the three Scandinavian monarchs met to discuss the situation in Russia, worried that revolution would spread to their own countries. Worse, if Russia negotiated a separate peace, the chances of a German victory would increase.

For the Norwegian monarch, there was another concern. The meeting was taking place in Kristiania, where demonstrations against the high cost of living had taken place in June. King Haakon was worried about the reaction of his hard-pressed people when they learned that he was entertaining two fellow monarchs. King Christian and King Gustav arrived in the Norwegian capital on 28 November to meet King Haakon and senior government ministers. The meeting achieved nothing.

In Petrograd it was rumoured that the Germans had entered Riga on the Baltic, where the kaiser had arranged for an Orthodox service to be held with prayers said for the tsar. A newspaper reported that the tsar had left Tobolsk and was returning to Petrograd after Lenin and Trotsky had arranged it with Grand Duke Paul.

Although a Danish newspaper thought it 'obviously inconceivable' that a gang of Bolshevik anarchists and criminals could govern the country,[2] in Petrograd Harald Scavenius was certainly under no illusions about the kind of ruthless regime with which he was now dealing. In January the Danish Embassy had been invaded by a mob who rushed through the rooms trying to remove reserves of food despite the protests of Scavenius. 'In spite of showing them documents from Smolny [Bolshevik headquarters] and even red seals, which up to now have produced such a good effect, they would not listen and said they didn't care a damn for embassies or Smolny either,' he told Louis de Robien.[3] The Winter Palace had also been ransacked, magnificent pictures destroyed and the wine cellar plundered.

Little could be done for the tsar in distant Tobolsk but Scavenius warned the Danish government that the dowager empress was now in great peril.

* * *

At Ai-Todor Empress Marie and her family were completely isolated. In December Commissar Vershinin was replaced by Zadorojny, a representative of the Sevastopol Soviet, who moved in with new guards. The Romanovs were placed under house arrest, watched by their loutish guards and under constant threat from the Yalta and Sevastopol Soviets, who were arguing over who had the right to execute them.

In February 1918 Scavenius received a desperate letter from Prince George Schervashidze, Chamberlain of the dowager empress's household, which had been brought to Petrograd by one of the foreign tutors of Grand Duchess Xenia's sons. He told Scavenius about the dire conditions under which they were living and asked that the dowager empress's journey out of Russia be accomplished 'officially', accompanied by a representative of the Bolshevik government and a member of the Danish diplomatic corps, but he stressed that she would not leave without Xenia and her family. (Olga and her husband had already decided to remain in Russia.) The details of the route would also have to be worked out and he had no idea how it could be accomplished. 'I am in despair to find myself in such a sorrowful situation,' he continued, 'and I am happy to know that Her Majesty ... possesses in you an energetic and chivalrous protector who is always ready to defend her interests. In your capacity as Denmark's Minister you are at the moment the only person who we can ask for help and support in our endeavours to lighten Her Majesty's lot...'[4]

The Danish newspapers reported that the dowager empress would soon be leaving for Denmark. The rumours proved to be false.

In February the Bolsheviks changed the calendar. 1 February now became 14 February, to bring Russia in line with the western, Gregorian calendar. Many members of the Romanov family, however, continued to use the Old Style dates in letters and diaries.

* * *

In March the dowager empress and her family were moved under guard to Djulber, the nearby home of Grand Duke Peter Nicolaievich, Grand Duchess Militsa and their unmarried children Roman and Marina. (Their elder daughter Nadejda, Princess Irina Youssoupov and Grand Duchess Olga Alexandrovna, who were all married to 'commoners', were not considered members of the Romanov family and were allowed to go free.) Also there were

Peter's brother, Grand Duke Nicholas Nicolaievich the former commander-in-chief of the Russian army, and his wife Anastasia, who had been brought from their nearby estate of Tchair.

With its white towers and Moorish-style minarets Djulber resembled something from the Arabian Nights but it had the advantage of high, stout walls. Conditions were cramped and the large party had to fit in where and how they could. The only visitors allowed were Xenia's two-year-old granddaughter Princess Irina Youssoupov, who toddled in with letters pinned inside her coat, and Dr Malama.

They were guarded by sixty men with machine guns in a tense, uncertain atmosphere. A local government had been formed in the Crimea with its seat at Simferopol but, in reality, power was in the hands of the local Soviets. Every second week a detachment from the rival Yalta Soviet arrived but Zadorojny, who was a secret supporter of the imperial family, always told them he was under orders from the Sevastopol Soviet not to release the family to them without proper orders. The Romanovs never knew if and when these would come.

* * *

In Tobolsk, Nicholas was shocked to hear that Lenin was now the ruler of Russia. 'I then for the first time heard the tsar regret his abdication,' Pierre Gilliard recalled.[5] Nicholas now realised that it had all been in vain and the idea that he had done Russia a bad turn haunted him more and more.

At first there was little effect on the Romanovs' daily lives. Colonel Kobylinsky and the other officials appointed by the Provisional Government remained at their posts, the tsar's children continued their lessons and the family maintained their daily routine.

Apart from an outbreak of German measles, which also affected his sisters, Alexei was well throughout this time and he still had the company of his young friend Kolia Derevenko. The English tutor Sydney Gibbes arrived, as did a consignment of carpets, curtains and blinds in preparation for the winter. Another tutor Claudia Bittner (Kobylinsky's lover) and the lady-in-waiting Baroness 'Isa' Buxhoeveden moved in with the retainers at the Kornilov House.

At Christmas the family were permitted to walk across the public garden to the church. Unfortunately, at the end of the service the priest said the prayer for the imperial family's health and long life, which had been dropped after the revolution. The guards took exception to it. Henceforth the Romanovs were refused permission to attend church and were subjected to closer supervision.

As temperatures dropped well below zero, Alexei went into the yard every morning with his father, at least once on a pair of makeshift skis. The children built an ice hill to slide down as an improvised toboggan run. This gave the family endless fun, as they tumbled pell-mell down the hill shrieking with laughter.

One evening a guard saw Nicholas wearing his Cossack uniform, complete with a Circassian dagger in his belt. He reported the incident, saying that the family was armed. Colonel Kobylinsky had to ask Nicholas to hand over the dagger. The guards became increasingly hostile. A soldiers' committee was elected and Kobylinsky found more and more of his authority being eroded. When the committee voted to forbid officers from wearing epaulets Nicholas refused to comply, saying he had been awarded them by his father. Kobylinsky was powerless to overturn the ruling and finally General Tatishchev and Prince Dolgoruky convinced the tsar to obey, in order to avoid hostile demonstrations or even violence against his family. However, he continued to wear them in his room, concealing them under a Caucasian cloak when he went outside. Alexei burst into tears when told he had to remove his. It was the first time he really realised the gravity of the situation.

To the Romanovs it seemed as if the outside world had forgotten them. Just before Christmas they made a bid to obtain help from the British royal family. On 15 December Gibbes wrote a letter to Miss Margaret Jackson. He had never met her but the letter was ghosted by Gibbes on behalf of Empress Alexandra, in the hope that it would more likely reach its destination in London.

Margaret Hardcastle Jackson was born in Kensington in 1835 or 1836 and had been a tutor to the tsarina when she was Princess Alix of Hesse. In the 1911 census she was listed as a woman of independent means living at 8 St Katherine's Precinct, London N.W., with a parlour maid and a cook. By 1917 she was said to be living at a home for retired governesses in Regent's Park, also in north-west London.

The letter written by Gibbes gave Miss Jackson a brief outline of the transfer to Tobolsk, a description of the house occupied by the imperial family complete with a floor plan, and an account of their daily routine. He then continued: 'It is ages since you wrote, or maybe your letters have not arrived! Try and write again, perhaps the next will reach its destination. Send news of everybody... I hear David is back from France, how are his father and mother? And the cousins, are they also at the front?'[6] 'David' was the Prince of Wales and the reference was a heavy hint to pass the letter to King George and Queen Mary at Buckingham Palace.

Many authors have seen significance in the fact that the letter is not in the Royal Archives, suggesting that it was removed from the files, but the explanation is much simpler. On 24 January 1918 the empress's sister the Marchioness of Milford Haven told a friend that Miss Jackson was 'ill in bed, with a nurse, and her heart is weak.'[7] Four days later, on 28 January, Margaret Jackson died aged eighty-two. She probably never saw the letter. On 1 March probate was granted to Miss Emily Jackson, who was quite probably her sister.[8] Emily would doubtless not have understood the significance of this missive and the reference to 'David'.

In December a telegram from Scotland was delivered to the Marchioness of Milford Haven, saying 'Tatiana has arrived!' It caused great excitement. The family initially thought that the tsar's daughter had escaped from Tobolsk but in fact the telegram was from Victoria's son George and his wife, announcing the birth of their daughter.

As 1918 began the imperial family waited, hoping that the letter would prompt some course of action. Alexei recommenced his diary but the words 'everything is the same,' or 'today passed as yesterday' show the increasing frustration and boredom of a thirteen-year-old boy in captivity.[9]

* * *

In late January 1918 the Bolsheviks issued an order demobilising all the old soldiers of the former Imperial army. 'All the old soldiers (the most friendly) are to leave us. The tsar seems very depressed at this prospect,' Gilliard wrote in his diary, foreseeing that it could have disastrous results.[10] Pankratov, who had been appointed by Kerensky, also handed in his resignation to the soldiers' committee. Now that Kerensky had gone he concluded that his duties had finished. He and

Nikolsky were ordered out of the Kornilov House by the committee but, for the moment, Kobylinsky remained.

Up to this point the Bolsheviks had been involved with more pressing concerns than worrying about the ex-tsar and his family. The Soviet authorities in Petrograd now authorised Omsk (the capital of the West Siberian region) to bring Tobolsk under regular control. They were to pay particular attention to the residence of the imperial family.

Kobylinsky was running out of money to pay the men because the sums formerly provided by Kerensky were no longer forthcoming. Credit was also wearing thin with the local suppliers and the family were only saved by 20,000 roubles advanced by Yanushkevich, a Tobolsk merchant. A foreign ambassador also donated a large sum, enough to keep the family for several months. Then Kobylinsky was informed by telegram that from 1 March the family would be placed on soldiers' rations, with each family member allowed 600 roubles a month from the interest of their personal estate. A budget was drawn up. To the Romanovs' dismay, some of the servants had to be dismissed and items such as butter and coffee became luxuries.

When the family climbed the ice hill to wave goodbye to some friendly soldiers from the 4th Regiment of Sharpshooters, the soldiers' committee ordered the hill to be demolished to prevent the tsar and tsarina being shot from the street or signalling to passers by. Alexei and his sisters were inconsolable at losing one of their favourite games. Their only distraction now was sawing and cutting wood.

'We continue to saw and cut logs and it is nice to go out. We mended our swing and now we can once again start to use it,' Olga wrote to a friend. '... In our little yard is a lot of water and mud. My brother has a little boat in which we go rowing. It is more in imagination as there isn't enough water after all, and we therefore move sticks and hands. Of course there is really nothing but this is small entertainment ...'[11]

In place of the old, friendly soldiers came younger men already imbued with revolutionary ideals. They enjoyed carving obscene words into the grand duchess' swing and drawing lewd pictures and inscriptions on the fence. Baroness Buxhoeveden had already been evicted from the Kornilov House by the soldiers and forced to find lodgings; now Countess Hendrikova, Catherine Schneider, General Tatishchev, Prince Dolgorouky and Sydney Gibbes were also evicted and moved into Freedom House on 13 April.

Yet there was still no representative of the Bolshevik government at Tobolsk. 'Never was the situation more favourable for escape,' wrote Gilliard. '... With the complicity of Colonel Kobylinsky, already on our side, it would be easy to trick the insolent but careless vigilance of our guards. All that is required is the organised and resolute efforts of a few bold spirits outside.'[12]

The shock of the Bolshevik revolution prompted some of the monarchists to think about rescuing the family, despite the enormous risks involved. Various dubious characters converged on Tobolsk but even if they did free the imperial family, they could not reach Tyumen in the south or the Arctic Ocean in the north until the end of April when the spring thaw occurred. The only other options were by carriage or sleigh and they would undoubtedly be intercepted as soon as the alarm was raised. The forests west of the town were also fraught with difficulties and there was nowhere safe for the family to go. There was also the problem that Nicholas, fearing a hostage situation, insisted that the family must all be rescued together. Alexei and Alexandra were not able-bodied and this in itself would cause complications. And what about their loyal servants? How could they leave them behind?

The family's best hope still lay with the diplomatic channels of the royal families of Europe – but they seemed disinclined to act.

* * *

On 3 March 1918 Russia signed a separate peace with Germany at Brest-Litovsk. A quarter of Russia's territory, including some of the richest crop lands, now came under German occupation as the Ukraine, the Baltic States, Finland, Poland, the Caucasus and the Crimea were all surrendered. A third of the railway network, half of Russian industry, three-quarters of its supply of iron ore, nine-tenths of its coal and much of its food supply now fell into the hands of Germany. As the German troops marched in, one third of the population of Russia found themselves in German-occupied territory. The terms were harsh but Lenin needed peace at any price.

The Allied embassies left for Vologda, 300 miles north-east of Moscow; the British left a skeleton staff in Petrograd and decamped to London. With the treaty still not ratified the Bolsheviks, afraid that the Germans would reach Petrograd, moved the government to Moscow, which now became Russia's capital.

Lenin still feared that the Germans would rescue members of the imperial family. The only certain way of avoiding this was to remove the grand dukes from Petrograd. In early March, all male members of the imperial family were therefore ordered to register with the Cheka, the Bolshevik Secret Police founded in December 1917. They were then sent into internal exile.

Grand Dukes George and Nicholas Michaelovich and Grand Duke Dmitri Constantinovich (brother of Queen Olga of Greece) were sent to Vologda. Grand Duke Paul, who was ill, remained for a while at Tsarskoe Selo. Princes Ioann, Constantine and Igor Constantinovich, Grand Duke Sergei Michaelovich, his secretary Feodor Remez and Prince Vladimir Paley, the twenty-one-year-old son of Grand Duke Paul's second, morganatic, marriage were sent to Vyatka in the Urals.

Grand Duke Sergei Michaelovich was born in the Caucasus in 1869, one of the six sons of Alexander III's uncle Grand Duke Michael Nicolaievich. Sergei was tall with blue eyes but unfortunately became prematurely bald. Although he was clever, with a keen sense of the ridiculous, he had a tendency to be moody. After graduating from the Michaelovsky Artillery School he joined the Life Guards of the Cavalry Artillery Brigade, becoming an ADC to Alexander III in 1891. At the request of Nicholas II he acted as protector to his one-time mistress, Mathilde Kschessinska. Sergei was at *Stavka* in 1917 when Nicholas II went there to say goodbye to the army. He remained there for a while in voluntary exile, returning to Petrograd at the beginning of June wearing unaccustomed civilian clothes. He moved into the New Michaelovsky Palace where his brother Nicholas Michaelovich was also in residence. In October, a friend obtained permission for Sergei to go to Finland. Unfortunately, the permit was made out only in Sergei's name, with no mention of his manservant and secretary Remez. The grand duke, who was ill, was unable to travel without him. He also feared repercussions for the tsar if too many grand dukes tried to leave Petrograd. It was his last chance of escape.

The Constantinovichi princes were the sons of the late Grand Duke Constantine Constantinovich (a noted poet and playwright who wrote under the pseudonym K.R.) and Grand Duchess Elisabeth Mavrikievna ('Mavra'). The grand duchess had already lost one son, twenty-two-year-old Oleg, who was mortally wounded in September 1914. He was the first Romanov to die in the war.

The eldest son Ioann, born in 1886, was the first member of the family to be affected by Alexander III's new family statutes, becoming a prince instead of a grand duke. Despite the fact that many in the family thought him more suited to a monastic life, in 1911 he married Princess Helen of Serbia. She decided to travel with her husband, leaving their children Vsevolod and Catherine with her mother-in-law Mavra at the Marble Palace.

Prince Constantine, born in 1890, served in the Izmailovsky Life Guards. During the war he was awarded the St George's Cross 4th Class for saving the regimental colours, as well as receiving several citations for bravery.

Prince Igor, born in 1894, had also been at military headquarters with the tsar. He was back in Petrograd when the revolution broke out and he telephoned the Alexander Palace to offer assistance to the empress and her children. This was politely declined by Grand Duchess Maria Nicolaievna after consultation with her mother.

Another son, Gabriel, born in 1887, was ill and for the moment also remained free.

They set out on 4 April and after two days' travelling reached Vyatka. The town, situated on the European side of the Urals, was hardly touched by the revolution. They were allowed to find their own lodgings, so Helen and Ioann spent a few days at an inn before moving to a small house in the town. Their food was prepared by nuns from a local convent and the people were sympathetic, which was not at all to the liking of the local Bolsheviks.

One morning while the princes were in church some uncouth Red Guards burst in to Helen's lodgings and demanded to know their whereabouts. Insisting to Helen that they would wait for the men's return, they sat down with their boots on the table and took out their cigarettes.

When the princes returned they were informed that the following day they would be transferred under guard. The nuns provided food for the long journey and, as a thank you for their help, Helen left her only fur coat behind with the Mother Superior.

On 30 April they were all loaded into a battered railway carriage escorted by Red Guards. Their destination this time was Ekaterinburg.

***

After the tsar's abdication, the tsarina's sister Grand Duchess Elisabeth (Ella) had declined an offer from the Provisional Government to seek refuge in the Kremlin. She remained in her Moscow convent throughout the Bolshevik revolution.

The red flag now flew over the Kremlin, the churches were desecrated and Ella's community of nursing sisters tended wounded from the running battles on the streets. The Cheka were established in Moscow and one word out of place was enough to have a charge levied. Ella felt responsible for her Sisters and for the sick entrusted to her care but any of the strangers coming daily to the clinic could be a Cheka spy.

One day the Cheka arrived with a search warrant. Ella explained that there were sick and aged people in the buildings and asked that the search be carried out with as little disturbance as possible. This was done and the men quietly departed. 'It looks like we are not yet quite worthy to receive a martyr's crown,' Ella remarked.[13]

Some time later an official from the Food Commissariat came to assess the convent's needs, saying that special rations would be allowed for the patients. 'That promise was kept, and supplies arrived with a staggering punctuality.' Lengthy questionnaires arrived, 'demanding ages and the social status of all the nuns and the patients.' These were completed and returned. No more was heard. 'The Health Commissariat made spasmodic allocations of quinine, aspirin, surgical spirits, lint and bandages.' Twice a week a lorry arrived with food and provisions. People continued to smuggle in butter and eggs but tea had become a distant memory.[14]

Soon the Bolsheviks tightened their grip. Patrols along the road were doubled, all visitors were questioned before they could enter the convent and some of the patients were transferred to another hospital.

Then during Easter 1918 Ella was arrested and informed by the Cheka that for her own safety she would be immediately removed from Moscow. With only half-an-hour to put the convent's affairs in order, there was no time to visit the hospital but Ella asked Father Mitrofan to continue working in the community for as long as he was allowed to do so.

Only two of the weeping sisters were allowed to accompany her, Catherine Yanisheva and Barbara Yakovleva. The remainder were forcibly separated from Ella as she was taken to the waiting vehicle. Just before entering, she turned and made the sign of the cross. Ella and her companions were moved first of all to the Convent of the Assumption in Perm, before the Ural Regional Soviet decided that they would join Grand Duke Sergei and the Constantinovichi princes in Ekaterinburg.

* * *

Grand Duke Michael Alexandrovich was also in prison. Troubled by stomach pains once again, the grand duke had been living quietly for the last few months and his request to Lenin to be allowed to change his name to Mr Michael Brasov was rejected.

On 7 March a group of armed men burst into Michael's house at Gatchina and informed him he was under arrest. By order of the Petrograd Cheka, he and his secretary Nicholas Johnson were taken to the capital and imprisoned in the Smolny Institute, the former exclusive school for girls of the nobility which served as Bolshevik headquarters.

Natasha followed them to Petrograd and the next morning, accompanied by Princess Putiatin, she went to the Smolny and was permitted to see Michael. After a few moments the door opened and Moisei Uritsky, head of the Petrograd Cheka, entered. Johnson asked if the grand duke could have better food on account of his illness; this was refused. Natasha tried to get him transferred to a hospital but Uritsky was non-committal. Their visit the following day lasted less than half-an-hour. The day after that they were not allowed to see Michael at all.

On 10 March the grand duke was informed by Uritsky that he would be moved to Perm under guard the following morning. It was mid-winter and he was given no time to gather together warm clothes or even a change of linen.

At 1.00am on 11 March Michael and Johnson were driven to the Nicholas Station with a six-man armed escort. Eight days later, after a bitterly cold journey in an unheated compartment with little food, they arrived in Perm.

* * *

'Grand Duke Michael arrested and sent alone to Perm,' Scavenius reported to the Foreign Office in Copenhagen on 12 March. 'He is very badly treated and must be said to be in absolute danger of his life.'[15] Scavenius received his information from Poul Ree, the Danish Vice-Consul in Perm. Ree was obviously finding the job too much, as he had recently put in a request to be transferred. Scavenius recommended a replacement be found as soon as possible.

Scavenius further reported that the emperor, empress and their children were at the mercy of ill-disposed guards at Tobolsk, and that he had heard from Prince George Schervashidze, the dowager empress's chamberlain that the family in the Crimea were under the 'surveillance of bands of sailors and soldiers,' they lacked provisions and were unable to draw on their bank accounts.[16] The telegram from Scavenius was immediately given to King Christian. Scavenius wanted the government to ask the kaiser to put pressure on the Bolsheviks and warn them against any ill treatment or violent action against the tsar and his relatives.

King Christian decided to make an urgent appeal to the kaiser in Berlin. German military might had crushed the Russians and Germany had recognised the Bolshevik government. William was surely the one person who could help. Christian telegraphed him, reporting the information about the imperial family's conditions and asking if he could do anything to help his unfortunate relatives.

William's reply on 15 March was disappointing. An intervention by Germany would worsen the situation for the tsar and his family, as the Bolsheviks would see it as a wish to restore the monarchy. The same conditions would also apply to England and France. He suggested the most practical solution would be a humanitarian initiative by the three neutral Scandinavian kingdoms of Denmark, Norway and Sweden. It is obvious from this that the kaiser had no idea about the kind of people who now wielded power in

Russia, although he did make a marginal note on one document saying, 'Cannot feel myself able to have anything to do with those swine.'[17]

However, he told King Christian, 'I cannot deny the imperial family my compassion from the human point of view, and when it lies in my power I will gladly do my part to ensure that the Russian imperial family has a safe and suitable situation.'[18] Karl von Bothmer, the German Military Attaché, thought that the kaiser was afraid of the German left-wing parties.

The royal family of Sweden also sent a similar message to the kaiser, asking him to use his influence to obtain an improvement in the tsar's living conditions. This request was also rejected.

'Conditions keep worsening,' Scavenius reported. 'They have absolutely no money.'[19] Christian did not think an appeal by the small Scandinavian powers would help and he authorised Harald Scavenius to try and alleviate the Romanovs' lot.

There was one thing, however, that the Danish monarch *could* do.

***

In letters to his wife, Grand Duke Michael hinted that he was uneasy for their seven-year-old son's safety. The fact that George was technically a commoner was no guarantee of protection. Even Prince Vladimir Paley had recently been arrested and exiled with other members of the Romanov family.

On receipt of Michael's letter Natasha asked Prince Paul Putiatin to go to Harald Scavenius at the Danish Embassy, which was near the Putiatin's apartment on Millionaya Street, and see if Denmark could help to get George out of the country.

The first thing Scavenius did was to arrange for the embassy to 'rent' part of Michael's house at Gatchina to secure it from the mob. Every morning two Danish officials arrived at the house and a Danish flag fluttered from the flagstaff.

Scavenius, as the representative of a neutral country, then made arrangements to smuggle little George Brasov out of Russia. He contacted forty-five-year-old Captain Frits Cramer, a Dane charged with overseeing the exchange of Austrian prisoners of war on behalf of the Red Cross. Denmark was looking after the interests of Austria-Hungary, and Captain Cramer agreed that George could stay with him at the Austrian Legation until a reply had been received from Denmark.

Natasha was unable to go with George, she could not leave Michael and she also had her daughter Tata Mamontov to think about. To get George out of the country Natasha needed the help of the children's governess Miss Neame, one of that remarkable breed of plucky Englishwomen who could cope with any situation.

Margaret Neame was born in Littlehampton, Sussex, in 1878, one of the thirteen children of George Neame, a boarding-house keeper. At least three of Margaret's sisters became governesses, so it was little surprise when she followed the same profession and was working for a London barrister by 1911.

She had met Grand Duke Michael's family in Cannes during the spring of 1914 and the following year replaced Edith Rata as governess to the grand duke's twelve-year-old stepdaughter Natasha (Tata) Mamontov and his five-year-old son George. Tata hated Miss Neame. 'I must say that when later I fell into the hands of the Cheka,' she wrote in her memoirs, 'I personally considered my treatment by them as considerate and humane, compared to what I suffered at the hands of governesses.'[20] George got round Miss Neame by flattery, calling her 'Pussy Darling.'[21]

Despite the risks, Miss Neame agreed to help get little George to safety. On 16 March George and Miss Neame went to the Austrian Legation on Sergeyevskaya Street in Petrograd, which was under Danish protection, where they were given a room. In the flat above them was Captain Frits Cramer. He proved to be a good companion during the five weeks Miss Neame and her charge remained there. 'Captain C has given me a book,' George wrote to his mother in an undated note which appears to date from this period. 'I run in the corridor... We have dinner downstairs with the Captain. He took me for a nice walk yesterday morning. Thank you very much for all the nice things. It is a pity what [sic] you have not seen our room. Best love and kisses to Mamma from Georgie.'[22]

With civil war raging in Finland, their only escape route to Denmark was through Germany but this proved a problem. Margaret Neame was English and Germany was an enemy country. If caught, she would be shot as a spy.

They waited in vain for orders to leave in disguise. On 3 April Scavenius reported to Denmark that George and his governess were still living in the Austrian Legation. Finally, it was arranged that they would leave on a Red Cross train carrying repatriated Austrian prisoners of war. Margaret Neame showed great courage. She knew the risks involved but also knew it was her duty to save the grand duke's only son.

On 25 April Captain Sørensen arrived to take them to the station. This was probably thirty-seven-year-old Engineer Einar Sørensen who had been working as a courier between Russia, Finland and Sweden and now was responsible for repatriating Austro-Hungarian prisoners of war. They were also accompanied by the Austrian Consul and an Austrian officer called Silldorf. Miss Neame had been told to bring enough food for one week. She would be travelling on a false passport, which showed her to be the English wife of a repatriated Austrian officer travelling with her son. She spoke a little Russian but no German. George, who had been told they were going to the seaside, was instructed to remain silent.

It was a nightmare journey on a slow train which took more than twenty-four hours to reach Pskov, the Russian-German frontier under the Treaty of Brest-Litovsk. Here, thankfully, Miss Neame and her party passed through without incident.

The train continued on via Dvinsk (now Daugavpils, Latvia) and Warsaw to Berlin, where they went straight to the Danish Embassy. The Ambassador Count Carl Moltke let them stay there while he raised the delicate subject with the Germans of whether they should be allowed to cross the border into Denmark. To do this, he had to disclose the true identities of Miss Neame and her 'son'. The kaiser was immediately informed.

'He not only kindly allowed us to go on,' wrote Miss Neame to a friend, 'but we had a reserved first-class carriage. Orders were sent ahead that on the frontier we were to be passed and neither we nor our luggage were to be searched.'[23]

They arrived in Copenhagen on 7 May and were met by a court official and a royal car. To Miss Neame's amazement, she was informed that they were to be guests of King Christian X and Queen Alexandrine at Sorgenfri, their country palace half-an-hour's drive from the capital.

Queen Alexandrine and her younger son, sixteen-year-old Prince Knud, welcomed George and Miss Neame and conducted them to their rooms. When the king returned the next morning his welcome was equally warm. 'You and the boy must settle down and be happy with us,' he told the governess. 'I admire you for undertaking such a dangerous journey.'[24]

Before he returned to Russia Einar Sørensen received a 14 carat gold cigarette case with a cabochon sapphire lock as a thank you gift. Inside, it was inscribed 'With love from Georgie, May 1918'.[25]

When Miss Neame took to her bed for a few days with a bad throat, Queen Alexandrine took care of little George. Luckily, Sorgenfri was surrounded by a beautiful park.

King Haakon learned of George's arrival in Copenhagen on 13 May, telling the Foreign Minister Niels Claus Ihlen that, in accordance with the promise given to Wrangel, the boy could come to Norway. He also informed Ihlen that he 'would ask the newspapers not to announce his [George's] arrival.'[26]

On 31 July, Wrangel arrived in Kristiania to 'talk about Misha's boy'. There were now three proposals for his place of residence and, King Haakon wrote in his diary, 'my promise therefore must be considered to be lifted.'[27]

George remained at Sorgenfri and continued writing to his father. 'Darling Papa, we are longing to go to you. Pussy [Miss Neame] and I are very sad without you, Mama and Johnny [Johnson]. I love Mr Sørensen very much. And am very sorry he is going away. I hope you are quite well... Best love and kisses to papa and Johnny.'[28]

Unfortunately, Miss Neame soon got off on the wrong foot with King Christian, who found her quite unpleasant and awkward. They had regular altercations over the upbringing of George, who seems to have been a precocious little boy. Having witnessed the revolution at an impressionable age he tried to persuade the king to forbid the guards from presenting arms when he passed. After all, George said, they were probably opposed to the idea and doubtless would prefer to sit and play cards. He also expressed surprise that all the people greeted the king as he drove past. Although astonished by these remarks from such a young boy, Christian became fond of George.

George and his governess later met other members of the royal family – the king's uncle Prince Valdemar and his daughter Princess Margrethe, and daughter-in-law Matilda Calvi dei conti di Bergolo.

Nevertheless, the little boy missed his family. 'How are you. Here it is very, very, very bad,' he wrote in Russian to his mother. 'I want so very much, and so does Miss Neame, to go to you, we are very lonely here. Or to Mr Sørensen. I have not forgotten dear papa...'[29]

Via a letter from Prince Valdemar to Queen Alexandra, news of George's journey eventually reached the dowager empress in the Crimea. 'You say that Valdemar writes that my poor Misha's [Michael's] son is staying with Christian and Adini [Queen Alexandrine],' the empress wrote in astonishment on 27 October, 'that is so nice of them, only strange that Valdemar did not tell me that. However, I would like to know how that happened, from where did you know he was in Copenhagen?'[30]

In July King Christian and Queen Alexandrine moved to their summer palace by the sea in Jutland and, as was traditional, scratched the dates of their arrival and departure, 5 July – 24 August, on a windowpane. George and his governess stayed with them, all the time waiting for news of Grand Duke Michael.

'Pity you were not here at Marselisborg for my birthday. It was a nice day,' George wrote to Natasha. 'I write my letters by myself now. I am in my room alone. Where is papa?'[31]

7

Germany's role

'We Germans have the situation well in hand...'

Nicholas II's relationship with Kaiser William II had always been tricky. The men were both descendants of Frederick William III of Prussia, making them second cousins once removed, but the closest family link was between William and Empress Alexandra who were both grandchildren of Queen Victoria. Despite this close relationship Alexandra hated William and could barely bring herself to be polite to him, privately referring to him as 'an actor, an outstanding comic turn, a false person.'[1]

William was born in Berlin in 1859 after a difficult delivery. As doctors fought to save his English mother Princess Victoria, wife of Prince Frederick William of Prussia, they scarcely noticed that the baby had not cried. William was slapped vigorously into life but his neck was damaged and the left arm hung limply from its socket. This would have a lifelong effect on his character. As William grew, photographs were posed to hide his withered arm, which remained slightly shorter and very weak. He came to the throne at the age of twenty-nine in 1888 following the deaths, in quick succession, of his grandfather and father. Determined to rule as well as reign, he had a terrific ego – wanting, it was said, to be the bride at every wedding and the corpse at every funeral. He travelled round Europe making theatrical speeches, embarrassing the German government and stirring up trouble in his wake. He was rarely seen out of uniform and thanks to a flood of official photographs was one of the world's most recognisable figures. With his waxed moustache and glittering orders, his portrait at the German Embassy in Paris, remarked a French general, looked like a declaration of war.

Nicholas had always felt somewhat intimidated by the bombastic William who, as soon as the tsar came to the throne began writing to him monarch to monarch, bombarding him with advice in the famous 'Willy-Nicky correspondence'.

In 1905 the Kaiser manipulated the tsar into signing a treaty of alliance between Russia and Germany while they were on a private sailing trip in their respective yachts at Björkö off the coast of Finland. Nicholas duly signed but afterwards both governments were appalled and refused to ratify the Treaty of Björkö, which broke Russia's alliance with France.

Their last meeting was at the wedding of William's only daughter Victoria Louise in 1913. Among the guests who travelled to Berlin were the tsar, King George and Queen Mary. Alexandra was conspicuous by her absence. One thing Nicholas and George shared was a distrust of William. Despite the kaiser's efforts to keep them apart, the cousins did manage to have a few quiet talks, although the king was convinced that William's ear was glued to the keyhole to check whether they were plotting against him. Before Nicholas left Berlin that evening he and George were photographed together wearing their German uniforms – but within fifteen months Germany was the enemy in a bitter war.

* * *

Then in 1917 Nicholas abdicated. 'I am sorry for the tsar and tsarina, and it is horrible that nobody intervenes and they are left to their own fate,' the kaiser's sister Princess Margaret of Hesse-Cassel wrote to British-born Princess Daisy of Pless on 24 March 1917. 'I hope they will be spared. They are such kind, lovely people, however too weak and completely unsuited to their position.'[2]

Once the kaiser was informed that the offer of asylum in Britain had been withdrawn he could do little to help Nicholas, as their countries were still at war. Later that year, in August or September, William's proposals for acceptance of his assistance were conveyed to Nicholas at Tobolsk via 'Russian officers of the type that moved in the circles from which the centre of the [Germanophile] organisation was formed...'[3] The offer was rejected. But by the spring of 1918, the situation had changed and the kaiser was now little more than a figurehead.

Generals Hindenburg and Ludendorff had been in command of the army since August 1916. William admired the enormously popular duo but he also resented them, afraid of their influence. With the war at stalemate and food shortages and falling wages in Germany, the Imperial General Staff was convinced that the war must be won against Russia on the eastern front. By early 1918 Hindenburg and Ludendorff had succeeded in removing William's most trusted officials, leaving Hindenburg to take the kaiser's title of Supreme War Lord.

The signing of the Treaty of Brest-Litovsk brought the Germans large swathes of Russian territory. Momentarily, the peace treaty served both sides – with Russia out of the conflict Germany would no longer have to fight the war on two fronts and could concentrate on beating the Allies in the west. Lenin gained time to consolidate his new regime.

Over the years there have been persistent rumours of a secret clause in the treaty by which the imperial family would be handed over to the Germans but such claims have never been substantiated. 'Why didn't the German Emperor make the release of the tsar and family a condition of the Brest-Litovsk peace?' an outraged Lord Stamfordham asked Lord Esher many months later.[4]

* * *

In April 1918 Count William von Mirbach was formally appointed German Ambassador to Moscow, with instructions from the kaiser to guarantee the imperial family's safety. At the same time Adolf Joffe became the Russian Ambassador in Berlin.

Mirbach was a forty-seven-year-old career diplomat from a wealthy and aristocratic Prussian Catholic family who had previously served as counsellor in the German Embassy in pre-war St Petersburg. His assistant, thirty-six-year-old Kurt Riezler, was a former philosophy student also experienced in Russian affairs. Neither spoke Russian.

Many Russians now looked to the kaiser for assistance, expecting him to save Nicholas. Russian monarchists, already alarmed at the seeming lack of effort to free the tsar, soon began calling at

Mirbach's office to lobby for the Germans to exert pressure on the Bolsheviks. Mirbach's reply was vague: 'Be calm. We Germans have the situation well in hand, and the imperial family is under our protection.' He further assured them that his government would 'take the necessary measures' when the time was right.[5]

With Allied forces already landing at Vladivostock, it suited Germany's interests to have a weak, unstable Russia bound to the Treaty of Brest-Litovsk. If Lenin's fragile regime could be toppled, Germany could set up a puppet government with a ruler of their own choice.

Mirbach now received a personal letter from Count Paul Benckendorff, Grand Marshall of the Russian Imperial Court and now the monarchist representative in Moscow. He had been prevented from following the family into exile because of his wife's health and had been replaced at Tobolsk by General Tatishchev. Benckendorff concentrated on pleading with government offices and even foreign ambassadors for money for the imperial family's daily keep, much of which fell into the wrong hands and never actually reached them. Benckendorff's letter prompted an icy response: 'The fate of the tsar is a matter for the Russian people. We now have to concern ourselves with the safety of the German princesses on Russian territory.' The German princesses were Empress Alexandra and her sister Grand Duchess Elisabeth Feodorovna.[6]

* * *

At the age of sixteen the kaiser had fallen in love with his beautiful eleven-year-old cousin Princess Elisabeth of Hesse and By Rhine (Ella), 'the most beautiful girl I ever saw'. He wrote to his mother, 'if God grants that I may live till then I shall make her my bride if you allow it.'[7] However his mother, Queen Victoria's eldest daughter Vicky, already had another princess in mind. It made no difference. All through his years at Bonn University, when he regularly spent Sundays with the Hesse family at Darmstadt, William still dreamt of making Ella his wife. Then in 1878 he suddenly forgot about Ella and declared he loved Princess Augusta Victoria of Schleswig-Holstein-Sonderburg-Augustenburg, the princess his mother always hoped he would marry. The couple were married in 1881. Three years later,

Ella married Grand Duke Sergei Alexandrovich of Russia. William studiously avoided her from then onwards.

In 1917 William suddenly showed concern for the safety of his former love. After the tsar's abdication he sent the Swedish Ambassador to convey his offer to help Ella leave Russia, with William's assurance of a safe passage. Ella refused to leave the convent. 'I could never leave my Sisters,' she said and continued to tend her patients.[8]

In 1918, with the Bolsheviks now in power, the kaiser once more was concerned. With diplomatic relations between Germany and Russia restored, he sent Count von Mirbach to Ella's Moscow convent to try and persuade her to leave while there was still time. The ambassador called there twice. Both times she refused to see him.

The kaiser was not the only German who was concerned for the safety of Alexandra and Ella. Their brother Grand Duke Ernest Ludwig of Hesse was also active on their behalf. He later claimed that the tsarina was 'a victim of circumstances' who had always been denigrated by the Russian court and that her life there had become impossible. He also said that the kaiser had taken a 'sadistic pleasure' in her downfall when the revolution came.

The revolution had been encouraged by the Germans, whose government had permitted Lenin and his followers to travel through Germany to Petrograd.[9]

On 13 March 1917, the twenty-fifth anniversary of his accession, Ernest Ludwig had received a telephone call from William. 'Ernie' had never had any love for his cousin the kaiser; in fact he 'genuinely loathed him.'[10] Now the kaiser told him bluntly that revolution had occurred in Russia and the tsar and his family were prisoners. 'Happy anniversary,' he added, before hanging up without even a word of sympathy or concern. The incident left Ernest Ludwig outraged. Two months later he received a telegram from William, who was at military headquarters, saying that 'the tsar's family had now been murdered.' The rumour was false but Ernest Ludwig was furious at the kaiser's insensitivity.[11]

The Germans had made undercover approaches to Nicholas, tied to political considerations, perhaps with a view to getting him to endorse any member of the family who would be restored by the Germans as a puppet tsar. Germany had offered the Russian throne to any Romanov who would counter-sign the Treaty of Brest-Litovsk. All refused, even Prince Felix Youssoupov, who was only married to a Romanov. As far as the Romanovs were concerned, the war continued and Germany was still Russia's enemy.

The intermediary the Germans used in their dealings with the tsar was his brother-in-law Grand Duke Ernest Ludwig of Hesse. Ernie was a general in the German army, serving at the kaiser's headquarters. While the imperial family were at Tobolsk he called on Adolf Joffe, the Bolsheviks' representative in Berlin, 'offering to mediate between Germany and Russia' during the peace negotiations at Brest-Litovsk.[12]

Lieutenant Sergei Markov of the Crimean Cavalry, a Russian monarchist officer, contacted the grand duke in 1918 through the German Embassy, offering his services to help the Romanovs. With the kaiser's permission Ernest Ludwig wrote a letter to his sister Alexandra offering German help to rescue the family. The letter was given to Markov and he was told to contact two German agents in Russia 'who served German intelligence during the war.'[13] Markov did so, reached Tobolsk and made contact with the imperial family. Alexandra sent a reply to her brother to explain why they could not accept German help. Major-General Vladimir Kislitsyn later said that he met Sergei Markov in Berlin and was shown the sealed reply. He was 'confident' that the writing on the envelope was Alexandra's. Kislitsyn testified in 1919 that the kaiser 'had earlier offered to spirit Alexandra and her daughters off to Berlin but that Alexandra had point-blank refused.'[14]

In February 1918 the French diplomat Louis de Robien reported rumours that the Germans would insist, as part of the Brest-Litovsk treaty, that Alexei be restored to the throne with his uncle the Grand Duke of Hesse as regent.

Nicholas refused to have any dealings with the Germans, considering such conduct dishonourable. He was depressed by the peace of Brest-Litovsk, calling it 'a disgrace for Russia... I should never have thought the Emperor William and the German Government could stoop to shakes hands with these miserable traitors,' he said.[15]

According to historian Robert Service, the Grand Duke of Hesse worked under the name of Major Haase and 'had important responsibility for foreign and security affairs under General Herman von Eichhorn.' In late May Paul Milyukov, the former

Foreign Minister in the Provisional Government, secretly crossed the Russian-Ukrainian border. His aim was to appeal to the German occupying authorities to help Russian officers from the Volunteer army overthrow the Moscow government. To approach the Germans he used an intermediary, a minister in the Ukrainian government, and this man's contact in the German camp was none other than Major Haase. Milyukov and Haase met on 21 June. Milyukov said that he wanted Russia and Ukraine united in a 'loose linkage' and he indicated that he would like the throne restored under Grand Duke Michael, who he believed was still under arrest. Failing Michael, he favoured a marriage between the tsar's daughter Olga and Grand Duke Dmitri Pavlovich in connection with a plan to create a Ukrainian state 'protected' by Germany and Russia. The commander of the Volunteer army, General Alexeyev, then made it clear that he 'had no intention of adopting a German orientation.'[16]

Milyukov had a further meeting with Haase on 10 July to press the need for Germany to co-operate with the anti-Bolshevik factions in Russia. The Russian peasants, he said, 'would welcome a new tsar.' But without either Alexeyev's backing or German agreement, Milyukov and his followers could not hope to mount a coup against the Bolsheviks in Moscow. There was also the further factor that a restoration of the monarchy under anybody but Nicholas would not help Ernest Ludwig's sister Alexandra.[17]

The Hesse family's involvement is further strengthened by the fact that the kaiser's brother Prince Henry was deputed to deal personally with matters relating to the Romanovs. Henry's wife was yet another member of the Hesse family, Princess Irene, the sister of Grand Duke Ernest Ludwig, the tsarina and Grand Duchess Elisabeth.

Alexandra and her brother had corresponded throughout the war via the good auspices of the Swedish crown princess and her mother-in-law Queen Victoria of Sweden. Daisy had faithfully forwarded letters right up to the end of 1916.

***

On 10 May Mirbach went to see Lev Karakhan and Karl Radek, the senior Bolshevik officials dealing with foreign affairs, and delivered 'a statement regarding our expectation that the German princesses will be treated with all possible consideration, and specifically that unnecessary petty annoyances, as well as threats against their lives, will not be permitted.' Both officials, said Mirbach, understood the situation and seemed willing to 'insist that such action be prevented.'[18]

At the request of the German imperial family and the Spanish royal family Mirbach then approached Yakov Sverdlov, the Chairman of the Central Executive Committee, with a view to getting the tsar's family transferred to Petrograd. Sverdlov told him, 'I will do all possible to bring the emperor to Petrograd, but cannot answer for the results because the local authorities do not make it possible to insist.'[19] Mirbach's continued insistence on the well-being of the family, however, did result in the central committee granting permission for money to be sent to Nicholas.

Germany was also supporting the Soviet regime by providing large sums of money to help crush resistance. Yet they were keeping their options open by enforcing the Treaty of Brest-Litovsk so that Russia would remain unstable, which would likely result in the overthrow of Lenin. The German Embassy in Moscow was not particularly in favour of the restoration of an imperial regime but, as Mirbach told the Foreign Ministry, it might be unavoidable.

There was one other consideration. Before the war Nicholas and his family had placed large deposits in Berlin banks, which the Russian Minister of Finance was unable to liquidate in time before war was declared. These deposits remained untouched and it could not have escaped the notice of the Germans that the Romanovs had immense value as hostages.

Towards the Urals

'There were plans, ... and they involved King George V and others...'

With the tsar still at Tobolsk, and Lenin and other extremists in control of his fate, there is now the first hint that King George V might have secretly backed a plan to rescue the Romanovs. By this time British Intelligence had learned of a German plot to kidnap the tsar and use him as a puppet to gain a foothold in Russia by promoting anti-Bolshevik feeling. Germany had to be prevented at all costs from getting to Nicholas.

In the spring of 1918 a Norwegian called Jonas Lied was summoned to London. Thirty-six-year-old Lied was the Norwegian Consul for Siberia before the revolution. He had made a considerable fortune out of timber and mining concessions in the area and been granted honorary Russian citizenship by the tsar through Nicholas's brother-in-law Grand Duke Alexander Michaelovich (Sandro). In 1913, with Fridjtof Nansen, he established a new trading route through the Kara Sea to America and Western Europe. He also formed the Siberian Steamship Company, navigating the rivers from the Kara Sea south towards Tobolsk. It was this connection that led him to London.

Jonas Lied had been in Russia in November 1917, where he met Lenin and Trotsky and also saw Sir George Buchanan shortly before the ambassador's recall. It may have been then, after the British had withdrawn the asylum offer, that the idea of a rescue mission was raised. It became more urgent with news of Germany's plans.

In February 1918 Lied received a wire from Henry Armitstead, head of the Hudson Bay Company's operations in Archangel and Murmansk, asking him to come to London to discuss an expedition to Siberia. The Hudson Bay Company was one of the oldest trading companies in the world and 'acted as purchasing agents for France, Russia and Romania'. It seems that both Armitstead and Lied were being paid by Mansfield Cumming, the head of MI1c (later MI6), a personal friend of George V.[1]

Lied duly crossed the North Sea to Aberdeen and arrived in London on 2 March, the day before Russia and Germany signed the Treaty of Brest-Litovsk. Colonel Frederick Browning, the personal assistant to Mansfield Cumming, had arranged for him to stay in a suite at the Savoy Hotel. The next morning he saw Colonel Browning and Henry Armitstead to discuss the expedition. Over the next few days he also met Sir William Mitchell-Thompson, the Director of Restriction of Enemy Supplies in Lloyd George's Coalition government, 'who was not very helpful', the Foreign Secretary Arthur Balfour and Lord Robert Cecil, the Parliamentary Under Secretary of State for Foreign Affairs who dealt with enquiries about the Russian imperial family.[2] On 8 March Lied had dinner with Armitstead and the head of Naval Intelligence, Sir Reginald Hall, 'who worked closely with MI1c' and whose involvement would be essential to getting the Romanovs away by sea. 'What is all this about?' Lied wrote in his diary.[3]

A few days later he was at the Marlborough Club having dinner with Sir Ernest Shackleton. During the meal the Prince of Wales stopped by their table. It was obvious that Lied had been called to London for some particular purpose that involved more than just an ordinary Siberian trading expedition. On 20 March he was taken to see Sir Francis Barker, the head of Vickers, the armaments engineers who supplied the Admiralty and the Ministry of War. Their St Petersburg agent before the war had been none other than the 'Ace of Spies' Sidney Reilly. In the adjoining office was Grand Duke Michael Michaelovich, a director of Vickers with a salary of £800.

They discussed rescuing the imperial family. According to Lied's friend Ralph Hewins, he was asked 'to berth a British boat at his sawmill depot at the mouth of the Yenisey [river] and to transport the imperial family downriver in one of his cargo boats.' On reaching the Kara Sea they would board a Royal Navy torpedo boat, which would head into the Arctic away from the minefields and any pursuing Bolsheviks.[4]

Lied, the man who had organised Fridtjof Nansen's expedition through Siberia, thought there would be no obstacle to bringing the family on a fast motorboat from Tobolsk to the mouth of the River Ob but both Barker and the grand duke asked Lied to keep their names out of it. This makes it unclear whether the scheme was Lied's and he was seeking support, or whether he had been called to London to see if a rescue was feasible. According to Summers and Mangold, Lied's diary was compiled after the war from 'surviving notes, papers and memory. On inspection, it has clearly been heavily edited ... to avoid contemporary scandal.'[5] He would certainly be the man to know how much of the river would currently be open to navigation after the long winter.

Lied wrote in his diary that 'Hagen would give £500.' Who was Hagen? Was this the Norwegian business friend who Lied says offered him a 'substantial sum'? Or was it an abbreviation of 'Meinertzhagen?' As we shall see, Colonel Richard Meinertzhagen claimed to have been involved in a later rescue attempt. Alternatively, given the fact that in an earlier diary entry Lied had abbreviated Norway's capital Kristiania to 'Kria',[6] could Hagen be an abbreviation for Copenhagen? Was the Danish royal family also involved in the scheme?

During the autumn of 1917 construction had begun at Archangel on a house that was to be erected at remote Murmansk (formerly Port Romanov) on the northern tip of Russia. Once the spring thaw arrived it would, in theory, be possible to transport the family by river from Tobolsk to Murmansk, which was sparsely populated and already had an Allied presence. The house was being assembled by the Hudson Bay Company and financed by the Admiralty in Britain under the supervision of Henry Armitstead, who was also in the pay of the British Secret Service. Construction was to be completed by November. Moreover, everything inside the building was to be provided in luxury, not standard issue, and in quantities of seven – sufficient for the tsar, tsarina and their five children.

It now appears that this building was intended as a safe house for Nicholas and his family once they had been liberated. This is corroborated by a telegram of 10 August 1918 from Francis Cromie, the British naval attaché in Petrograd, to the senior naval officer in Murmansk, which mentions a house near the British Consulate 'formerly intended for the late tsar.' Here Nicholas could live while the outcome of the war was decided, or until a British ship could pick him up.[7]

The construction of this house was kept so secret that when Lloyd George wanted to publish a book about Russian events during the First World War, parts of it were censored by George V. The king also insisted that the chapter about British involvement in northern Russia be removed from the published work and forbade any reference to a house for the tsar at Murmansk. Thomas Preston, the British Consul at Ekaterinburg, later confirmed that rumours were circulating in the spring of 1918 that the imperial family would be rescued. The Bolsheviks were also aware that the spring thaw would increase the chances of the Romanovs being freed.

In the 1970s Grand Duke Vladimir Cyrillovich said in an interview that 'there were plans, distinct from monarchist plots, while the imperial family were at Tobolsk and they involved King George V and others...' According to Ralph Hewins, 'King George backed the [rescue] plan, but the Prime Minister, Lloyd George, had no use for the tsar...'[8]

In his memoirs, written in the 1950s, the Duke of Windsor said that 'it has long been my impression' that before the Bolshevik take-over, King George had planned to send 'a cruiser' to rescue the tsar 'but in some way the plan was blocked. In any case, it hurt my father that Britain had not raised a hand to save his cousin Nicky.' He laid the blame firmly at the door of the politicians.[9]

Lloyd George was anxious to normalise relations with the Bolshevik government and he was hoping that some compromise could be reached. He had no wish to endanger this by an intervention on behalf of the tsar. The king, reluctantly, had to bow to his government's decision and, whatever the king's scheme was, the plan was not put into action.

***

In April the Romanovs' peaceful existence was shattered by the arrival of a new detachment of 150 horsemen under Commissar Vassili Yakovlev. His real name was Constantine Myachin and he was born in 1883 near Ufa. He first used the alias of Yakovlev when he fled to Europe, having been involved in revolutionary activity in Russia. In 1905 he joined the Bolshevik party but found the Socialist Revolutionary Party more in line with his own principles and left to join them. Like many others he returned to Russia following the tsar's abdication. Using the alias of Captain Tarasaov-Rodionov he was one of the men sent to the Alexander Palace to arrest Nicholas and his family and take them to the SS Peter and Paul Fortress in Petrograd. As we have seen, the men eventually agreed to leave the palace after 'inspecting' Nicholas as he walked along a corridor.

Under the alias of Yakovlev he was then appointed military commissar of the Urals by the Central Executive Committee in 1918 but Ekaterinburg rejected him in favour of their own man Filipp Goloshchokin.

Yakovlev arrived in Ufa with two mandates to transfer the Romanovs from Tobolsk. One was signed by Sverdlov, the other by Lenin, and both stated that he was on a 'mission of special importance'. Neither stated where the family would be taken. At a meeting with Goloshchokin (who a few days earlier had been assured by Sverdlov that the Romanovs would be sent to Ekaterinburg), Yakovlev was reluctantly assured that the Ekaterinburg and Regional Ural Soviets would obey him on penalty of death. By now two rival Soviets – the relative moderate Omsk and the hard liners in Ekaterinburg – were claiming jurisdiction over the Romanovs and both had their men in Tobolsk.

Yakovlev arrived on 22 April with his party of horsemen. Producing his mandates to Colonel Kobylinsky, he announced that he was acting under orders from Yakov Sverdlov in Moscow and asked to see the tsar and Alexei.

The tsarevich was ill in bed. In a daredevil bid to relieve the crushing boredom he had hurtled downstairs on his sledge, fallen off and injured his groin. He also developed a bad cough and the result was another haemophiliac crisis unlike anything since he had nearly died at the imperial hunting lodge at Spala in 1912. This time there was no Rasputin for the tsarina to turn to. At Yakovlev's insistence an army doctor was summoned to examine him and it then became obvious that Alexei was very ill. This news forced Yakovlev to reconsider his plans. He communicated with Moscow via his personal telegraph operator and then announced that he had received an order to just take the tsar away. The imperial family were given no idea of the planned destination.

A frantic discussion now ensued among the family. Nicholas was convinced that they were going to make him counter-sign the Treaty of Brest-Litovsk. Alexandra was horrified at the thought of Nicholas being alone as he was when, as she saw it, he was forced to sign his abdication. She wanted to accompany her husband. But what were they to do about Alexei? Suppose a complication set in when she was not there?

Pierre Gilliard insisted that if she went with the tsar, Alexei could be entrusted to his sisters and the rest of the household. Finally, the girls decided that as Olga's health was not strong and Anastasia was too young, Maria would go with her parents, leaving Tatiana in charge of Alexei.

Very early in the morning of 26 April the tsar, tsarina and Maria left with Yakovlev, sitting in uncomfortable peasant *tarantasses* with no springs or seats, on the first part of their 200 mile journey to the railway station at Tyumen. With them went Prince Vassili Dolgoruky, Dr Botkin, the valet Terenty Chemodurov, the footman Ivan Sednev, and the maid Anna Demidova. The rest of the children and household would follow when Alexei was well.

* * *

The news that the tsarevich and three of his sisters were now separated from their parents alarmed the children's aunt Victoria, the Marchioness of Milford Haven. From her home at Kent House on the Isle of Wight, she dashed off a letter to Arthur Balfour at the Foreign Office full of concern that her nephew and nieces were 'without a single relation to take care of them'. Although Alexei might not be allowed to leave Russia for political reasons, Victoria now wondered if the girls at least might be placed under her guardianship on the Isle of Wight. After all, she reasoned, they could be 'of no value or importance as hostages to the Russian government.'[10]

Balfour replied at the end of May. Although officials at the Foreign Office had considered approaching Trotsky to request he give 'his secret consent', one of the problems was finding a suitable escort for the young and pretty grand duchesses. It would be impossible to entrust them to the Bolsheviks, and sending British officers to bring them out via Vladivostok 'would leave the government open to accusations of a tsarist conspiracy', thus putting many more lives in danger. He promised to let Victoria know if any other opportunities presented themselves.[11]

News of the tsar's move had obviously not reached King George. By early May 1918 he was 'distressed at news of the imperial family's conditions in Tobolsk.' He asked Lord Cromer to request that the Foreign Office ask the British Consul in Moscow, Robert Bruce Lockhart, to raise the matter with Leon Trotsky. 'The request was sent but, once again, nothing further is recorded in the files.'[12]

On 23 May *The Mercury* in Hobart, Tasmania, reported that the move from Tobolsk had been allegedly due to the discovery of a plot 'in which the local peasantry had been bribed to effect the release of the deposed monarch.' After his escape Nicholas was to be accompanied by one of his daughters, Prince Dolgoruky and the Bishop of Voronezh. A search of Freedom House was said to have revealed £8,000 in cash, which according to the newspaper had been confiscated.

* * *

It has been suggested that the Yakovlev mission was either an escape attempt that was foiled, or a humanitarian arrangement with the Germans (or even the British) in return for 'vital concessions' for the new Soviet government and which later fell through.[13]

Colonel Kobylinsky was convinced that the tsar would be taken to Moscow, from where after a brief show trial the family would be transported via Petrograd to Finland, Sweden and finally to safety in Norway. Others believed they would be taken to the port of Riga, before leaving for Scandinavia. One thing everyone agreed on is that Yakovlev was unfailingly polite and solicitous towards the tsar.

Although Moscow seems a more likely scenario, the problem was the hard line Soviet of Ekaterinburg, the regional centre for the Urals. The Soviet there was determined to bring the ex-tsar, dead or alive, to Ekaterinburg. The Fourth Ural Regiment of the Red Army had been ordered by the military commissar Filipp Goloshchokin to attack the convoy during the journey to Tyumen. Luckily Yakovlev was warned and cabled Tyumen to request that an armed escort meet him along the road.

They reached Tyumen on the evening of 27 April escorted by the armed soldiers requested by Yakovlev. At the station the Romanovs were transferred to railway carriages, where Yakovlev left them to sleep while he went to the telegraph office. They would leave, he said, in the morning. Using his personal telegraph operator, Yakovlev contacted Sverdlov in Moscow asking permission to change the route to go via Omsk and await further instructions there.

Omsk lay to the east of both Tyumen and Ekaterinburg. From there it would be possible to double back on the southern railway line to Moscow, avoiding Ekaterinburg completely. Alternatively, to the east of Omsk, some 2,686 miles away, lay Vladivostok from where they could, in theory, reach Japan. What happened next depends on whether the plan was really to take the tsar to Moscow, as authors Greg King and Penny Wilson believe, or whether Yakovlev was a foreign agent trying to get the imperial family to safety abroad, the version preferred by Anthony Summers and Tom Mangold. Sir Charles Eliot, in his later report for King George V, scented a conspiracy between the Bolsheviks and the Germans to take the tsar to Germany.

According to King and Wilson, when Yakovlev telegraphed Moscow about the change of route he used the Russian word *mashrut,* which has a very specific meaning in Russian. It conveys a change of the *manner* in which Yakovlev was to reach the planned destination, rather than an actual *change* of the destination. Therefore the original destination, Moscow, did not change. There would have been no need for this telegram had Moscow originally told Yakovlev to take the Romanovs to Ekaterinburg.[14] The only way to avoid the family ending up in the hands of the Ekaterinburg hard-liners was to employ a deception. This is now what happened.

On 28 April, at five o'clock in the morning, Yakovlev's train with the Romanovs on board steamed out of Tyumen heading west in the direction of Ekaterinburg. It then reversed back through

Tyumen towards Omsk with all its lights out. Unfortunately, news of Yakovlev's plan had already reached Ekaterinburg by telegraph and, as the train continued towards Omsk, Ekaterinburg asked the Omsk Soviet to turn the train back, calling Yakovlev a traitor to the revolution.[15] Both Omsk and Ekaterinburg feared that the Romanovs would escape via Japan.

Yakovlev, warned that he could expect a hostile reception committee at Omsk, uncoupled the engine at Lyubinskaya station and proceeded into town to use the telegraph to communicate with Sverdlov. Meanwhile, Ekaterinburg was still demanding that Omsk turn the train around, despite receiving Sverdlov's assurances that Yakovlev was acting on instructions from Moscow and his warning that they must follow his orders.

Yakovlev then received a telegram from Sverdlov saying that, having 'reached an understanding with the Ural Soviet,'[16] he was to hand the Romanovs over to Alexander Beloborodov, Chairman of the Ural Regional Soviet at Ekaterinburg. 'Omsk Sovdep would not let us pass Omsk, as feared one wished to take us to Japan,' Alexandra wrote in her diary.[17] Nicholas's comment was more succinct. 'I would have gone anywhere but to the Urals. Judging from the papers, the workers there are bitterly hostile to me.'[18]

* * *

For generations of political exiles and criminals, Ekaterinburg on the eastern side of the Ural Mountains marked the point of no return, known even today as 'the last city before Siberia.' Slightly to the east lay the border between the European and Asian parts of Russia. Beyond to the west were the vast tracts where the tsars had exiled men, women and even children in their hundreds of thousands. The city was named after Peter the Great's wife and successor Catherine I and had been a thriving industrial city before the revolution, where miners had discovered rich deposits of gold, platinum and semi-precious stones. By 1918 it was a major centre of Bolshevik activity filled with militant young radicals.

On 30 April the tsar's train was greeted by an angry mob baying for the Romanovs' blood. Faced with this, Alexander Beloborodov ordered the train to proceed to Ekaterinburg's freight station No. 2 on the eastern outskirts of the city, which would be easier to guard.

Here Yakovlev had no choice but to surrender the family to the Ural Regional Soviet.

The Romanovs were taken to one of the city's finest private residences, the Ipatiev House on the corner of Voznesensky Prospekt and Voznesensky Lane, renamed the House of Special Purpose by the Bolsheviks. Ironically, Ipatiev was the name of the monastery where Michael, the first Romanov tsar, had been offered the throne in 1613. The house had been requisitioned from Nicholas Ipatiev, a retired army engineer and his wife Marie, who had bought it ten years earlier. The house had three bedrooms, a dining-room, salon, reception room, kitchen, bathroom and lavatory, all with electric lighting and hot running water. The semi-basement, part of which ran down the hill below road level, was empty as Ipatiev had intended to use it as a business office. It consisted of fourteen rooms, including a storeroom, another small vaulted room and a hallway approached from a separate door to Voznesensky Lane. Outside was a small garden and some outhouses, one of which was used as a storeroom for the imperial family's belongings. The small cottage used by Ipatiev's servants became the guardhouse. The commandant, thirty-year-old Alexander Avdeyev, a former factory worker, had an office on the house's upper level.

There were four machine gun posts and ten guard posts, patrolled twice an hour and manned by young men quickly pulled from the local prisons and factories to act as guards in the Special Detachment. Most had no army training and had volunteered to guard the Ipatiev House to avoid an army training course followed by inevitable conscription. A crude fence screened the house from curious passers-by; a further tall palisade was erected after all the Romanovs had moved in.

Having been thoroughly searched on her arrival at the Ipatiev House, Alexandra was afraid that the jewellery left behind at Tobolsk would be confiscated when Olga, Tatiana and Anastasia joined them. Many of the large pieces had been hidden or given for safety to local monasteries around Tobolsk, to be used by sympathisers to raise funds for an escape. She now sent coded instructions to her daughters to conceal the jewellery.

Back at Freedom House the girls busily began wrapping large jewels in wadding and black silk to disguise them as buttons, which were then substituted on their clothes. Rubies, pearls and sapphires were secreted inside corsets and specially constructed double brassieres, also covered with wadding. More jewels, including a large pearl necklace, were sewn into hats. In this way some eight kilograms of stones were concealed.

Writing to his children in Tobolsk, Nicholas made a clumsy attempt to enclose a plan of the Ipatiev House by concealing it in the lining of an envelope. It was confiscated by Avdeyev.

On 19 May the tsar celebrated his fiftieth birthday. A telegram of congratulation from the Scots Greys, of whom Nicholas had been appointed colonel-in-chief by Queen Victoria in 1894, was not forwarded. It had been intercepted by the censors in Britain and sent to the Foreign Office, who decided it would be inappropriate for it to be transmitted.

***

In Petrograd Harald Scavenius was scathing in his criticism of Berlin when he reported to the Danish Foreign Ministry. He asked his government to inform King Christian about the crude manner of the tsar and tsarina's transfer to Tyumen in simple peasant wagons so that King Christian could make one more attempt via the kaiser to save the tsar's family. Whether this report ever reached the king is unknown. It is quite possible it was withheld, but a translation *was* sent to the government in Berlin. The Germans then enquired whether the Danish government wished to request anything from them. The reply was blunt: 'We do not request anything from the German government, but merely inform the facts in connection with a German request to begin discussions on the subject!'[19]

***

It took three days for Princess Helen of Serbia and her Romanov companions to cross the Ural forest by train and reach Ekaterinburg, where they arrived on 3 May. Helen found rooms at a small hotel run by the Atamanov family; the others lived at the Palais Royale Hotel on Vosnesensky Prospekt, where they were allowed a certain amount of freedom by the guards. Helen soon learned that the tsar, tsarina and one of their daughters had arrived four days earlier and were imprisoned in the Ipatiev House. Every day Prince Vladimir Paley wandered along to see if there was a possibility of getting in touch with the imperial family but the high wooden palisade surrounding the building made it impossible to see anything. Nevertheless, Helen, who was not under arrest, hoped to make contact with them.

Soon after Helen's arrival the tsarina's sister Grand Duchess Elisabeth (Ella) arrived, with Sister Barbara and Sister Catherine. They are also believed to have lodged at the Atamanovs' hotel. Ella was not permitted to see Alexandra, and had to be content instead with sending small gifts of coffee, eggs and chocolate to the family through the good auspices of the nuns at the local convent. A note of thanks from Grand Duchess Maria arrived soon afterwards.

The circumstances of their confinement being somewhat lax, the Ekaterinburg *bourgeoisie* soon began inviting the Romanov princes to their dinner parties. A secret organisation was formed which included White officers and various officials from the St Petersburg Academy of the General Staff, which had been transferred to Ekaterinburg. This organisation of right-wing extremists and monarchists was led by Captain Dmitri Malinovsky. He was able to meet several members of the family while they were in Ekaterinburg and plots were discussed.

This large gathering of Romanovs at Ekaterinburg so near to the Ipatiev House was becoming unwelcome to the Bolsheviks. On 20 May they were moved.

* * *

There were twenty-three days of separation and uncertainty for Nicholas and Alexandra before the rest of the children joined them in Ekaterinburg on 23 May. The family's isolation was now complete. There were no daily newspapers and even the windows were whitewashed so that they could not see the outside world. Left with only a handful of devoted servants – Dr Eugene Botkin, the maid Anna Demidova, the cook Ivan Kharitonov, the Tsar's old valet Terenty Chemodurov, Ivan Sednev the grand duchess' footman, his nephew Leonid Sednev the kitchen boy, and the footman Alexei Trupp – they can have had very little real hope for the future.

Prince Vassili Dolgoruky was arrested immediately on his arrival in Ekaterinburg, as was General Tatishchev, who shared a cell with the tsarina's valet Alexei Volkov. Before they left Tobolsk, Tatishchev had contacted the Serbian Minister in Petrograd to tell him of the imperial family's situation. Spalaikovich had sent approximately 75,000 roubles to Tobolsk with a Serbian officer called Maximovich. What remained unspent when they moved to Ekaterinburg was divided between Tatishchev and Dolgoruky and kept for use in an emergency. Volkov believed that they still had this money and that Dolgoruky used part of his share to bribe his way out of prison. (It did him no good. In July he was rearrested and found to be in possession of maps of the region and money. He was shot, as was Tatishchev.) Chemodurov, who was ill, was taken to the prison hospital along with Catherine Schneider and Anastasia Hendrikova.

Gilliard, Gibbes and Baroness Buxhoeveden were freed. They were not permitted to join the imperial family in the Ipatiev House and were only grudgingly allowed by the authorities to remain in town because the rail line was cut and it was impossible to leave. Alexei's sailor attendant Klementy Nagorny was admitted to the house but was taken off to prison with Ivan Sednev on 27 May. They were also shot. Dr Derevenko was allowed to set up a medical practice in the town.

Alexei was still unable to walk and Nicholas now carried his son everywhere, although his leg did slowly improve. It was often left to young Leonid Sednev to sit with him when he ventured outside. Apart from evening games of chess, bezique or draughts with his parents, playing with toy soldiers with Sednev, or collecting nails and bits of string, which he stuffed into his pockets, Alexei had few distractions.

The family were sustained throughout by their fervent religious faith. In July when the priest arrived to conduct a service he found Alexei 'looking pale and thin, lying in a white nightshirt with a blanket covering him up to the waist. His eyes, looking up, were still clear but sad and distracted.'[20]

Before leaving Tobolsk on 20 May Alexei had written a last letter to his friend the doctor's son Kolia Derevenko. '...I believe we will not see each other again before our departure,' he said. '... I embrace you and bless you. Your Alexei.'[21]

* * *

In March 1918 Harald Scavenius managed to arrange for Carl Immanuel Krebs, a twenty-nine-year-old former Guards officer and Red Cross delegate to visit the dowager empress while she was under house arrest at Djulber. Interestingly, Carl Krebs's brother Ove, a delegate working to help prisoners of war, was living in Ekaterinburg near the Ipatiev House.

Through one of the foreign tutors to Grand Duchess Xenia's sons, Krebs managed to get money, provisions and a letter to Empress Marie. Shortly afterwards, the commissar at Yalta gave permission for Krebs to see her on condition that only Russian was spoken, the guard commander was present and any letters exchanged were censored. Despite the commissar's orders, the empress insisted on speaking Danish. She spoke of the loutish behaviour of the Bolsheviks and the theft of her private papers and expressed her gratitude to Harald Scavenius and his wife for all they were trying to do. Although she did not want to discuss the tsar, Krebs thought that the visit of a fellow countryman seemed to do her good.[22]

Shortly afterwards the dowager empress suffered a cruel blow when Prince George Schervashidze, who had been in poor health for some time, was found dead in bed in early April. He was buried in the little chapel in the park at Ai-Todor.

Carl Krebs reported back to Copenhagen and on 16 April Scavenius received a joint telegram from King Christian and Prince Valdemar insisting that a date of departure from the Crimea for the dowager empress and her family be speedily arranged. It would be too dangerous for any of the Romanovs to travel overland through Russia, so a sea route from Yalta to Constanza on Romania's Black Sea coast would be the safest option. A sum of 60,000 roubles had been allocated by the Danish royal family for the preparations.[23]

In the meantime, in accordance with the terms of the Treaty of Brest-Litovsk, the Germans began marching towards the Crimea. Zadorojny was warned that the Yalta Soviet planned to eliminate the Romanovs before they could be liberated by the kaiser's army. Despite its high walls, it was impossible to defend Djulber completely from an armed band so Zadorojny returned the weapons taken from the imperial family and told them to be prepared.

Bands of Yalta men now descended on Djulber under the pretext of acquiring gold for the revolution. Luckily the jewels belonging to the empress and Xenia had been left with Grand Duchess Olga, who hid them in cocoa tins by the seashore at Ai-Todor at the first sign of trouble.

With the Yalta contingent expected to arrive at any moment, machine guns were positioned and every gate and exit was locked. Zadorojny decided to go to Sevastopol to summon help. It would be a race to see who arrived first – the firing squad from Yalta or the reinforcements from Sevastopol.

After a tense, anxious night they were saved by a totally unexpected development. A party of German soldiers, sent personally by the kaiser, arrived at Djulber. The Romanovs had been freed by Russia's enemies. 'Everything is so beautiful and everything is spoiled by the German invasion,' wrote Xenia in her diary. 'This is some kind of terrible dream, I cannot take it into my head.'[24]

Both the dowager empress and Grand Duke Nicholas declined the kaiser's invitation to go to Germany and they resolutely refused to receive the German officer who had saved them from the firing squad. But the Romanovs asked the Germans to spare Zadorojny, who had performed several acts of kindness towards the family.

The Germans now occupied the Crimea. On 15 May Count Carl Moltke, the Danish Ambassador in Berlin, reported to his government that Germany considered the departure of the dowager empress undesirable. According to Joffe, the Russian Ambassador in Berlin, the Soviet government were insisting that all members of the Romanov family remain in Russia 'for their own safety'.[25]

First Victims and First Escapes

'Tell me why...?'

In June 1918 Grand Duchess Xenia and her family returned home to Ai-Todor, while the dowager empress moved to Harax, the nearby English-style house of Grand Duke George Michaelovich. The grand duke was under arrest in Petrograd, as we shall see later, and his wife the former Princess Marie of Greece, the dowager empress's niece, was in England. After returning to their estate of Tchair for a few weeks, during which time Stana angrily drove away a visiting German general with a broom, Nicholasha and Stana sold the house to an industrialist from the Urals. They then returned to live with Grand Duke Peter at Djulber.

With the Crimea now under German control the Danish royal family were active in their efforts to save the various members of the imperial family living in the region. At the end of June a report reached King Christian from the German Ambassador in Kiev saying that the dowager empress and her daughters were well. Ulrich, Graf Brockdorff-Rantzau, the German Minister in Copenhagen, had received similar information.

In mid-July Brockdorff-Rantzau handed Foreign Minister Erik Scavenius a letter from the kaiser's military cabinet addressed to King Christian, giving information about the members of the Romanov family in the Crimea. The king felt that Germany was becoming 'unfriendly'. He now explored the possibility of communicating with the dowager empress by air mail via Vienna, which was under the jurisdiction of the Austro-Hungarian military authorities. This would have the advantage of by-passing Berlin.[1] The Germans were opposed to the dowager empress returning to Denmark for political reasons. They feared she might become 'a rallying point for Russian émigré agitation against the Bolsheviks and against the German/Bolshevik connection.'[2]

The Dowager Empress Marie and her relations in the Crimea were now at least able to live a more peaceful existence. Their life, however, was soon to be disturbed by rumours from the north of Russia concerning the fate of other members of the family.

***

Grand Duke Michael and his secretary Nicholas Johnson were still living in relative freedom in the Korolov Rooms, a hotel in Perm. Michael had received some visits from his wife Natasha and one evening when they went to the theatre, flowers were thrown in their direction. The grand duke had even been making arrangements to rent an apartment in the town. Then just before midnight on 12 June 1918 two armed men, Nikolai Zhuzhgov and Ivan Kolpashchikov, arrived at the office of the hotel commissar Ilya Sapozhnikov saying that they had 'orders to evacuate Michael,'[3] whose life was in danger. They refused to allow Sapozhnikov to phone the Cheka for confirmation. In fact, the orders were forged and the telephone line had been cut.

Upstairs they found Michael in room twenty-one. His valet Vassili Chelyshev tried to bar the way but Zhuzhgov pulled out a revolver and, brandishing his piece of paper, ordered Michael to come with him. The grand duke refused, saying that first he needed to speak to the chairman of the local Cheka (who unbeknown to him was in on the plot). Neither the gun nor the piece of paper bothered Michael, who was demanding to see a doctor. While they all stood there arguing, a third man, Andrei Markov, appeared from downstairs.

Realising that resistance was useless, Michael began to dress. Johnson was permitted to accompany him (which was not part of the original plan) and they were told their belongings would be sent on later. As the grand duke was leaving, the faithful valet tried to give him his bottle of medicine. Chelyshev caught a last sight of his master through the window as Michael was pushed into a phaeton with Zhuzhgov. Johnson, Markov and Kolpashchikov occupied a second one. A fourth member of the gang, Gabriel Myasnikov, was left behind to catch the party up later. All the men were members of the Perm Cheka.

The carriages set off eastwards towards the Siberian highway in the direction of Motovilikha. When they reached a designated spot they turned right into the woods beyond Malaya Yazovaya and stopped. Michael was ordered to get out and walk, one of the men telling him 'it was a short cut to the railway crossing.' When they got out of the carriages, Zhuzhgov pulled out his revolver and shot Michael, while Markov fired at Johnson. Michael, who was only wounded, realised that Zhuzhgov was about to shoot him again and rushed forward with arms outstretched 'begging to say goodbye to his secretary.' He was felled by a bullet fired at close range. Both men were then finished off by a bullet in the temple as they lay on the ground. It was two o'clock in the morning.[4]

The Perm Cheka then informed Moscow that Michael had been 'abducted by persons unknown in military uniform' and, despite the most energetic measures, the search for the grand duke had so far proved unsuccessful.[5] The valet Vassili Chelyshev and Michael's chauffeur Peter Borunov were among thirty-seven innocent people shot in October 1918 for supposedly helping Michael to escape.

Foreign newspapers later published reported sightings of the grand duke in Kiev, Omsk and Vladivostok. Reports circulated that he was at the head of an army in Siberia and that he was the most popular candidate for the restoration of the monarchy. Prince Henry of Prussia even forwarded a report to his brother Kaiser William to this effect. In fact Michael and Johnson were buried somewhere in the woods outside Perm.

***

Queen Olga of Greece had been reluctantly forced to move out of Pavlovsk Palace in mid-November 1917. While she was alone there one night, a group of armed revolutionary sailors arrived to search for weapons. Quickly alerted by the servants, Olga came to meet the hostile band, saying she had always loved the Russian navy, had met many of the sailors when she visited the ships at Piraeus in Athens and wanted to see if any of her acquaintances were among the group. The sailors, disarmed by the queen's warm words, left quietly without doing any damage. Shortly afterwards the sympathetic commissar of the palace called on Olga. 'I had to confess to Her Majesty that ... my work [of saving Pavlovsk] would be easier if, in the eyes of the people, there were no more links with the imperial family,' he wrote.[6] Olga therefore moved to the Marble Palace in Petrograd where her sister-in-law the widowed Grand Duchess Elisabeth Mavrikievna (Mavra) was living with members of her family.

Queen Olga's dowry payment of one million roubles had been given to Greece by the Provisional Government in April 1917, all property had now been nationalised, they had very little money and food was scarce. The women resorted to stealing what were effectively their own possessions in order to sell them to buy whatever food was available.

In March 1918 Mavra's sons Ioann, Constantine and Igor were sent into internal exile. Mavra remained in the Marble Palace with her younger children George and Vera. With them also were Helen and Ioann's children Vsevolod and Catherine.

Queen Olga's son-in-law Grand Duke George Michaelovich visited her twice before he left for enforced exile in Vologda. He did his best to persuade the queen to get out of Russia as soon as she could but for many months she refused to leave her native land.

It was almost impossible to receive news from Greece and it was several months before Olga learnt that the Greek royal family had been forced into exile. Hearing that her son King Constantine was dangerously ill in Switzerland, she finally decided to join the rest of her family.

The queen's late husband King George I of the Hellenes (a brother of the Dowager Empress Marie Feodorovna) had been a Danish prince before he was elected to the Greek throne in 1863. The Greek royal family were therefore princes of Greece *and* Denmark. It was consequently Denmark who now came to the queen's assistance.

With the help of Harald Scavenius, Olga obtained a visa, although the authorities refused to recognise the title 'Queen of the Hellenes'. They compromised with the name of 'Mme Olga Hellenes'. Olga was now anxious to get her jewels safely out of the country. Realising that their luggage would undoubtedly be searched, she and her lady-in-waiting came up with a plan.

One day a Greek student called to see Mme Baltazzi bringing a package of books. The guards carefully examined the parcel and admitted him to the Marble Palace. Sometime later he left the palace carrying a box of the same size and shape made by the resourceful lady-in-waiting. It contained Olga's jewels, including a particularly magnificent set of emeralds. The guards, having searched him when he came in, saw no need to examine his parcel again. He delivered the jewels straight to the Danish Legation, from where they were sent to Copenhagen. Scavenius then organised the queen's departure.

Olga left Russia with Mme Baltazzi, a maid and a Secretary from the Danish Legation in a private carriage attached to the end of a military train carrying repatriated German prisoners-of-war. During the night the train was stopped and the local Soviet tried to uncouple the queen's carriage and leave it standing on the line, where an express train was due to pass through ten minutes later. Only the quick action of the Secretary, who woke in the night and heard what was happening, saved Queen Olga. He managed to have the carriage hooked into the middle of the train and they reached the border safely.

At the German frontier she was received with full military honours and every courtesy was extended to her throughout her journey. It was a bitter contrast to the way the queen had been treated by her own Russian countrymen. In Berlin she spoke to the kaiser's daughter-in-law Crown Princess Cecilie, the sister of Queen Alexandrine of Denmark. According to Sir Horace Rumbold, the British Ambassador in Berne, Queen Olga was told by the crown princess that 'the tsar says he will not be saved by Germany at any price. His [the tsar's] attitude much disturbs the German emperor, who spends sleepless nights in mourning over the Romanovs' fate.'[7]

By 7 July Queen Olga was safely in Lucerne. 'It is such happiness to be with my chicks [children] again after so long,' she wrote to her nephew King George V, ' – but the going away from my old home was terribly hard!'[8]

* * *

By the summer of 1918 a Bolshevik organisation was occupying a floor of the main wing of the Marble Palace in Petrograd and Mavra was forced to leave. She and her children, fifteen-year-old

George and twelve-year-old Vera, as well as Ioann and Helen's children Vsevolod and Catherine, moved in with the Zherebtsov family, who lived just along the road near the American Embassy.

The situation was becoming dangerous. George was tall for his age and already looked sixteen; there was a great risk that he could soon be drafted into Trotsky's Red Army.

One day Edvard Brandström, the Swedish Ambassador, brought a letter to the grand duchess from her friend Queen Victoria of Sweden, the wife of King Gustav V. The queen was born a princess of Baden and, showing concern for German-born Mavra, a princess of Saxe-Altenburg, she invited her to come to Stockholm.

Mavra had not converted to Orthodoxy on her marriage so it was therefore through the auspices of the Protestant Bishop Freifeldt and the Swedish Embassy that she and her family were permitted to leave Russia. With them went Prince Vsevolod and Princess Catherine with their Irish nanny Miss Irwin, the grand duchess's major-domo, her lady-in-waiting Emma Schadewitz and Prince Shakhovsky, the former adjutant to Mavra's late husband Grand Duke Constantine Constantinovich. They were each permitted to take one trunk but no gold or silver could leave the country.

They boarded the steamer bound for Kronstadt, where they spent the night. The next day the boat travelled to Reval (now Tallinn) on the Baltic where, Princess Vera recalled many years later, it was approached by 'a battered German destroyer. On board was Reval's commander the German General von Seckendorff – a Saxon and our mother's childhood playmate.'[9] After crossing the Baltic they reached Helsingfors (Helsinki) but an outbreak of Spanish flu in the city meant they were not allowed to go ashore.

Instead they boarded the ship *Ångermanland* for a journey which was fraught with danger. The passengers were searched as they embarked, there was a Soviet agent on board who took a little too much interest in Mavra's party, and the ship was halted and searched by both the Soviets and the Germans – but if they were looking for the grand duchess's jewellery they were disappointed. She had given her valuables to a Swedish diplomat who carried them to safety.

At Mariehamn on Finland's south-west coast (ironically named after Empress Marie Alexandrovna of Russia in 1861) there was a two-hour stop. General Mannerheim, who led the Whites in the Finnish civil war, came on board to speak to the grand duchess.

The *Ångermanland* continued its journey in weather so rough and foggy that the voyage took eight days instead of the expected four. Finally, they reached Stockholm where Crown Prince Gustaf Adolf met them at the harbour. The grand duchess, her family and companions remained in Stockholm as guests of the Swedish Royal family.

* * *

After twelve uncomfortable hours in a train, on 20 May the tsarina's sister Grand Duchess Elisabeth Feodorovna (Ella), Grand Duke Sergei Michaelovich, Prince Vladimir Paley, Princess Helen of Serbia, and Princes Ioann, Constantine and Igor Constantinovich reached Alapayevsk, a small town on the Asian side of the Ural mountains. They were taken in rough carts to the now deserted Napolnaya School, a six-room red brick building on the outskirts of the town. The place was dirty and they spent the first night sleeping on benches because the beds had not arrived. Sergei shared a room with Vladimir Paley and Feodor Remez. It became the communal dining room, where their cook Alexandra Krivovna served meals. Helen and Ioann shared a room, as did Constantine and Igor. Ella and her companions Sister Catherine and Sister Barbara had the largest room.

Although guarded by Latvian soldiers and members of the local Soviet, for the first few weeks they had a little freedom. Helen made early morning tea and coffee for everyone and, as she was there voluntarily and not under arrest, she was able to go shopping in town. Local children played football or skittles with the younger princes and there was a monastery nearby where on Sundays the Romanovs were allowed to attend church. A kitchen garden gave them something to do and provided food. It also helped them to get fresh air, as they were never allowed to open any windows. Apart from this there was little contact with the outside world, although occasionally a newspaper or magazine would be dropped to them over the hedge. The evenings were passed reading Russian novels delivered from the local library. A doctor also came to tend Sergei, who was in severe pain from rheumatism.

Sergei became close to Vladimir Paley, a talented poet and playwright, who was fulsome in his praise of the grand duke.

'What a beautiful soul, what intelligence, what a memory, what culture!' Vladimir wrote to his family. '... He talks quite openly with me and I know now that this man, who outwardly is so cold and haughty, is a man of tender heart and that all his life has been profoundly unhappy.'[10] Sergei also chatted to the guards, giving them his views on equality and the impossibility of equal land distribution. Some were friendly and sympathetic; others were coarse and enjoyed bursting into the rooms in the middle of the night to conduct searches. Although Sergei protested, no notice was taken.

Helen had written to the Serbian Embassy in Petrograd asking for news of Vsevolod and Catherine. The letter was smuggled out by the cook Krivovna, who hid it inside her corset. Then in early June a newspaper was clandestinely brought into the Napolnaya School from which Helen and Ioann learnt with dismay that all the palaces had been requisitioned and famine and cholera were raging through the city. They became increasingly worried about their young children, who were believed to be living in Petrograd with their grandmother.

A family council decided that Helen must make use of her safe conduct signed by Trotsky and return to Petrograd to bring the children back to Alapayevsk. The local commissar told her she would have to go to Ekaterinburg and appeal to the chairman of the Ural Regional Soviet, Alexander Beloborodov, for a permit.

On 20 June the family were allowed to go outside the compound to see Helen leave. She later recalled the terrifying moments of her departure: 'I saw all those I loved standing between the guards. For a moment, terror took over, and it seemed to me that they were lined up for execution,' she wrote dramatically in a magazine article some years later. '"I don't want to go any more," I shouted to the driver. "Stop now!" Without doubt my dear ones realised how I felt. After making encouraging signals to me, they all turned back to the house. The door closed behind them. I was alone. I had left them.'[11]

* * *

Grand Duke Michael's alleged escape from Perm on 12 June was used as an excuse and had repercussions for the Romanovs at Alapayevsk. On 21 June their regime was tightened. A barbed wire fence was erected, they were put on soldiers' rations, the games of football were stopped. Most of their belongings were confiscated, they were forbidden to write letters or to take any exercise outside the school compound. They were permitted one last telegram to inform their relatives. 'Transferred to prison regime on soldier's rations,' Prince Vladimir Paley telegraphed to his parents.[12] Prince Igor used his last message to enquire after his mother Grand Duchess Elisabeth Mavrikievna, who the princes had heard was seriously ill, although this does not appear to have been true.

Sergei sent a telegram to the head of the Ekaterinburg Soviet asking for the lifting of the prison regime, as they had done nothing wrong. Up to this point Feodor Remez, the servants, the doctor and the two Sisters who had accompanied Ella were not under arrest. On 21 June a telegram was sent from the Alapayevsk Soviet deputies to the Ekaterinburg Soviet asking if the Romanovs' servants should be arrested or permitted to leave. The answer came from Belobodorov the following day. 'Do with the servants as you wish. Any departure forbidden without permission from either Dzerjinsky [Head of the Cheka] in Moscow or Uritsky [Head of the Cheka] in Petrograd or the Ekaterinburg Local Soviet. Announce to Sergei Romanov that his imprisonment is a preventative measure against escape because of the disappearance of [Grand Duke] Michael from Perm.'[13]

Sister Barbara and Sister Catherine were taken back to Ekaterinburg, with Prince Vladimir Paley's Polish valet Ceslav Kronkovsky and Ivan Kalin, the valet to the Constantinovichi princes. They were all set free. Sister Barbara then returned to Alapayevsk to share Ella's fate. The faithful Remez, who had been with Sergei since 1905, had remained with him at Alapayevsk.

***

After a terrifying train journey surrounded by coarse soldiers, Princess Helen of Serbia arrived in Ekaterinburg on 21 June and took refuge in the Atamanovs' hotel. Here she was forced to burn the letters she had smuggled out from the Alapayevsk prisoners after Mrs Atamanov told her their discovery would mean her certain death. The next day, still wearing her nurse's uniform, Helen went to the Cheka Headquarters in the Hotel Amerika on Voznesensky

Prospekt and demanded to see Alexander Beloborodov. He refused to let her find her children, or to return to Ioann in Alapayevsk, saying that rail travel was impossible because of the military situation.

Just along the 3-mile-long Voznesensky Prospekt from the Ipatiev House was the British Consulate, opened in 1913. The French, Swiss, Americans, Germans, Swedes and Danes also had consulates in Ekaterinburg. Trapped in Ekaterinburg, Helen visited the British Consulate almost daily to see the Consul, Thomas Preston, and reel off a long list of demands. She wanted him to intervene on behalf of her imprisoned husband, 'speak to the Presidium of the Ural Regional Soviet and guarantee her continued freedom,' and obtain a travel pass for her so that she could get to Petrograd and find her children. Most important of all, she wanted him to obtain permission for her to visit the tsar and his family at the Ipatiev House.[14] Helen was convinced that the Germans planned to kidnap Nicholas and force him to sign the Treaty of Brest-Litovsk and she was insistent that Britain must make arrangements to free the family.

Thirty-two-year-old Thomas Preston had been British Consul since 1916. Fluent in Russian (and with a Russian wife) he had formerly been the Siberian representative of a Leeds mining company. As Consul in Ekaterinburg he had been instructed by the War Office to keep an eye on the Urals platinum industry. Preston was in a difficult position. He was 'resident in a town which was the seat of a Bolshevik government' whilst maintaining contact with the White army and the Czech legions who were closing in on the town.[15] He was also in touch with secret agents who told him to support the Czech revolt.

Helen continued to pay frequent visits to the Hotel Amerika in an attempt to see Beloborodov. Finally, the Ekaterinburg Cheka warned her that unless she desisted she would be thrown into prison. Undeterred, she simulated a wound and went to see Dr Derevenko, who had arrived with the rest of the imperial children on 23 May, to see if he would intervene on her behalf and obtain permission for her to see the tsar's family.

Dr Vladimir Derevenko was a pragmatist who had his own family to consider. He had maintained a good relationship with the Bolsheviks and is said to have cured Beloborodov's wife when an epidemic of Spanish flu swept through Ekaterinburg. In gratitude the doctor was given his freedom and allowed to set up a practice in the town. Conversing in whispers while Derevenko dressed her wound, Helen learnt that security around the Ipatiev House was tight, he never saw the family without a guard and could therefore not pass on a message.

This was not strictly true. Derevenko is believed to have been the conduit who supplied information to monarchist factions, including a group of Serbians under a Captain Stepanov. The doctor provided these monarchist plotters with weekly reports on conditions in the Ipatiev House as well as floor plans. Others, noting the deference with which the Bolshevik guards treated Dr Derevenko, suspected him of collaboration.

Still Helen did not give up. She walked straight up to the Ipatiev House and asked to see the commandant. Avdeyev came out to the gate to see her. 'I am the wife of a Romanov interned at Alapayevsk,' she told him, 'but I am also the daughter of the King of Serbia... As a relative of the tsar, I have come to hear news of him and, if you will allow it, to see him.'[16] He refused to let her in but later that evening she received a message of thanks from the tsar and tsarina saying they needed nothing. There is no mention of this in the tsarina's published diary.

On 4 July four more Serbs arrived in Ekaterinburg – Major Jarko Michich (the adjutant to the Serbian military attaché), Prince Ioann's former steward at Pavlovsk Serge Smirnov, and two soldiers, Sergeant Major Bojitchitch and Captain Abramovich. After visiting the princess at the Atamanovs' house Michich and Smirnov presented their credentials at the Hotel Amerika, saying they were on an official mission from Miroslav Spalaikovich, the Serbian Minister, sent to bring Princess Helen back to Petrograd. Although communications were unreliable and difficult, the Ural Regional Soviet sent a telegram to Petrograd to check. When the answer finally arrived some four days later the deception was uncovered. The Serbian Minister's request for Helen to return to Petrograd had already been refused by the Petrograd Cheka.[17]

Belobodorov sent a telegram to Sverdlov in Moscow on 9 July, saying that Michich and Smirnov had been arrested on a charge of 'misleading the Soviets' and asking where they should be sent.[18] The Ural Regional Soviet were nervous. Riots and demonstrations had broken out in Ekaterinburg and they feared an attack on the Ipatiev House.

Helen was also arrested.

The princess's memoirs were written and published some forty years later. Confusion now sets in as she muddles the dates and events of her two visits to Ekaterinburg, so it is not always possible to work out exactly what happened next.

Helen says that she was taken to the Hotel Amerika to face a military tribunal, where to her utter astonishment she was given a pass to return to Petrograd. She was then released and, on returning to the Atamanovs, found Michich and Smirnov there. Helen then says that Michich had been ordered to reunite her with her children and take them all north to Murmansk, from where they could leave Russia. Helen refused. She would not leave Russia without Ioann and declared she would accept their help only as far as Petrograd.

The next day they all boarded a train to the capital. While they were waiting to leave, their carriage was silently uncoupled. As the rest of the train pulled away, Helen and her companions found themselves surrounded by soldiers. Helen was taken before Yurovsky (soon to be the tsar's executioner), who ordered her to be stripped, searched and locked up in the city prison.

On 19 July an urgent telegram purporting to be from Helen (but obviously not written by her, as the new Soviet spelling was used) was sent from Ekaterinburg to Lev Karakhan, Deputy Commissar for Foreign Affairs. 'Having relied upon negotiations with you and your permission given to me to leave for Petrograd, the Serbian Ambassador Spalaikovich sent on my behalf a mission of four persons of which he informed you via the Petrograd Commune. Until now I have not been given permission to leave, I and the despatched persons being kept under arrest. I beg of you to urgently clarify this misunderstanding with the local Soviet.'[19]

***

Apart from the kaiser's representations on behalf of the German-born Ella, no foreign effort seems to have been undertaken on behalf of the Romanovs at Alapayevsk. Although the tsarina's sister was imprisoned there, they seem to have been forgotten. Ella's sister the

Marchioness of Milford Haven received news of her from time to time and passed it on to King George, but it was always out of date.

As the White army closed in, the Bolsheviks decided to act. During the afternoon of 17 July the guards were replaced by Bolshevik workers from Ekaterinburg, who took the prisoners' remaining money and told them they would be transferred that night to the Verkhne-Sinyachikhensky works about 10 miles away. After a hurried supper the prisoners were blindfolded and put into carts outside with their hands tied behind their backs. When Sergei barricaded himself behind a cupboard one of the guards shot him in the arm. He offered no further resistance.

As the carts rumbled out of town, Sergei repeated that he knew they were going to die. 'Tell me why?' he asked. 'I have never been involved in politics. I loved sport, played billiards ... was interested in numismatics...'[20]

At about one o'clock in the morning of 18 July the carts approached Sinyachikha, where the prisoners were made to walk several hundred yards to the disused Nizhny Seliminsky mineshaft. There Grand Duchess Ella, Grand Duke Sergei Michaelovich, Princes Ioann, Constantine and Igor Constaninovich, Prince Vladimir Paley, Feodor Remez and Sister Barbara were hit on the head with blunt instruments and thrown alive down the mineshaft. Sergei resisted and was shot in the head.

It was officially announced that the prisoners had been abducted by persons unknown and that full searches for them were underway.

In London it was believed that the men had escaped. Victoria Milford Haven heard the news from Mavra, who at that point was still in Petrograd and reported all the rumours and reports from the Consul. Victoria wrote to the king, 'I hope that Ella may be at Alapayevsk, where there are evidently people who were still kindly inclined toward the prisoners – but Elisabeth [Mavra] did not know whether Ella and Helene of Serbia were there still or not.' Victoria promised to pass on any further news.[21]

But Ella and the other Romanovs at Alapayevsk were dead.

* * *

Princess Helen of Serbia was still in prison. After two weeks, the woman who brought her food said that the White army had freed the Alapayevsk prisoners and was heading towards Ekaterinburg. Only the second statement was true.

The next morning Helen was ordered to dress. In the street were armed guards who claimed they were waiting to take her to Moscow. But they drove into the forest instead. Helen thought that she was to be shot in retaliation for Ioann's escape and as they stopped in a forest clearing she prepared herself for the worst. Instead she was pushed towards the only two women there – Countess Anastasia Hendrikova, the tsarina's lady-in-waiting, and Catherine Schneider, her reader, both pale and emaciated from weeks in prison. They were all herded into a barred railway carriage, which then set off for Perm, where they were forced to walk 3 miles from the station to the prison. Here the women were placed in a single cell.

Five weeks later the guards came one night for Countess Hendrikova and Catherine Schneider. As they left, the Countess pressed a message for her sister into Helen's hands. After a sleepless night pacing her cell, Helen learnt the next morning that her companions had been shot.

Helen was then moved to a cell with twelve criminals, 'to allow her to meet the real people' while her own fate was being decided.[22] Most of these women were prostitutes and all had committed (or were accused and convicted of) murder but gradually they became curious and began talking to her. In return Helen learned about the violence and misery of their lives. During the five months she spent in their company the Serbian princess had her eyes opened to a whole new world.

10

Ekaterinburg

'We may be rescued only by force...'

By June, in both Moscow and Berlin, Germany was emphatically demanding assurances about the safety of *all* the Romanovs. There were already Germans in Ekaterinburg. Ostensibly members of a Red Cross mission concerned with the repatriation of the former prisoners-of-war, they had arrived during May and June and were living aboard a luxurious train drawn up in the city's main station. The group, which included nurses and some German generals, had been welcomed by the local commissars and, reported *The Times*, they were there 'to ascertain all about the life of the residents of the Ipatiev House.....'

General Michael Diterikhs, the White Russian General who later supervised the original investigation into the imperial family's deaths, believed that a German proposal may have been passed to the tsar by Colonel Ivan Siderov. He was a former imperial aide-de-camp who arrived in Ekaterinburg from Odessa in June 1918 and spent three weeks in the city. Siderov brought letters for the imperial family from their friends, which he passed to the family via Dr Derevenko. Through him he then made contact with the nuns from the Novotikhvinky Monastery and Convent who brought provisions to the family every day. In this way he was able to smuggle notes to the imperial family but whether these involved a proposal from the Germans is another matter. Diterikhs also speculated that Siderov may have transmitted 'a communication with respect to the imperial family's pending removal from Ekaterinburg' orally through Dr Derevenko,[1] but this is pure conjecture.

Another route, which the White investigator Sokolov believed was used, was that messages were communicated through the priests Father Meledin and Father Ioann Storozhev, one of whom was occasionally permitted to conduct a Sunday service at the Ipatiev House. With the commandant continually watching them during these services this seems unlikely.

The tsar, like many other members of his family, did not recognise the legality of the Treaty of Brest-Litovsk and considered that Germany and Russia were still at war. He could not be thought to have co-operated with the Germans, whose army the Russians had fought with such a great loss of life and at great expense to the Russian nation. Even an *involuntary* arrangement, whereby Nicholas was transferred to German control, would incite suspicion that he had been party to some sort of deal. The family lived in dread of such an arrangement. Germany's interest in the tsar may have been purely political – the wish to set up a chain of puppet monarchies on their eastern front.

* * *

Anti-Bolshevik forces were gathering in Samara, about 480 miles south-west of Ekaterinburg. It had been taken on 8 June by a combination of the Czech legion and the advancing White army, who had now joined forces. A month later, 'nearly the whole of the Trans-Siberian railroad from Penza to Vladivostock lay in Czech control.'[2]

With the railway line cut by fighting, the Russian Ambassador Joffe told State Secretary William von Kuhlmann that 'it was important to them [the Russians] to look after the emperor's family and put them in a suitable place.' It was impossible to do anything about bringing them to Moscow until the rail connection was reopened, even though the decision to move them had been made. Even without the co-operation of Nicholas, the Germans had done some sort of deal with the Bolshevik government for the safety of the family.[3]

The kaiser was deeply upset and concerned that Nicholas had refused his country's offers of help and sent constant questions to Mirbach about the situation. Mirbach, who had been at the heart of German efforts on behalf of the tsar, went to see Georgi Chicherin in the Kremlin to demand an explanation about foreign press reports that the tsar had been assassinated. Although he was given assurances that the rumours were false, the Russians were unable to establish the current situation in Ekaterinburg.

By now Lenin was so worried that he sent Reinhold Berzin, military commander of the Northern Siberian Ural front, to Ekaterinburg to personally verify that rumours of the tsar's execution were false. Berzin was told in no uncertain terms that if any violence was done to the family he would pay with his own life. It was clear now that Moscow was not solely in charge of the Romanovs' fate. Authors Greg King and Penny Wilson have speculated that rumours of the tsar's murder were spread by Ekaterinburg to test Moscow's reaction.[4]

Only on 28 June were the Russians able to assure Germany that the tsar was safe and the counter-revolution had been crushed. Such was the chaotic situation that Mirbach suggested that the German government now 'consider switching to rival political groupings in support of the restoration of a monarchy' under Grand Duke Michael.[5]

Mirbach had no idea that the tsar's brother was dead.

* * *

In the summer of 1918 Count Alexander Mossolov, former head of the tsar's Chancellery, was in German-occupied Kiev where he met Prince Kotchubey (a former colleague) and Duke George of Leuchtenberg. Duke George and his elder brother Duke Nicholas were second cousins of the tsar and were also related to the royal family of Sweden through the Swedish queen, Victoria. Together they concocted a plan to rescue the tsar with German help.

Duke George spoke to General Herman von Eichorn, commander-in-chief of the occupying army, and also to his Chief-of-Staff General Groener. The Germans promised 'machine-guns, rifles and motor-cars' which would be loaded on to two vessels and sent along the River Volga and its tributary the River Kama.

They would stop 40 miles from Ekaterinburg to receive further instructions. Two officers would be sent into Ekaterinburg to get in touch with German secret agents who were already hiding there. The plan was apparently to take the tsar and his family to Berlin. Duke Nicholas went to the German capital for consultations in the summer of 1918.

Meanwhile Alexander Mossolov, knowing that the tsar would never consent to be freed by the Germans, asked Count Werner von Alvensleven, the kaiser's ADC in the Ukraine (and also ADC to General von Eichhorn) to deliver a letter to the kaiser. In it, he asked William to write a letter to the tsar guaranteeing that he would be sent to the Crimea 'without having to submit to captivity in Germany.' Mossolov would arrange for it to be delivered to the tsar. The answer, when it eventually came, was that 'the kaiser was unable to reply without consulting his government'[6] and furthermore, when the imperial family heard about the plan they rejected any hint of German help.

Kiev, the capital of German-occupied Ukraine, was the setting for another curious episode. On 5 July, in a meeting with the White General Prince Alexander Dolgorukov and a member of the Ukraine State Council Feodor Bezak, Count Werner von Alvensleben accurately predicted the date of the tsar's execution. He told Dolgorukov and Bezak that the news of Nicholas's death would come between 16 and 20 July and would be a diversion, because the kaiser wanted to save the tsar. He said it was important that they act as though they believed the tsar was dead. Von Alvensleben then asked them to send some Russian officers to ascertain Nicholas's exact location. Why, when the Germans had their own well informed intelligence network? What was going on here?

Historian Karina Urbach thinks that Prince Max of Baden may also have supported a German Foreign Ministry plan to rescue the tsar, although it has so far proved impossible to verify this.[7] The prince was another relation of the Romanovs. Through his mother he was a great-grandson of Tsar Nicholas I; his wife Princess Marie Louise of Cumberland was a niece of the Dowager Empress Marie Feodorovna. Before the war Max had been a regular visitor to Russia where he met Nicholas II.

Middleton Edwards, the British Consul in Geneva, was briefed about a German plot to free Nicholas and his family, move them across German-occupied Russia and then across the Baltic to Denmark in a neutral ship. Although the tsar had refused all German offers, the Germans were planning to kidnap him and take them to Germany whether Nicholas wanted to go there or not. The rescue would be for humanitarian reasons. The Swiss Section of the League for the Restoration of the Russian Empire had been asked whether they agreed to this plan. Edwards' source for this report was Maurice Poznanski, the pre-war Commercial Attaché at the Russian Embassy in Berlin, and Swatowski, a diplomat in Vienna. Edwards sent the report to Berne, from where it was forwarded to London marked 'secret'. By the time it arrived at the Foreign Office on 21 July the first reports of the tsar's murder were circulating and the report was filed.

The French Secret Service in Switzerland had also received this report but, according to Summers and Mangold, there is no more mention in the files of London or Paris about this scheme.[8]

* * *

Early in July Mirbach was present at the 5th All-Russian Congress of Soviets held in Moscow's Bolshoi Theatre, where members of the Left Socialist Revolutionary Party (rival extremists opposed to Lenin and his policies) unleashed their wrath against the Treaty of Brest-Litovsk. Their anger was especially directed at the German ambassador.

On 6 July two men announced themselves at the German Embassy on Denezhnyi Pereulok claiming to be members of the Cheka who wanted to speak to Mirbach about a relative detained on suspicion of espionage. Mirbach reluctantly came down to see them. A moment later both men pulled out revolvers and fired at Mirbach and his assistant Kurt Riezler. Both shots missed. As the ambassador tried to escape one of the men fired at the back of his head and the other threw a bomb. Mirbach died later that afternoon. The men were Left Socialist Revolutionaries.

Riezler, who was already a sick man, now assumed charge of the embassy and he demanded that Lenin 'appear in person with an explanation and an apology.' There was no choice. The Germans had so much influence that he had to obey.[9]

The Germans demanded that they be allowed to send a battalion to Moscow, and Lenin now feared that they would use the murder as an excuse to invade Russia.

In Moscow chaos reigned. The Bolshevik regime seemed to be on the verge of collapse and the threat of a Left Socialist Revolutionary counter-revolutionary coup was only averted by the intervention of the Latvian Rifle division, skilled troops from Trotsky's Red Army.

***

On 16 July, the Danish newspaper *National Tidende* sent a cable to Lenin in the Kremlin. They had heard rumours that the tsar had been shot and wanted to know if the news was true. Lenin had a reply drafted denying the rumour but later it was returned undelivered because the telegraphic connection to Denmark had failed.

In London on 3 July *The Times* had published a dispatch from their Petrograd correspondent. The report, dated 23 June, spoke of the rumours purportedly spread by Moscow to test public reaction to the murder of the tsar: 'Every time this kind of public prominence is given to the Romanoff family people think that something serious is on foot. Bolshevists are getting impatient of these frequent surprises about the deposed dynasty, and the question is again raised as to the advisability of settling the fate of the Romanoffs, so as to be done with them once for all.'

This was not long in coming.

***

The situation around Ekaterinburg had changed and by June the Romanovs were no longer in the middle of a Bolshevik stronghold. The Czechs controlled Omsk, Cheliabinsk and Samara. The province of Perm was now in danger and the Romanovs were close to an area of fighting from which the Bolsheviks were in retreat. As the Czech army closed in on Ekaterinburg the situation had a direct bearing on the family's fate.

Thomas Preston was frequently urged by the foreign tutors Gibbes and Gilliard, who had remained in Ekaterinburg, to bring pressure to bear on the Bolsheviks regarding the tsar. 'Our only hope was diplomatic pressure,' Preston said in a BBC interview in 1971. 'I used to visit the Soviet daily ... saying that the British government was interested in the situation of the imperial family. They always assured me they were in perfectly good health, well treated, and they were certainly in no danger.'[10] His frequent representations were resented but Preston continued, saying that he did so because of their close relationship to the British royal family.

There had been a panic on 13 June, when Avdeyev told the family to quietly pack and be ready to leave. The family did so, hoping that they would be taken to Moscow and then eventually on to England – but once again the crisis passed and their hopes came to nothing. It appears that the Bolsheviks feared that either anarchists or an underground monarchist organisation would attack the Ipatiev House and free the prisoners. Such an attempt may well have succeeded. Later, various guards or their relatives were quoted as saying they probably would not have used their rifles in the event of an attack, the men in charge of the machine guns had not practiced how to use them and, anyway, most of the men were 'half-wits who knew nothing'. Paul Bykov, a member of the Ekaterinburg Soviet, maintained that many of the more rigorous security measures were not in place. He believed that 'it was not out of the question that a rescue could have succeeded,' especially during the spring.[11] The family would have co-operated fully with any organisation that would free them provided that they could all be taken away together, as is shown by the incident of the officer letters. Between about mid-June and the first week of July, the tsar's family received four letters purporting to be from supporters who hoped to free them. The first one was written in French and concealed among provisions brought by the nuns from the Novotikhvinsky Convent. The cook for the Special Detachment, to whom the provisions were delivered, discovered it concealed in the top of a bottle of cream and handed it to Avdeyev. It came from a monarchist group consisting of Dmitri Malinovsky (who, as we have seen, had already met the Romanov party who were afterwards transferred to Alapayevsk) and others. Malinovksy was in regular contact with Dr Derevenko, who had given him a floor plan of the Ipatiev House.

The discovery of the letter gave the Bolsheviks an idea. Peter Voikov, the Commissar of Supplies, spoke French fluently, so the Cheka had him alter the text slightly, then it was copied out and handed to the Romanovs. It was signed 'An Officer of the Russian Army' and requested a sketch of their rooms, the time they all went to bed and told them to be ready. 'One of you should not sleep between two and three o'clock all the following nights. Reply in a few words, but give, I beg you, all useful information to your friends outside.'[12]

The reply, probably written by either Olga or Tatiana, came a couple of days later and was confiscated by the Cheka. It pointed out that all the windows were sealed shut and that Alexei was ill in bed, unable to walk. 'It is important not to risk anything without being absolutely sure of the result. We are almost all the time under watchful observation.'[13]

A second letter was handed over by a member of the interior guard on or around 24 June. The previous day, in response to frequent representations from the family who were suffering in the intense summer heat, a single window in the tsar and tsarina's bedroom was finally unsealed by Avdeyev. The letter from 'An Officer' rather conveniently asked if a window could be unglued and told them to indicate which window it would be. Alexei's illness complicated matters but the letter writer did not see it as an insurmountable problem. The family's reply the following day gave details of the window, the location and routine of the guards and asked them not to forget the servants, who had voluntarily followed them into captivity. If they had to stay behind, could they be sure that nothing would happen to them?

'We spent an anxious night,' Nicholas confided to his diary on 27 June, 'and kept up our spirits, fully dressed. All this was because a few days ago we received two letters, one after the other, in which we were told to get ready to be rescued by some devoted people, but days passed and nothing happened and the waiting and the uncertainty were very painful.'[14]

By this time the guards of the Special Detachment had begun to view the Romanovs as normal human beings. Only fourteen of the 105 guards who served at the Ipatiev House at this time were over twenty-five. Many had fallen into easy conversation with the tsar's daughters, looking at the photo albums of their former life while the girls drank tea in the guardroom. Inevitably sexual tension was rife as these young men were exposed to the proximity of four beautiful young women.

Things came to a head on 27 June when one of the young guards, a former factory worker called Ivan Skorokhodov, was apparently found with one of the grand duchesses. No name is mentioned in any of the sources, none of which are first hand, but King and Wilson guess at Maria, the most beautiful, sincere and flirtatious of the girls, who was celebrating her 19th birthday that day. Details of the actual incident are hard to come by, as the pages of the guards' duty book covering the incident are 'unavailable,' but it is generally agreed that Skorokhodov smuggled a cake into the Ipatiev House and was later found consorting with one of the younger grand duchesses during an inspection of the house by Alexander Beloborodov and Filipp Goloshchokin, respectively chairman and military commissar of the Ural Regional Soviet. Skorokhodov was carted off to the city prison, after which no more is heard of him.[15]

The following day another letter was received by the family asking for further details of the guards and detailing the plan. 'Upon the expected signal you close and barricade with furniture the door separating you from your guards who will be blockaded and terrorized in the interior of the house. By a rope made specially for this purpose you descend through the window. You are expected below...' The family were expected to provide the rope and it was some days before they replied.

'We do not want to and cannot flee. We may be rescued only by force as it was by force that we were taken from Tobolsk. Therefore do not count on any active aid on our part...'[16]

For several more nights the family had little sleep, perhaps expecting some sort of rescue attempt but the tension was now showing. Nicholas even stopped writing his diary, which was a most unusual occurrence, and from June the entries were made only periodically.

Soon afterwards there was a tightening of security, caused, Nicholas wrote, after things belonging to the Romanovs had been stolen from the shed. Avdeyev was dismissed and new specially selected guards were appointed inside the House of Special Purpose, all dedicated Bolsheviks from the Verkh-Isetsk factory volunteer battalions. Most were foreigners.

The change of guard prompted one final letter, clearly a forgery by the Cheka. 'We are a group of officers in the Russian army who have not lost consciousness of our duty to emperor and country. We are not informing you in detail about ourselves ... but your friends D and T [possibly Dolgoruky and Tatishchev] who are already safe [they were not] know us. The hour of deliverance is approaching...'[17]

No response to this letter has been preserved. The Cheka now had all the evidence they needed to justify the execution of the family to the Central Executive Committee in Moscow because of the discovery of a plot to free them.

* * *

On 4 July, Yakov Yurovsky was appointed Commandant of the Ipatiev House. The Germans, whose ambassador was still making representations that the family be well-treated, were assured that discipline had been restored. After 1 July Dr Derevenko paid no more visits to the imperial family.

One of Yurovsky's first acts was to order the family to hand over their jewellery, ostensibly for safe keeping. If he hoped that the fabled Romanov jewels would be handed over, he was disappointed. A minor collection of rings, brooches, earrings, necklaces and bracelets was given to Yurovsky and all were catalogued. The women were allowed to keep bracelets which were too tight to take off, as was Nicholas's engagement ring. Alexei was also permitted to keep his watch.

On 9 July the guards' duty book recorded that a bomb had gone off near the Ipatiev House. This incident, caused by the carelessness of a guard who was throwing grenades from his post on the upper terrace out of boredom, gave rise to various garbled accounts in the newspapers. According to the *New York Times*, the guard had mistakenly pulled the ring out and, finding the grenade was hissing, quickly threw it into the lane where it exploded. This led to several similar reports stating that Alexei had died of fright.

Poul Ree, the Danish Vice-Consul in Perm, heard about the incident when he visited Ekaterinburg. 'While I was there, a bomb was thrown over the fences around the tsar's villa,' he told his mother. 'Lots of noise – little damage. The man got away in the smoke and the dust. Next day there was nothing to see....'[18] Ree also heard that Alexei had died of fright, although he told his mother that he didn't believe it.

On another occasion loud noises and shouts were heard from the garden while the family were taking their daily exercise.

ИХЪ ИМПЕРАТОРСКІЯ ВЕЛИЧЕСТВА И АВГУСТЪЙШІЯ ДЪТИ.

Above: The Imperial family at the time of the centenary of the dynasty, 1913.
Seated: Grand Duchess Olga, Nicholas II, Grand Duchess Anastasia, Tsarevich Alexei, Grand Duchess Tatiana.
Behind: Grand Duchess Maria, Empress Alexandra. (Collection of Ian Shapiro)

Below left: Grand Duke Michael Alexandrovich, the Tsar's brother, whose refusal of the throne in 1917 ended the 304-year-old Romanov dynasty. He was exiled to Perm and killed by the Bolsheviks in 1918. (Collection of Mark Andersen)

Below centre: The Dowager Empress and her sister Queen Alexandra: The Danish-born sisters, close since childhood, were distraught at not being able to communicate freely after the revolution. (Collection of Ian Shapiro)

Below right: Nicholas II and George V at their last meeting, Berlin 1913.
Although the cousins had been close, George reneged on the government's offer of asylum to the Imperial family. (Collection of Ian Shapiro)

The Hesse family, 1903.

Empress Alexandra remained close to her siblings but the war put them on opposing sides.

Left to right: Grand Duke Ernest Ludwig of Hesse, Empress Alexandra Feodorovna and Tsar Nicholas II of Russia, Princess Irene and her husband Prince Henry of Prussia, Grand Duchess Elisabeth Feodorovna (Ella) and her husband Grand Duke Sergei Alexandrovich of Russia, Princess Victoria and her husband Prince Louis of Battenberg. (The Eurohistory Photo Archive)

Nicholas and Alexandra in captivity, 1917.

Nicholas adapted well to their new circumstances but Alexandra, whose health was poor, was bitter at the family's downfall. (Courtesy of Galina Korneva)

The family of Grand Duchess Xenia and Grand Duke Alexander Michaelovich ('Sandro'), 1909. Left to right: Prince Nikita, Princess Irina, Princes Andrei and Dmitri, Grand Duchess Xenia holding Prince Vassili, Princes Feodor and Rostislav and Grand Duke Alexander Michaelovich. All except Irina were held under house arrest after the revolution. (Private collection)

Ai-Todor, the Crimean home of Grand Duke Alexander Michaelovich and Grand Duchess Xenia. The Dowager Empress was held under house arrest here with Xenia and her family in 1917. (Private collection)

The family of Grand Duke Constantine Constantinovich, 1909.
Back: Princess Tatiana, Princes Gabriel and Ioann, Grand Duchess Elisabeth Mavrikievna (Mavra) and Grand Duke Constantine Constantinovich (died 1915).
Front: Princess Vera, Prince George, Princes Igor, Oleg and Constantine.
Oleg was killed in 1914, Grand Duke Constantine died the following year, and Princes Ioann, Constantine and Igor were killed by the Bolsheviks. Mavra escaped with her youngest children George and Vera. (The Eurohistory Photo Archive)

Above left: Prince Ioann and Princess Helen, 1911.

Prince Ioann Constantinovich and Princess Helen of Serbia at the time of their engagement. Helen voluntarily followed her husband into internal exile. She survived but he was killed by the Bolsheviks. (Marlene A. Eilers Koenig collection)

Above right: Nicholas II in captivity at Tsarskoe Selo, 1917.

The well guarded Tsar is sitting by the bridge marking the furthest limit in the Alexander Park to which the family were allowed to walk. (Courtesy of Galina Korneva)

Below: The Tsar's children at Tsarskoe Selo, 1917.

Olga, Alexei, Anastasia and Tatiana taking a rest after working in the kitchen garden in the Alexander Park, May 1917. (Courtesy of Galina Korneva)

King Christian X and
Queen Alexandrine of
Denmark.

They could do little
to help the king's cousin
Tsar Nicholas, or save
three of the Queen's
uncles from death at the
hands of the Bolsheviks
but they looked after
Grand Duke Michael's
young son until he could
be reunited with his
mother. (Collection of
Mark Andersen)

Harald Scavenius
(1873-1939).

The Danish Minister
in Petrograd from
1912-1918. The
Dowager Empress
said that he was the
only one who helped
the Romanovs but he
was recalled by his
government at a critical
moment. (Courtesy of
Peter Scavenius)

Queen Olga of Greece.
The magnificent jewels of the Tsar's Russian-born aunt were spirited out of Russia by the Danish Embassy. (Collection of Mark Andersen)

King Haakon VII, Queen Maud and Crown Prince Olav of Norway.
Despite their close family links with Nicholas and Alexandra, there was little the Norwegian monarchs could do to help as the Norwegian government had little sympathy for monarchies. (Collection of Mark Andersen)

Left: King Gustav V and Queen Victoria of Sweden.

The pro-German sympathies of the Swedish sovereigns were well-known and, although they could not help the Tsar, they were able to assist other members of the Romanov family. (Collection of Mark Andersen)

Below: The semi-circular hall of the Alexander Palace.

In the summer of 1917 Nicholas II and his family left the palace for the last time through the central doors to go into an uncertain future in exile. (Margaret Guyver)

Above left: Grand Duchess Elisabeth Feodorovna (Ella).

The Empress's sister became a nun after she was widowed in 1905, but her care for the poor and needy did not save her from the hands of the Bolsheviks; she was killed at Alapayevsk with other members of the family in 1918. (Collection of Ian Shapiro)

Above centre: Grand Duke Sergei Michaelovich.

One of the three Michaelovichi Grand Dukes killed by the Bolsheviks. Sergei was killed at Alapayevsk, while his brothers George and Nicholas were executed in the Saints Peter and Paul Fortress in January 1919. (Private collection)

Above right: George Brasov, son of Grand Duke Michael Alexandrovich. Although Michael was killed by the Bolsheviks in Perm, his young son was smuggled to safety in Denmark where he lived for a year with King Christian and Queen Alexandrine. (Kongernes Samling, Amalienborg)

Above left: 'Georgie, 11 April 1919.'

The photo of George Brasov that King Christian X of Denmark kept in his office. (Kongernes Samling, Amalienborg)

Above right: King Alfonso XIII and Queen Victoria Eugenie (Ena) of Spain. Alfonso did his best to help the Romanov women, who he believed were still alive in August and September 1918. (Private collection)

Nicholas II and the Kaiser.
Although the relationship between them was difficult, the Kaiser suffered sleepless nights when the Tsar refused his offers of German help. (The Eurohistory Photo Archive)

The Ipatiev House, Ekaterinburg, from a 1920s postcard. The arched windows are the basement where the Imperial family were murdered. (Collection of Ian Shapiro)

Grand Duke and Duchess George of Russia, 1900.
The former Princess Marie of Greece lobbied monarchs all over Europe in an effort to free her husband from a Bolshevik prison. She was unsuccessful. Grand Duke George Michaelovich was shot in January 1919. (The Eurohistory Photo Archive)

Grand Duke Paul Alexandrovich and family.

The Tsar's uncle was shot in the SS Peter and Paul Fortress in January 1919. He is pictured with his wife Olga, his children and step-children.

Left to right: Olga, Princess Paley; her son and daughter Alexander and Olga von Pistolkors; Grand Duke Paul; his and Olga's daughters Irene and Natalie Paley and son Prince Vladimir Paley; Olga's daughter Marianne Derfelden.

Prince Vladimir was killed by the Bolsheviks at Alapayevsk but Olga, Natalie and Irene escaped to Finland. (The Eurohistory Photo Archive)

Right: Grand Duke Dmitri Pavlovich, his sister Marie and Prince William of Sweden.

Dmitri and Marie were the children of Grand Duke Paul by his first marriage. Marie Pavlovna and Prince William married in 1908. Although they divorced in 1914, Marie's status as a former member of the Swedish royal family was of great help to her during the revolution. (Private collection)

Princess Catherine Yourievsky.
As the youngest daughter of Tsar Alexander II's morganatic marriage, she was in great danger during the revolution. She escaped with her second husband Prince Sergei Obolensky and died in England in 1959. (The Eurohistory Photo Archive)

Grand Duke Cyril Vladimirovich and his wife Victoria Melita ('Ducky').
The couple reached relative safety in Finland but as civil war erupted they were in a precarious position. They declined King Gustav of Sweden's offer of help and finally reached Europe in 1920. (Collection of Mark Andersen)

Queen Marie of Romania
('Missy'), 1917.

Missy was concerned for her sister Ducky and other relatives trapped in Bolshevik Russia but failed to persuade her aunt, the Dowager Empress, to leave for Romania.

However, in 1919, having failed to save the other Romanovs, George V sent a warship to evacuate his aunt and members of her family from the Crimea. (Marlene A. Eilers Koenig collection)

Grand Duke Nicholas Nicolaievich ('Nicholasha') on board HMS *Marlborough*.

The former Commander-in-Chief of the Russian army and his brother Grand Duke Peter were among those evacuated, with the Dowager Empress, on HMS *Marlborough* in 1919. (Collection of Ian Shapiro)

Grand Duke Dmitri Pavlovich.
When the Grand Duke arrived unexpectedly in England at the end of 1918, he was angry and appalled at remarks made by King George V. (Private collection)

The British royals: King George V and Queen Mary, with their family. Left to right: Albert (later George VI), George, Duke of Kent; Queen Mary (May of Teck); Henry, Duke of Gloucester; King George V; and Princess Mary. King George's failure to help his cousin Tsar Nicholas preyed on the minds of both the King and Queen. (Flickr Commons project, 2017)

Grand Duchess Olga Alexandrovna and her family.
Olga and her second husband Nicolai Kulikovsky left the Crimea for the Caucasus and reached Denmark in 1920. Their sons Tihon and Guri (in his father's arms) were born after the revolution. (Private collection)

Quickly investigating, Yurovsky found Alexei and the kitchen boy Leonid Sednev, who was two years younger than the tsarevich, lighting fireworks and tossing them at the guards and over the fence, where they exploded. It transpired that Alexei had been allowed by Avdeyev to keep a box of fireworks for his amusement. They were immediately confiscated.

Thomas Preston was urging London to get the tsar out to prevent him from falling into German hands but with the unreliable nature of communications his messages did not always reach London. He paid frequent visits to Sergei Chukazev of the Ekaterinburg Soviet to stress that he and his diplomatic colleagues were concerned about rumours that the tsar and his family were not being well treated. Chukazev's assurances to the contrary were not convincing.

Inside the Ipatiev House the monotony and uncertainty of daily life continued.

* * *

With the imperial family now firmly under guard at Ekaterinburg there have been rumours for many years that King George V mounted a last-minute rescue attempt, which failed. It has long been suspected that the king had been having meetings with British secret service agents and it is believed that a member of the Royal Naval Air Service was involved in a plan to rescue some of the family by air.

The man who was asked to plan an escape for the family was Air Commodore Peregrine Forbes Morant Fellowes.[19] Born in 1883 at South Yarra, Melbourne, Australia, he originally served as a Lieutenant Commander in the navy. He later joined the Royal Naval Air Service and obtained his flying certificate at the Royal Naval Air Station, Chingford, in 1915. In 1918 he was shot down while bombing the Ostend canal. The official version is that he was 'rescued by the Germans and spent the remainder of the war as a POW, later receiving a Mention in Despatches for valuable services while in captivity.'[20] This was in connection with preparatory work for the Zeebrugge and Ostend raids in April 1918. Other sources say he was taken prisoner and later escaped.[21]

According to Prince Michael of Kent, the plan to fly an aeroplane into Ekaterinburg could not take place due to logistical reasons, which prevented a plane from flying in there.[22] The corroborating documents of the proposed rescue plan are apparently 'not available'.[23]

The report of Sir Charles Eliot, British High Commissioner for Siberia, who arrived in Ekaterinburg in September 1918, spoke of a plane seen flying over the city on 14 July. 'There is some evidence that they [the Bolsheviks] were much alarmed by an aeroplane flying over the garden of the house and I fear it is comprehensible that in a fit of rage and panic they made away with His Imperial Majesty,' he reported.[24]

If Air Commodore Fellowes *was* involved in any failed mission his career did not suffer. According to the *London Gazette* of 1 January 1926, in 1925 he was appointed ADC to King George V, in which capacity he served until 1929. In 1933 he became the first pilot to fly over Mount Everest.

Another story surfaced from the family of Sergeant John Taylor Waite of the 20th Hussars. They say that in March 1918 about thirty men from the regiment were given 'top secret orders' emanating from King George V to try to rescue the tsar and his family. The plan involved meeting up with White Russian Cossacks loyal to the tsar and taking the family to Constantinople, from where they would go by ship to America. By the time the party arrived in Russia, the tsar and his family had been murdered at Ekaterinburg. 'During this mission a number of brave men were fatally wounded' but they did apparently rescue some of the tsar's relatives.[25] Who and where these relatives were remains unspecified.

If nothing else, these stories indicate that many people still *believe* that King George V tried to do something to help his relatives.

Yet another story involves Colonel Joseph Whiteside Boyle, a Canadian who was working for British Intelligence. His daughter Flora maintained that her father was 'one of the last men to be seen with the ill-fated Tsar Nicholas of Russia and his family'. Boyle had allegedly 'had a plan all ready for their escape' from Ekaterinburg but Nicholas refused to leave Russia. The story was published in *Maclean's Magazine* on 1 June 1938 but, unfortunately for Flora, at the time the imperial family were killed Joe Boyle was miles away in Kishinev, having suffered a 'massive heart attack'.[26]

Boyle, however, *was* involved in efforts to rescue other members of the imperial family, as we shall see later.

* * *

As rumour and counter-rumour flourished, monarchist groups and secret agents converged on Ekaterinburg and began watching the Ipatiev House.

A French agent was hiding in the British Consulate. On 9 July he sent a telegram to the French Consul in Moscow: 'Arrived Ekaterinburg. At present living at British Consulate. Rumours about Romanovs false. *Boyar*.'[27] The word '*Boyar*' in Russian meant aristocrat.

The American journalist Carl Ackerman from the *New York Times* reported that people were watching the imperial family from the window of a building opposite the Ipatiev House. 'A private telephone in this house was connected with the house of a certain prominent businessman. The man in the attic and this merchant communicated with each other day and night, and I remember learning from one of them some of the secret phrases they used in talking, so that if anyone should by chance overhear them the Bolsheviki [*sic*] could not understand. When the observer under the roof of the house across the street saw the tsar in the garden he would phone, "the baggage is at the station" and then messages would be communicated to the tsar.'[28]

Several of the agents in Ekaterinburg were British.

Stephen Alley was born near Moscow in 1876. His father John Hyder Evans Alley was an engineer; his mother Victoria Ruffel was also born in Russia. The family had a country estate and also a town house. Stephen was educated at Moscow's prestigious Fiedler school, before returning to England to study at King's College, London. He later took a degree in engineering at Edinburgh University before becoming an engineer in the family firm of Alley & McLellan. After falling out with his cousin, he set up his own company. Later he 'joined the Imperial Yeomanry, a reservist unit, and qualified as a interpreter in Russian, French and German.'[29] Finding himself almost bankrupt, he returned to Russia in 1910 and worked on the construction of the oil pipeline to the Black Sea.

A fluent Russian speaker who could pass for a native, he was recruited by Military Intelligence on the outbreak of war and sent to Petrograd, where he was privy to the plan to murder Rasputin in 1916. Early in 1918 he was fired by Mansfield Cumming, the head of the Secret Intelligence Service (MI1c), in circumstances that are unclear. Alley later said it was because of his refusal to assassinate Stalin. Whatever the reason, his journey back to London took him via Murmansk and, if he had been fired, he was soon back in harness.

Alley was briefed on a plan to rescue the imperial family and transport them to the safe house in Murmansk, the idea first mooted back in March. The journey overland from Ekaterinburg would be long and arduous.

On 24 May Alley sent a cable to the headquarters of MI1c in London naming four officers who he would like to have under his orders for a mission. All were fluent Russian speakers able to pass as natives and all were told they might be required to ditch their uniforms and don civilian attire. Capture could entail them being shot as a spy. They were Lieutenant George Edward Hill, Lieutenant John Hitching, Lieutenant Ernest Michelson and Lieutenant Commander Malcolm McLaren, a former sea captain and member of the Royal Navy Volunteer Reserve who wore gold earrings 'that gave him the look of a pirate'. Alley requested that London provide him with a grant of £1,000 a month due to 'increased requirements for intelligence purposes'.[30]

Once again liaison for the mission was to be in the hands of Henry Armitstead of the Hudson Bay Company, to whom expenses for his trip would be fully reimbursed, but this time Jonas Lied was not involved. 'I have made it clear to Armitstead, in no uncertain terms, that his role is strictly liaison and that he must leave all arrangements for the journey to Murmansk to us,' Alley wrote in an undated note. 'We are responsible for securing and delivering the valuables, he is responsible for their safe passage out of Russia.'[31]

By June Stephen Alley was in Ekaterinburg doing reconnaissance work. He obtained a sketch of the outside of the Ipatiev House and its location on the corner of Voznesensky Prospekt and Voznesensky Lane, noting that in order to effect a rescue he needed details of the roads – their 'width, how constructed, what materials available on the spot for repair … any particular steep gradients such as would affect movement of carts.' What were not marked on the sketch were the machine gun posts all around the building, including one on the Cathedral of the Ascension opposite, and the numerous guard posts.[32]

All the time, he and his local agents were watched by the Cheka and 'it is believed Alley's telegrams to London may have been intercepted,' leading to tighter security around the house. The rescue plan was aborted. A relative of Alley later explained in an interview that it was called off 'because it wasn't possible to achieve it.' The Ipatiev House appeared impregnable. There are also 'strong indications' that he was 'involved in a special assignment in Murmansk ... which may ultimately have resulted in failure.'[33]

What Alley probably didn't know, of course, was that in June the guards were not what they seemed. As we have noted, they were young, at least one of them was flirting with a grand duchess and they were not experienced in the handling of rifles and machine guns. Not until the beginning of July was the regime tightened. This is not to say it would have been possible to rescue the family, but a bit of British bulldog spirit might have gone a long way. Whatever happened, Alley was recalled to Britain.

Another agent arrived on 16 July and was billeted at the British Consulate. Captain Charles Kenelm Digby-Jones of the Royal Engineers was a fluent Russian speaker who arrived in civilian clothes, having come 'through the lines from General Poole's expeditionary force at Archangel,' ostensibly as a liaison officer for the advancing Czech forces.[34] The name 'Jones' was later scrawled in the margin of Sir Charles Eliot's report alongside the description of shooting and uproar on the night of 16/17 July in the Ipatiev House. Digby-Jones died in Vladivostok on 25 September 1918. There was a secret intelligence organisation temporarily based at Vladivostok at that time 'under Shaw from Hong Kong who is in touch with Sir Charles Eliot.' Sir Charles was also said to have had details of Digby-Jones' death.[35]

Another possible rescue mission centred on a Royal Flying Corps Officer called Stephen Bertholt Gordon-Smith. The son of a British father and a Russian mother, he was fluent in the language and, in 1915 when invalided out of the British army, he joined the Royal Flying Corps. His fluency in Russian soon saw him seconded to the Imperial Russian Air Force.

During the war he worked with the later Dean of Windsor, the Rev'd Eric Hamilton, another fluent Russian speaker. Gordon-Smith was attached to the British Military Mission, where he was ordered to find a plane, 'rescue the Imperial family at all costs' and fly them to Archangel. A British submarine would be waiting there to take them to safety. This was the plan but then, for unknown reasons, orders suddenly arrived 'to abandon the project and return via Stockholm.'[36]

Then there is the mysterious diary entry of Colonel Richard Meinertzhagen, who claimed to have been asked by George V if anything could be done to rescue the imperial family by air. According to his account, 'On July 1st everything was ready and the plane took off. Success was not complete and I find it too dangerous to give details. One child was literally thrown into the plane at Ekaterinburg, much bruised and brought to England where she still is.'[37] Meinertzhagen has been described by many people as a fantasist, as all the family's bodies have been accounted for.

But did an abortive rescue mission actually take place? In 1974 British authors Anthony Summers and Tom Mangold were told by Sir Anthony Royle, a former Under Secretary of State at the Foreign Office, that after making enquiries, he had learned that 'there was a Naval Intelligence dossier on a mission that had been designed to bring the Romanovs out of Russia.' He was unable to say more, as he was bound by the Official Secrets Act.[38] Was this a botched rescue mission that went tragically wrong? Were the British co-operating with the kaiser's Germany over this? If that was the case, they would have every reason to want the attempt kept secret.

* * *

On 16 July the kitchen boy Leonid Sednev was removed from the Ipatiev house, having been told he was to go and see his uncle. 'Wonder whether it's true & we shall see the boy back again!' Alexandra wrote in her diary.[39]

The White Volunteer Army, comprising monarchists, counter-revolutionaries and anyone else who was opposed to the Bolsheviks, led by Alexander Kolchak, had been boosted by 25,000 Czech deserters. As the Whites made inroads into Western Siberia, many of the men assigned to guard the Romanovs had been sent off for military duty to protect the fledgling revolution, leaving Ekaterinburg with only a thin line of soldiers defending the city.

At eight o'clock that night a curfew was imposed on Ekaterinburg. Machine guns were placed on the roof of the Ipatiev House and on

Voznesensky Square; passers by were ordered at gunpoint to walk on the other side of the street from the house. The local population remained indoors as silence descended on the city. Before retiring for the night Alexandra finished writing her diary. 'Played bezique with Nicholas. 10.30 to bed. 15 degrees.'[40]

* * *

On 25 July the White army took Ekaterinburg. They found the Ipatiev House empty. There was only the sinister ground-floor room, with blood on the floor and bullet holes in the walls. It was obvious that something terrible had happened there and that someone, perhaps the servants, had been shot. As the Whites began an investigation only one thing was certain – the imperial family had completely disappeared.

11

The Trust of Kings

'The west are wishful thinkers, we will give them what they wish to think.'

– Lenin.

On 17 July 1918 the British Consul-General in Moscow, Robert Bruce Lockhart, sent a brief message to London: 'Ex-emperor of Russia shot on the night of 16 July by order of the Ekaterinburg local Soviet in view of approaching danger of his capture by Czechs ...'[1] Lockhart had received the news in a telephone call from Lev Karakhan, the Deputy Foreign Commissar.

In Ekaterinburg Thomas Preston also heard the news that morning and went down to the telegraph office to send a message to Arthur Balfour at the Foreign Office. His text read: 'Tsar Nicholas the Second was shot last night.' Before he could send it Goloshchokin snatched it away and substituted his own message. 'The hangman Tsar Nicholas the Second was shot today – a fate he richly deserved.' It was this version that was transmitted, although because the telegraph was so unreliable it probably never reached its destination.[2]

The announcement came the following day from the official Communist press bureau. Although it mentioned the tsar's death it stated that 'the wife and son of Nicholas have been evacuated to a safe place.'

Lockhart's telegram took several days to reach London.

Just days earlier, on 6 July, King George and Queen Mary had celebrated their silver wedding anniversary with a service at St Paul's Cathedral and an address from Parliament at the Guildhall. As tsarevich, Nicholas had attended their wedding in 1893. Nicholas and George had their photograph taken together; Nicholas sitting on a chair, George standing beside him, both with the same carefully trimmed Van Dyke beard and looking for all the world like brothers. Queen Victoria was one of many people who commented on the likeness. The public were deceived too, always mistakenly cheering the tsarevich when they caught sight of him along the route. 'Everyone finds a great resemblance between George and me, I am tired of hearing this again and again,' Nicholas wrote in exasperation in his diary.[3] At a garden party George was asked if he was enjoying his visit to London, while Nicholas was congratulated on his forthcoming wedding. Now Nicholas was reportedly dead. There is no record of King George's immediate reaction, or any note of contrition for his own part in the tragedy. Margot Asquith later recorded that his grief was obvious and that he had described his cousin's murder as 'abominable.'[4]

The Norwegian newspaper *Aftenposten* reported the news on 21 July based on secure messages from Moscow to Berlin but, according to this report, only the tsar had been killed. The Swedish press reported that Nicholas was killed because he was seen as a danger to the revolution. They also stated that Grand Duke Michael was free and working for the monarchy's restoration. A telegram from the British Ambassador in Berne reported that the tsar had died alone, in a military execution. This despatch was forwarded to King George.

The Times of London published the Russian government's official announcement on 22 July. With rumours about the fate of the imperial family swirling around, the British government tried to verify the information.

On the evening of 23 July Arthur Balfour sent a telegram to the British Embassies in Copenhagen and Stockholm marked 'urgent' and 'personal', asking if they had any definite information about the death of the tsar. He requested that any *reliable* news be telegraphed to London immediately.[5]

* * *

In Moscow the Senior Counsellor at the German Embassy Kurt Riezler reported Sverdlov's statement of 18 July about the tsar's execution to Berlin. The Germans immediately demanded reassurances as to the fate of the rest of the family and wondered whether they should repeat their former representations on behalf of the German princesses on Russian soil. 'To extend the representations to the tsarevich as well would be dangerous because the Bolsheviks are no doubt aware of the monarchists' inclination to put the tsarevich in the forefront,' a memo from Riezler to the German Ministry of Foreign Affairs said.[6]

Riezler went to see Karl Radek, head of the European Department of the Bolshevik Foreign Commissariat, to protest against the tsar's murder. With Nicholas's wife and children generally supposed to be still alive, he then 'gave urgent warning against further actions of this nature.'[7] He was informed that Nicholas was executed to prevent him from falling into the hands of the Czechs and that Alexandra had been taken to Perm (which he did not believe). 'Radek asserted the personal opinion that if we show special interest in the ladies of the Imperial family of German blood, it might be possible to grant them free exit. It might perhaps be possible to free the tsarina and the tsarevich (the latter as inseparable from his mother) as indemnification in the matter on a humanitarian basis,'[8] Riezler reported. Perhaps also the Germans could then give up their demand to send a battalion to Moscow.

Radek then continued: 'In case Joffe [the Soviet Ambassador to Germany] ... should really offer to make an immediate, strong move against the allies, with support from us [the Germans] against contingencies, our acceptance might be conditional on their undertaking to grant freedom, on humanitarian grounds, to the tsarina and tsarevich...'[9]

On both 23 and 24 July Riezler went to see Chicherin to demand further assurances. By this time the kaiser was reported to be having nightmares about his relatives' fate. 'I did all that was humanly possible for the unhappy tsar and his family, and was seconded heartily by my chancellor,' he told General Wallscourt Waters in the 1930s.[10]

The Germans had a highly developed intelligence network in the Urals by 1918 although, with fighting still going on, the Hughes telegraph (a primitive form of telex machine), the only means of communication, was difficult and often unreliable at the best of times. The telegraph line ran along the railway and the line was often cut by anti-Bolshevik forces. However, based on what their agents were reporting, the Germans had every reason to believe that the Romanov women, if not the tsarevich, were still alive.

In an effort to confirm that the tsarina had not been killed, Riezler asked the Bolsheviks to pass on a greeting from her sister Princess Irene of Prussia. He was informed that the local Perm Soviet had been asked to forward the telegraphic message but this action could endanger Alexandra's life. Although Chicherin said he would try to find other means of ensuring the tsarina received the message, Princess Irene never received any acknowledgement of her greeting.

Riezler was ill during the critical summer months and there is apparently no mention of the Romanovs in his papers. He was recalled in August and the efforts to free the Romanov women were continued by Dr Karl Helfferich, Mirbach's successor as ambassador.

On 31 July Helfferich reported that he had been told by the Soviet government that Grand Duke Sergei was in Perm and Grand Duchess Ella was in Petrograd, living impoverished in her own palace. Empress Augusta of Germany had received news of Ella from some of the grand duchess's German friends and she reported on 8 August that all Ella's wealth had been confiscated. In fact, both Sergei and Ella were dead; and anyway the grand duchess had no wealth, having used it to build the Convent of Martha and Mary in 1909.

Helfferich only remained in Moscow a short time. In August the German Embassy pulled out and went to Petrograd.

The kaiser blamed the British for the tsar's murder and he was anxious to exploit the Allies' abandonment of Nicholas for propaganda purposes. 'For the dethroned tsar, for whom England had no further use, neither the British government nor the Foreign Office did anything,' an official from the German Foreign Ministry noted.[11]

* * *

After receiving news of the tsar's death William immediately contacted King Christian of Denmark. Harald Scavenius appears to have missed the official Soviet notification of the tsar's murder. He reported the news to the Danish government from Petrograd on 24 July but, as Sir Ralph Paget told London, Denmark thought that the murder had occurred on 1 July, a date also reported by

The Times in London. Scavenius believed, as did most people, that only Nicholas had been killed and that Alexandra and the children had been moved, probably towards Perm. The Foreign Minister Erik Scavenius considered that events in Russia were an internal matter and no official statement was issued by the Danish government or the royal family.

King Christian informed the British ambassador, who later that day reported to the Foreign Office: 'Family here after making all possible enquiries are of opinion that there no longer exists any doubt as to death of the tsar.' Sir Ralph promised to telegraph any further news.[12]

Stockholm had no information but Sir Esme Howard replied that he would telegraph anything that could be ascertained.[13]

In Norway on 27 July, the national press and foreign legations were informed that three weeks' court mourning would take place. King Haakon and Queen Maud were both cousins of the tsar.

King Christian, who was at Marselisborg, his summer residence in Aarhus, also ordered three weeks court mourning from 26 July but this time the foreign representatives were not informed. They were, however, told about the memorial service for the tsar which took place in the Russian Church on Bredgade in early August and was attended by the royal family and members of the diplomatic corps accredited to Copenhagen.

Although the Danish royal family must have been deeply shocked, there was no instruction to Harald Scavenius to protest to Moscow about the murder of the king's cousin and neither did Denmark consider breaking off diplomatic relations. They did not expect the Bolsheviks to be in power for long and, in order to protect Danish commercial interests in Russia, the Danish government had recognised the Bolshevik government in May 1918. A permanent diplomatic mission was now established in Copenhagen. The Danish government had allowed these considerations to take priority over the king's family feeling.

* * *

After the White army retook Ekaterinburg in July the urgent question of what had happened to the family began to be examined. There were no bodies, just the statement that the tsar had been shot and his family taken to a safe place. As they searched through the debris at the Ipatiev House – icons, books, Alexandra's perfume bottle and other personal belongings – a White Russian officer appeared bringing some items found in Koptyaki Forest, about 9 miles north-west of the city. He told them that from early morning on 17 July the peasants had been turned away from the woods at gunpoint by soldiers of the Red Army. Only after Ekaterinburg had fallen to the Whites did they dare return. Near the Ganin Pit, an abandoned iron mine in an area known as the Four Brothers, they found evidence of bonfires, pieces of broken jewellery and some burnt clothing near the mouth of the shaft.

The next day one of the peasants returned to the site accompanied by the civilian court investigator Alexander Nametkin, Captain Dmitri Malinovsky of the St Petersburg Military Academy (who had already been involved in escape plots), Dr Derevenko and the tsar's former valet Terenty Chemodurov. The doctor and valet confirmed that the jewels had belonged to the tsarina and the grand duchesses – but if the tsar was dead, where were the family?

* * *

Meanwhile, the question of mourning for the tsar now occupied the British royal family and the government, who appeared to be worried about public reaction. Lord Stamfordham particularly thought that the king should not attend the memorial service 'for fear of irritating public opinion.'[14]

On 23 July a memo was sent to Stamfordham by Arthur Balfour at the Foreign Office. The prime minister, he said, was 'quite aware that some comment and criticism might be levelled against the king if he was represented at the requiem service and thereafter ordered court mourning for the late tsar. But he was clear that taking into account the close relationship between the sovereigns, and that the emperor was always loyal to the Entente and always most friendly to the king, no criticism need divert His Majesty from the natural course of treating the emperor's memory with the same respect as would be extended to other friendly sovereigns. The tragic circumstances of his death appear to render this course more consonant to natural good-feeling than it would have been...'[15]

The first *known* reaction from the royal family comes in Queen Mary's diary, where she wrote on 24 July that 'the news were [sic] confirmed of poor Nicky of Russia having been shot by those brutes of Bolsheviks last week.' She called this act 'too horrible and heartless', adding that 'Mama and Toria [Queen Alexandra and Princess Victoria] came to tea, terribly upset at the news.' A postscript added in pencil later says that 'His wife Alix, his son Alexis, & daughters Olga, Tatiana, Anastasia & Marie were shot as well.'[16] King George declared court mourning for one month from 24 July, with half-mourning to be worn from 14 to 21 August.

On 25 July a memorial service was held at the Russian Embassy Chapel. Among those present, *The Times* reported, were Queen Alexandra with her daughters the Princess Royal and Princess Victoria; the Duke of Connaught; Grand Duchess George of Russia with her daughters Princess Nina and Princess Xenia; the Marchioness of Milford Haven; the former ambassador to Russia Sir George Buchanan and his wife, and members of the embassy staff, diplomatic corps and prominent Russians.

'We attended the Memorial Service in memory of poor Nicky in the Russian Chapel Welbeck St at 12,' Queen Mary recorded in her diary. For once, the king's entry was more fulsome. 'May and I attended a service at the Russian Church in Welbeck Street in memory of dear Nicky who I fear was shot last month [sic] by the Bolshevists,' he wrote. 'We can get no details. It was a foul murder. I was devoted to Nicky, who was the kindest of men and a thorough gentleman: loved his country and people.'[17]

During July and August memorial services were also held in Paris, Rome, The Hague, Oslo, Corfu and Stockholm.

There was still no news about the fate of Alexandra and the children. On 25 July *The Times* published a Reuters report that Alexandra 'had been taken away from Ekaterinburg.' Another report which reached Berlin and was published by *The Times* on the same day stated that the tsarevich died of exposure a few days after his father's execution.

Many people believed that the tsarevich was also dead. But what of his mother, and his sisters Olga, Tatiana, Maria and Anastasia? The royal houses of Europe now tried to find out where they were.

* * *

The king of Spain now stepped back into the picture and, as part of his vast humanitarian war effort, tried to help the surviving Romanovs.

Queen Ena, a cousin of the tsarina, had already made her feelings plain in a letter to another cousin Queen Marie of Romania. The revolution was, she said, a very serious thing for all European monarchies but she was particularly scathing in her view of Alexandra: 'And to think that Alix is a great deal to blame for having brought ruin on her whole family,' she wrote in June 1917. 'I would not be in her place at the moment for anything.'[18]

The Spanish royal family were at their summer residence, the Palacio de la Magdalena in Santander, when news arrived of the tsar's murder. Alfonso cancelled his participation in a polo match in order to attend a bullfight – but this seeming lack of concern belied activity behind the scenes. Spanish mediators immediately made contact with Bolshevik agents and reached agreement in principle about the transfer of the surviving members of the family to Spain. A telegram was sent to Harald Scavenius saying that King Alfonso was prepared to receive the dowager empress, Empress Alexandra and Tsarevich Alexei and requesting 'that a way be found to communicate return suggestions for resolving the matter as soon as possible.'[19]

According to *The Times* of 3 August, on King Alfonso's initiative, 'the Spanish Ministry of Foreign Affairs has approached the cabinets of the belligerent countries with a view to the removal to Spain of the widow and daughters of the ex-Tsar Nicholas.'

Progress of the negotiations was confirmed by a report from the French *Deuxième Bureau* and Prince Maximilian von Ratibor und Corvey, the German Ambassador in Madrid, who informed Berlin on 3 August 'that King Alfonso was making a personal effort to obtain better conditions for the family.'[20]

On 4 August 1918 Alfonso Merry de Val, the Spanish Ambassador in London, wrote to the Minister of Foreign Affairs Eduardo Dato. The ambassador had good connections. His brother Cardinal Rafael Merry de Val was Secretary of State to the Holy See during the papacy of the previous Pope, Pius X. Spain now proposed a joint mediation between King George and King Alfonso, in an effort to get Britain to take action. Ambassador Merry de Val did not see any prospect of the tsarina being allowed to go to England. 'So profound and alive is the hatred towards the unfortunate empress ... that exclusive action in her favour could easily be interpreted as inspired from Berlin with the desire to protect the well-served German interests.' This resentment, he concluded, 'goes so far as to exclude any possibility of her residing in the United Kingdom.'[21] He also raised the question of the dowager empress and enquired whether it would be possible to include her in the negotiations. The British were concerned about her fate and, as the sister of Queen Alexandra, intervention in her favour could only make matters easier for the release of Empress Alexandra.

On 6 August *The Times* published a piece from Reuters in Amsterdam. They had picked up a news report, which said that 'it is declared in political circles in Moscow that the ex-tsarina is safe. It is, however, reported that the government intends to bring her before a revolutionary court owing to her relations with Rasputin.'

Luis Polo de Bernabé, the Spanish Ambassador in Berlin, offered the hospitality of King Alfonso to the surviving members of the imperial family as soon as they were free. Alfonso was anxious for other European sovereigns to publicly express support for his action in order that his hand might be strengthened. 'This will especially be the case if the Russian government demand, as they are not unlikely to do, official recognition by Spain as the price of their acquiescence in any such arrangement,' wrote *The Times* on 8 August.

On the same day Alfonso telegraphed King George V seeking approval of his action. 'May [Queen Mary] wires me she would be grateful for any assistance I can give to save the Russian imperial family – can I count on your approval?'[22]

With King George away, Queen Mary forwarded the message to the Foreign Office asking for Mr Balfour's approval to reply to Alfonso in the following terms: 'George is away. My telegram was sent with knowledge of Foreign Office.' The secretary at Buckingham Palace noted that 'It is evident that the king of Spain is afraid to act on his own initiative.' This was not the case, as soon became apparent.

In fact this telegram was not sent. The queen asked for it to be stopped because Grand Duchess George of Russia (who had telegraphed the Spanish for help in trying to free her own husband, who, as we shall see, was imprisoned in Petrograd) had sent Queen Mary a telegram she had received from the Spanish monarch. In it Alfonso wrote: 'Ena has given me your telegram. I am absolutely willing to add [Grand Duke George] to the request that I am making for the empress and her children but it would be of the highest importance that the king of England telegraphs me in this sense to give more force to my request which is not easy. Alfonso R.'[23]

In view of this, Queen Mary did not wish to compromise herself or King George when replying to Alfonso. It was therefore suggested that the following text be substituted: 'My telegram specifically referred to Grand Duke George [Michaelovich] and was sent with Mr Balfour's knowledge [King] George being away. I can only speak for myself but I feel sure that he would be very grateful for anything you feel you can properly do to improve the lot of his unfortunate relatives.'[24] The telegram was duly sent to the Madrid embassy on 8 August, with Mr Balfour agreeing to take full responsibility.

A despatch from Santander dated 6 August and published in *The Times* two days later confirmed that Alfonso was indeed continuing his efforts and was 'anxious to offer the neutral hospitality of Spain on condition that they [the Romanovs] remain in the country until the war is over...' The king's motive was humanitarian, not political; he wanted to lessen the family's sufferings in any way possible.

On the same day the Spanish Conservative newspaper *ABC* published the following news received from Paris. 'The Russian government agrees that the ex-tsar's family come to Spain. Telegraph from Amsterdam [reports] that the *Hamburger Frendernblatt* says that the Bolsheviks have consented to the departure to Spain of the ex-tsarina and her daughters. The negotiations regarding the requested guarantees are ongoing.' The guarantees referred to were that the surviving Romanovs would not be involved in any political activity undertaken by Russian exiles or White Russians.[25]

Rumours now reached the Germans via the Russian military attaché in Berlin that this offer had in fact come from the Allies, who did not want the tsarina to fall into German hands and wished Alexandra to be handed over to them at Archangel.

On 9 August, Agueros, the Spanish Ambassador in Norway, informed the Danish Foreign Minister Erik Scavenius that King

Alfonso had been engaged in talks both inside and outside Russia with the aim of 'bringing to Spain the Empress Marie Feodorovna and Alexandra Feodorovna and her children, and that His Majesty hopes this will be successful.'[26]

Three days later Moscow was informed that the kaiser had agreed to Alfonso's proposal. Alfonso explained to Ratibor, the German ambassador, that the Bolsheviks were un-co-operative and that it was impossible to achieve anything through the Entente powers.

King George returned from France on 14 August and immediately answered King Alfonso's earlier appeal: 'I shall be most grateful if you will exert all your influence in whatever direction you think best to rescue the imperial family of Russia from their present pitiable position,' he telegraphed.[27] Alfonso had also received support from the Netherlands, the Scandinavian kingdoms and other European countries.

＊＊＊

On the Isle of Wight Princess Victoria was frantic for news of her sister. Towards the end of May, after she heard the imperial family had been moved to Ekaterinburg, she had written to Arthur Balfour in a bid to get the British government to do something for them. The Foreign Office suggested that Victoria turn for assistance to the neutral Danish royal family, the Swedish crown princess or the Swedish legation in Moscow.

In July, with the tsar now reportedly dead, she thought of writing to Lenin's wife as one woman to another but Lord Robert Cecil at the Foreign Office thought this approach might do more harm than good. Once again the princess showed less concern for her sister Ella, who had no children and would want to return to her Moscow convent as soon as possible – but for Alix the situation was different.

Instead she wrote to King Alfonso of Spain. On 6 August she received his reply by telegram. 'Letter received. I have started negotiations to save empress and girls as tsarevich [I] think is dead. Proposition is to leave them to go to neutral country and on my word of honour they would remain here until the end of the war. Hope all the different sovereigns will assist me. Will let you know all news I get.'[28]

On 9 August, the day after Queen Mary's intervention, Victoria wrote to Mr Whitmore of *The Times*. 'Thank you so much for your letter & the trouble you have taken to talk with your Minister at Stockholm about my idea of writing to Lenin's wife... I have meanwhile had a telegram from the king of Spain confirming what the papers mention about the steps he has taken to have the empress & her daughters sent to him for the duration of the war & he promises to let me know any news he gets about them. He thinks it is true that the cesarevich [*sic*] is dead – my poor sister!'[29]

She also wrote to King George, telling him that Alfonso had sent a positive response to her request that he intervene on behalf of the imperial family and begging that his 'government may be quick in its support of Alfonso.'[30]

Orders had in fact been given the previous day via a telegram from the Director of Military Intelligence to General Poole in Archangel. 'King of Spain having offered the empress her children and the dowager empress his hospitality is believed to have asked Germans to help them to leave Russia. If you have a chance of helping and saving them Mr Balfour desires you should do so.'[31] Copies of all these initiatives were sent to Queen Alexandra by the Foreign Office.

* * *

The Vatican now entered the negotiations. As far back as January 1918 an appeal had been sent to Pope Benedict XV from the Czech writer and translator Jan Grmela, who was living in exile in Paris, asking him to intervene on behalf of the imperial family. He hoped the pope would add his influence to the appeals made by the British and Spanish to release the family. Pope Benedict had worked with Alfonso throughout the war on humanitarian initiatives and they remained in close contact.

Paolo Giovanni Battisa dell Chiesa, Pope Benedict XV, was a well-known humanitarian. He had become pope in 1914 and right from the start of the war had negotiated the exchange of prisoners and also of civilians in occupied zones, as well as arranging for the exchange of hostages and the repatriation of bodies. Now the pontiff stepped in to help the tsar's widow and children. Count de Salis, the British Ambassador Extraordinary to the Vatican, reported Pope Benedict's interest to his government.

On 11 August messages reached Monsignor Valpré, the Apostolic Nuncio in Vienna, and Archbishop Pacelli, the Apostolic Nuncio in Munich, instructing them to approach the Austrian and German governments and ask them to endeavour to secure the release of the empress and her children. The dowager empress's name was also added to the request. Their 'extremely sad fate' had aroused the pope's 'profound pity' the message said. Both nuncios pursued this course of action.[32]

The Austro-Hungarian Foreign Minister Count Burian informed Valpré that both King Alfonso and King Christian of Denmark 'were already pursuing the subject' but nevertheless, he would raise the matter with Emperor Carl. Pacelli also appealed to the German Chancellor Georg von Hertling for help but the Germans already knew about the move being made by the king of Spain and dismissed the pope's intervention. The Vatican anyway preferred to deal with the Catholic government of Austria-Hungary.

Alfonso's intervention even extended to contacting his distant cousin and rival for the crown, forty-eight-year-old Don Jaime de Bourbon, Duke of Madrid. Don Jaime was regarded by the Carlists (those Spaniards who did not recognise the right of the king's grandmother Queen Isabella to the throne) as the rightful king of Spain, a role for which he had no inclination. In his youth Don Jaime had fought in the Grodno Hussars during the Russo-Japanese War and had been received by Nicholas II in St Petersburg. Alfonso now asked for his help and for once the rival branches of the family were united. Don Jaime answered his cousin from his home at Schloss Frohsdorf in Lanzenkirchen, Austria. 'Don Alfonso. Waiting for quick result [for] salvation of unhappy Russian imperial family. Greet you. Jaime.'[33]

In a conversation with the French Ambassador, Eduardo Dato said that the kaiser would play a major role in the negotiations. Alfonso had a difficult relationship with William, another of his wife's cousins, whom he considered arrogant. During Alfonso's 1905 visit to Berlin, the kaiser gave orders that no hired vehicles were to be allowed inside the palace gates. Alfonso, having gone out incognito, hired a dilapidated taxicab to drive him back to the palace, where the sentry refused him admission. Insisting that the kaiser would make an exception for him, Alfonso delighted in telling the officious guard that the occupant of the old vehicle was the king of Spain. Things did not improve at the state banquet.

Having agreed that the monarchs would make their speeches in French, William threw away his notes and spoke in German, a language Alfonso did not understand. He replied in Spanish.

Diplomatic relations were also tricky, with hundreds of tons of Spanish shipping being sunk alongside Allied ships, even though Spain was neutral. Nevertheless, Alfonso now needed the help of the Germans, who were exerting heavy pressure on the Bolsheviks to free the surviving Romanovs, and on 13 August a personal message was sent to William asking him to join forces to help rescue the family. After the Treaty of Brest-Litovsk it was generally assumed that the Bolsheviks were under German control.

A communiqué was received in Spain on 16 August after the Spanish Ambassador in Berlin, Polo de Bernabé, had spoken to the Acting Secretary of State. 'In conversation today, the acting Secretary of State, told me that the [German] imperial government has ... no objection to the dowager ex-empress, the Russian imperial prince, and his sisters, enjoying the hospitality offered by His Majesty the King...'[34]

The Vatican's official newspaper *Osservatore Romano* reported that the pope had offered to pay the expenses of the family's transfer to Spain, Pope Benedict XV 'having asked the cabinets concerned to act as soon as possible on compassionate grounds.' The Apostolic Nuncio in Bavaria, Eugenio Pacelli (the future Pope Pius XII) was instructed by Pope Benedict to inform the German government that His Holiness 'supported all negotiations for the release of the tsar's family' and would provide them with dignified accommodation.[35] This initiative apparently had the backing of King Christian of Denmark.

The following day a report came via neutral Sweden. 'In the last deliberations held in the Kremlin, the petition from the pope was presented by the Archbishop Freiherr Dr Repp, requesting the liberation of the tsarina with her four daughters. According to reports from Stockholm, it seems that the national commissars were in agreement to accede to the wishes of the pope, with certain conditions. Resistance to the freeing of the tsarina has almost been overcome.'[36]

The Russians now began 'haggling over tsarist assets held in foreign banks' and it was not until 25 August that full agreement was reached. Alexandra and her daughters would be sent abroad, probably first to Denmark. Archbishop Freiherr Dr Repp was to accompany them and ensure that everything was carried out according to the agreed conditions.[37]

On 26 August the German Consul in Petrograd told Berlin that he was travelling to Moscow with the Spanish envoy the following week to negotiate with Chicherin. The following day, Baron von dem Bussche (the Under Secretary of Foreign Affairs) told Pacelli that the King of Spain had offered asylum. Also on 27 August King Alfonso suggested to Ratibor 'that vigorous steps should be taken in Moscow' to move the members of the imperial family to Spain.[38]

Two days later Commissar Radek suggested an exchange of the Romanov women for the Marxist revolutionary Leo Jogisches who was under arrest in Berlin. The proposal, said Radek, could be placed before Lenin that very day. If Radek knew he was dealing in ghosts he was playing a very dodgy game.

In Berlin, Joffe suggested to Nadolny at the German Foreign Office that they release Lenin's friend Karl Liebknecht as part of the exchange.

The acting Dutch Minister in Petrograd William J Oudendijk, a fluent Russian speaker, called on the Bolshevik Commissar for Foreign Affairs on 1 September. He was acting at the request of his monarch Queen Wilhelmina, the second cousin once removed of the tsar. Oudendijk asked Georgi Chicherin 'for the release of the tsarina and her children, and was told to convey to his government that they could not leave, but were safe.' Oudendijk, a diplomat of the old school, later said that Chicherin 'resembled some weird prehistoric lizard.'[39]

The Spanish *chargé d'affaires* in Petrograd, Fernando Gomez Contreras, accompanied by Oudendijk as a witness, went to the Ministry of Foreign Affairs in September for two meetings with Chicherin. He relayed the king's offer to bring the empress and her children to Spain, pay for their living expenses and guarantee that they would not enter into any anti-Bolshevik activity. Chicherin demanded that Spain recognise the Soviet government. Contreras stressed that this was a purely humanitarian initiative and assured Chicherin that Spain was not intervening in Russia's affairs. The Romanov women would remain there far from any counterrevolutionary movements. Chicherin replied that Spain would then become the focus of counterrevolutionary activity. The Spanish and Dutch diplomats protested against this statement.

'After very painful discussions and much effort, I secured his promise that he would submit our petition to the first session of the Executive Central Committee...,' the diplomat's report concluded.[40]

The German Ambassador was informed on 10 September that in principle Radek and Chicherin had no objection to the women's release on the basis of the discussion of 29 August. Germany was insistent that they be removed from danger in Perm and brought to Moscow. Radek said the Bolsheviks wanted to do this. 'In the light of the growing influence that he has won,' the ambassador reported, 'I hope that this step will be carried out.'[41]

The negotiations were now jeopardised by an outbreak of violence in Moscow. On 12 September Moisei Uritsky, the thirty-five-year-old head of the Petrograd Cheka, was murdered by members of the Right Socialist Revolutionary party, and on the same day Lenin was shot and severely wounded at point blank range by a woman called Fanny Kaplan. As Lenin struggled to survive, wholesale reprisals took place.

As late as 10 September the Germans were reporting that Radek still favoured releasing the Romanov women – but shortly afterwards Moscow became evasive on the subject of their whereabouts, saying all trace of them had been lost after Ekaterinburg was evacuated. Meanwhile Nadolny was saying that the negotiations should be left to Spain.

In mid-September news reports were still saying that a yacht sailing under the papal flag was expected to convey Alexandra and her children to a port in Spain. Gomez Contreras said that Chicherin 'will see to it that a solution is found to the situation of the imperial ladies in the sense of their being set free.'[42]

In Germany, in a speech before a parliamentary committee on 24 September, Paul von Hintz, Under Secretary at the Foreign Office, supported the plan for the tsarina and her children to go to Spain, which had been arranged with the Russian government. At the very least he thought it should be possible for them all to go to the former imperial palace in the Crimea.

* * *

In late September 1918, London asked Sir Charles Eliot, High Commissioner and Consul-General for Siberia, to go to

Ekaterinburg and investigate the fate of the missing Romanovs. Sir Charles, an erudite man with a qualification in law, met Thomas Preston and Judge Sergeyev (successor to Nametkin, who had been fired) and then went to the Ipatiev House. His full report reached London in January 1919. No bodies had been discovered, he said, and there were rumours that the tsar had not been murdered but placed in German custody. Furthermore, 'on 17 July a train with the blinds down left Ekaterinburg for an unknown destination and it is believed that the surviving members of the imperial family were in it.' Sir Charles was well aware of the activities of the Secret Intelligence Service around Ekaterinburg and he did not believe all the family were dead. This agreed with a report which reached London in August from Captain Voitkevich, who had been at Koptyaki with Nametkin's investigation and now said that Alexandra and the children had been taken north to Verkhoturye.[43]

There were also rumours that one of the grand duchesses had escaped. Princess Helen of Serbia, in prison in Perm, was asked by the Bolsheviks to identify a girl calling herself Anastasia Romanov. Was she the tsar's daughter, they asked. No, Helen said, she was not.

In mid-October Adolf Magener, who was working for Grand Duke Ernest Ludwig of Hesse, had a meeting with the monarchist officer Sergei Markov in Kiev. Magener told Markov that he had learnt from German intelligence agents in Perm that Nicholas was 'not with his family' but his wife and children were still alive. Markov later said that he had 'made the acquaintance of a Germany spy.... [whose] nephew had recently been operating in Perm province, and had reported to him that the imperial family was unquestionably alive and constantly being moved about within Perm province.'[44]

By the autumn of 1918 this is what many Germans believed but the Russians, knowing that the war would soon be over, were obviously stringing the Germans along.

***

'I fear that these disgusting brutes in Russia have killed poor Alicky, the lovely girls and the little boy,' King George wrote to Queen Alexandra on 5 September.[45] He had asked that the information be kept from the press until the empress's sister Victoria, the Marchioness of Milford Haven, had been informed.

Victoria received confirmation of this devastating news on 2 September in a letter from the king. It was brought to the Isle of Wight by her cousin Princess Marie Louise, who had been at Windsor in July when news of the tsar's murder broke. Enclosed with it was a copy of a letter from Lord Milner, the Minister of War, to Stamfordham the king's private secretary: 'I think I ought to let you know at once for His Majesty's information that we have just received a very distressing telegram from the Intelligence Officer serving under General Poole at Murmansk to the effect that there is every probability that the empress of Russia, her four daughters and the tsarevich were all murdered at the same time as the late tsar. The information reached the Intelligence Officer from a source which he has no reason to doubt. I am much afraid, therefore, that the news is only too likely to prove true...'[46]

George's letter to Victoria was one of commiseration. 'May and I feel most deeply for you in the tragic end of your sister and her innocent children. But, perhaps for her, who knows, it is better so; as after dear Nicky's death she could not have wished to live. And the beautiful girls may have been saved from worse than death at the hands of these horrid fiends... The awful part is that they might all have been saved if W [William] had only lifted a finger on their behalf.'[47] King George was now putting the blame squarely on Germany.

On 18 September Victoria telegraphed the crown princess of Sweden. Daisy had shuddered when she heard the news of the tsar's murder. It seemed 'too awful to have actually known and liked another monarch to whom these dreadful things have happened', she wrote to Lady Egerton.[48] Now Victoria reported the fate of his family. 'Have received information of news derived from trustworthy source that there is every possibility that Alix and daughters were murdered at the same time as Alexei and his father – fear it is likely to prove true. Inform brother and sister.'[49]

The brother and sister were Grand Duke Ernest Ludwig of Hesse and Princess Irene of Prussia, both living in Germany and with whom it was impossible for Victoria to communicate directly. The crown princess had been doing a sterling job receiving letters from belligerent countries, copying the contents in her own handwriting and then forwarding them to the intended recipient in the enemy camp. Now she duly passed this message on to Ernie and Irene.

In an uncharacteristic outburst to her former lady-in-waiting Nona Kerr, Victoria put the blame for her sister's death on Lloyd George and President Woodrow Wilson, who thought they could reform the Bolsheviks 'by moral persuasion'. She called them fools. '… You don't persuade such people except with cold steel, or leave them to devour each other, after they have slaughtered enough other people.' She then wrote a diplomatic letter to King George. 'It is easier to bear the sense of their loss to me, than the thought of what they have gone through and what might have still been in store for them,' she said.[50]

Yet privately she had no doubt where the responsibility lay for her sister's untimely death, nor to whom she should express her gratitude for assistance. On 22 September she wrote to King Alfonso.

> Now that there is alas nothing to hope for, for my dear sister Alix & her children on this earth & that it is now almost a positive certainty that death has released them from further suffering & that they have passed from the cruel hands of man into those of a just & merciful God, I feel I must just send you a few lines to thank you with all my heart for all you tried to do to save them from their enemies.
>
> The sovereign who had the most direct influence on the revolutionary government in Russia, the one who had known my sister as a child, who had the same blood as hers flowing in his veins, who formerly never failed to claim her as of his nationality, deserted her, I fear I must believe, in her distress, whilst you to whom she and hers were comparative strangers thought of and strove to help them. I shall never forget the gratitude I owe you for this.[51]

She had received a report, forwarded by King George, from Thomas Preston in Ekaterinburg, which made gruesome reading. They were 'stated to have been burnt alive,' although there was 'the possibility of their having being taken north by the Bolsheviks.' Victoria hoped that the 'horrid tale of their end' was based on nothing more than rumour and conjecture. On comparing the two sets of information the king had provided, one saying they were definitely dead, the other with these horror stories, she thought the probability was that Alix and the children 'were killed almost at the same time as Nicky and then their bodies, his too possibly, removed to another house which was set fire to, to remove all traces of the slaughter. I can but pray that I am right in this guess and that they were spared the other horror.'[52]

The most barbaric stories were now circulating, as Victoria's son, Lord Mountbatten, recalled many years later. 'About six months after the tsar's death, King George V showed me secret service reports that they had all been raped. The king advised me not to tell my mother.'[53]

***

On 27 September, three weeks after King George V had told Victoria that all the family were dead, she received a telegram from Daisy in Sweden passing on more news from the Grand Duke of Hesse. 'Ernie now telegraphs that he has heard from two trustworthy sources that Alix and all the children are alive,'[54] the crown princess reported. This was in line with Thomas Preston's report sent to London on 16 September, which stated that the tsar had been shot and his family taken away. At about this time the Minister of Foreign Affairs in Berlin reported to Cardinal von Hartmann, the Archbishop of Cologne, that 'the Russians have assured [the Germans] that they will not interfere in their affairs, that they will protect the grand duchesses from the people's fury and that they are planning to move them to the Crimea.'[55]

With conflicting reports coming out of Russia, announcements now came from London that the tsarina and her children had died at the same time as the tsar. The Vatican refused to believe it, thinking it probable that the pope would have been informed if the news was true. Madrid, where in mid-September preparations were being made for the family's reception, reacted similarly.

At the end of September a report from Vienna quoted Sverdlov as saying that the surviving Romanovs were well and that his government intended to send them abroad as soon as it became possible. The statement was signed by an official acting on behalf of King Alfonso and Pope Benedict. Yet in Moscow they were now claiming that they had lost trace of the family and were not certain where they were.

The Vatican finally received a reply from the Bolsheviks via the Austro-Hungarian Consul on 10 October, saying 'that they did not know where the tsarina and her daughters were.'[56] The Vatican doubted the validity of the report and asked an official to make enquiries.

King Alfonso was reported to be indisposed for several days during October and was not seen in public. It seems that he had finally accepted that the whole family had died and was devastated at the distress he had caused Alexandra's family. His son Don Juan, the Count of Barcelona, later told two British authors that, although only five years old at the time, he remembered that his mother 'was very sad' and his father 'lamented the lack of solidarity of the other monarchies.'[57]

As late as 5 December 1918 the American Ambassador in Rome, Nelson Page, was reporting that he had heard that in 'highest quarters here it is believed the tsar and his family are all alive.' In diplomatic parlance 'highest quarters' could only mean the pope or the king and queen of Italy, and it is significant that the day before this message was sent Page had visited Queen Elena, whose sisters Grand Duchesses Militsa and Stana were in the Crimea. They clearly believed the family were safe. A telegram was then sent to London from Washington asking for the opinion of the Foreign Office. They replied that reports that the tsar and tsarevich were dead seemed to bear the hallmark of truth but they were not so sure about the empress and her daughters.

Then, just after Christmas, telegrams arrived in London, Washington, Paris and Rome from General William Graves in Siberia which used the code word 'family' seven times. Seven times for seven Romanovs? A few days later the response came from the American Embassy in London, requesting the U.S. Department of State to 'verify "family" used seven times'. As Shay McNeal points out, when the original telegram arrived, President Wilson was visiting King George and Queen Mary.[58] Was somebody trying to find out whether a rescue plan had succeeded?

This was what the Dowager Empress Marie Feodorovna believed. In July King Christian had sent a letter to her in the Crimea, expressing his sympathy at the news of the tsar's murder. Her reply was dated 9 October. 'Thanks be to God the most terrifying rumours concerning my poor beloved Nicky seem to be untrue. After several weeks of terrifying suspense and proclamations, I have been assured that he and his family have been released and brought to a place of safety...' She carried on believing that the tsar was alive, even when faced with contrary statements. According to French *Deuxieme Bureau* reports, Prince Henry of Prussia, the kaiser's brother, was in contact with Marie and informed her in August that although the tsar was dead, the family was safe.[59]

On 28 October, even as the Austro-Hungarian Consul in Moscow was making last desperate attempts in favour of the Romanov women (to which the Bolsheviks were not responding) the Vatican recognised the White government in Siberia as Russia's legitimate rulers.

In Archangel, the French diplomat Louis de Robien heard details of the imperial family's end from a Czech officer who managed to get through from Ekaterinburg in September. After listing the various items of jewellery and effects found at the Four Brothers Mine he concluded: 'A glimmer of hope remains, which is that we may be faced with an act which is being staged in order to put people off the scent or to cover up an escape... But this glimmer is a very faint one.'[60]

* * *

In December 1920 King Christian and Queen Alexandrine visited the Vatican, the first visit by a Danish monarch for more than 500 years. During a 30-minute meeting in the pope's private library, the *New York Times* reported, 'Benedict thanked Christian for the king's assistance in the papal proposal that the Bolsheviks in Russia allow the Russian grand duchesses to leave their country and come to Rome to be maintained at the expense of the pontiff.' Clearly the royal families of Europe had not been idle, although several authors have questioned why no memorial service was ever held for the tsarina and her children.

* * *

The Marchioness of Milford Haven still had no definite news of her other sister, Ella. In September she learnt that an American consular official was about to visit Russia. Victoria gave him a letter for her in the vain hope that he might be able to make contact.

Not until November did Victoria hear from Lord Robert Cecil that Ella had died with the others at Alapayevsk. He had heard the news from Thomas Preston, who had learnt from the White army that 'the grand duchess was killed and that when Alapayevsk was taken by Russian troops on September 29 they found her body sufficiently preserved to be recognised. The bodies were also found of Princes Ivan, Igor & Constantine as also of the Grand Duke Sergei Michaelovich & a lady-in-waiting [*sic*]...'[61]

For some weeks Victoria had lived under the misapprehension that the men had escaped but that, perhaps, Ella was still at the schoolhouse. She had forwarded this information to King George V, who she was certain would inform her of any news that reached the palace. Now it was clear that all the Romanovs imprisoned in the Urals had been killed by the Bolsheviks.

* * *

Several people blamed King George for the imperial family's brutal end. In 1920, from his home in St Cloud, the tsar's cousin Prince George of Greece expressed his total disgust to Grand Duchess Xenia. 'Morals, principals [*sic*], heart and every Christian feeling has been done away with by this infernal war and those who are guiding the nation today are all without religion. There is one, who might have stuck to principal and to nobel [*sic*] acts, only one, and this is English Georgie, but he, hiding behind the words 'constitutional king' allows the evil to conquer over everything that is good and right, so as to stick to his d—d throne, which nowadays is no better than a W.C.'[62]

Escape of a Tsar's Daughter

'Now is the time to get out of here.'

When the reign of terror began in Yalta in January 1918 another member of the imperial family was also in the Crimea, although this was not immediately apparent from her name.

Princess Catherine Yourievsky was Nicholas II's step-aunt. She was the youngest daughter of Tsar Alexander II and his mistress Princess Catherine ('Katia') Dolgoruky, whom he had married in 1880, causing a scandal. Katia was the tsar's mistress for many years and gave birth to four children, three of whom survived infancy. Catherine, born in 1878 at Biuk Sarai, a large house near Livadia, was the youngest. In 1880 the tsar scandalised Europe by installing Katia and her children in the Winter Palace for security while his wife lay dying in another room. He married her morganatically just forty days after the empress's death that year, created her Princess Yourievsky and legitimised their children.

Little Catherine, now Her Serene Highness Princess Catherine Yourievsky, remained in the Winter Palace with her siblings George and Olga until a terrorist's bomb ended Alexander II's life in 1881. Catherine's half-brother Alexander III then gave them another palace but in 1882 Katia and the children left Russia.

In 1901 Princess Catherine Yourievsky married Prince Alexander Bariatinsky. They had two sons, Andrei and Alexander and enjoyed a lively social life. Then in 1910 Prince Bariatinsky suddenly died and Catherine took over the running of his Russian estate on behalf of her elder son.

During the war she opened a hospital in one wing of the house and gave concerts to raise funds. Catherine was a talented singer but her health was never good and in the spring of 1916 she moved to the milder climate of Yalta, where she met Prince Sergei Obolensky at a charity bazaar. They married in the St Alexander Nevsky Cathedral in Yalta in October and Catherine received an aquamarine necklace from her nephew the tsar as a wedding gift. After stopping briefly at the sixteenth century palace of the Crimean khans at Bakhchiserai, with its 'fountain of tears', made famous by Pushkin's poem, they returned to Petrograd where Sergei took up his regimental duties.

When revolution came, Sergei's regiment ceased to exist so he and Catherine rejoined her sons in Yalta. During the summer of 1917 they lived quietly in the Mordvinov Palace, which was surrounded by a magnificent park in the hills above the town.

To Catherine's dismay, when the Bolsheviks seized power in October Sergei left to join a rebel force of Tartars and she was left alone with her boys. Hours later Yalta was bombarded from the sea and Catherine sent her sons to the cellar for safety. As she sat singing by the piano, her usual refuge in times of stress, a group of Bolsheviks burst in and took control of the palace. The boys and their English governess Miss Pickens were allowed to leave the next day and found shelter with the Scherbatoff family. Catherine, the daughter of a tsar and the wife of a rebel, was only saved from the possible threat of a firing squad by a friend who bribed one of the guards to let her go. She was hurried under shell fire to another friend's house.

When the Tartar force recaptured Yalta Sergei arrived back at the Mordvinov Palace and found it ransacked. He feared the worst but luckily was told where to find Catherine. They were briefly reunited before the Bolsheviks recaptured the town and Sergei, a resistance fighter with a price on his head, was forced to make his escape.

Various people risked their lives to shelter Catherine for a few days at a time. Then, disguised as a nursemaid, she was taken to a country farm by her husband's former gardener and his wife. Here Catherine posed as one of the family, scrubbing the floors, doing farm work and cooking, all the while living in terror of being discovered. She had no idea what had happened to Sergei and only learnt some time later that he had been drugged to simulate illness and then smuggled to Moscow by friends.

These same people then helped Catherine. Despite her heart condition she walked for 20 miles to a boarding house, where she posed as Mlle Hélène, a French governess stranded in Yalta. Some Bolsheviks were among the guests but she kept her nerve, even teaching one of them French.

Finally, dressed in a nurse's uniform and with a bribed soldier as escort, she endured a terrifying journey to Moscow on a train full of Bolshevik soldiers. During the journey she recognised two of the men who had raided the Mordvinov Palace and the remainder of the trip became a nightmare. Convinced she was part of a trap to lead them to Sergei, Catherine slipped away from her soldier escort in Moscow and finally reached the house where Sergei was being sheltered by an employee of the Obolensky family.

Sergei and Catherine now had to pretend to be strangers to one another. Both found work and waited until they could rescue Catherine's sons from Yalta.

After the Crimea came under German control in the spring of 1918 Catherine and Sergei returned to Kiev in disguise as part of an official delegation to the Ukraine. It was another nightmare journey. The Cheka were everywhere, watching everyone and Sergei still had a price on his head. It was with some relief that they passed through the checkpoint at Pskov into German territory. The irony of feeling safe in land held by Russia's enemies did not escape them.

They reached Kiev and lodged in the flat of Catherine's former brother-in-law. Luckily Hetman Skoropadsky, nominal head of the Ukraine, gave permission for Catherine's sons, their governess and their servants to cross from Yalta into the Ukraine to join them.

While they were waiting for their official travel permits, news arrived of the murder of the tsar and the deaths of the Romanov captives at Alapayevsk. Catherine and Sergei attended the memorial service in St Sophia's Cathedral.

After three months in Kiev, Sergei applied to the Austrian legation for permission to go to Vienna on the first leg of their journey to Switzerland. This would exclude Miss Pickens and the coachman Albert Stanard, who had brought Catherine's boys to Kiev. Austria was still at war with England and they could not go through. They eventually reached England via Odessa with French help.

Catherine and Sergei arrived in Vienna just before the collapse of Austrian control in the Ukraine. Not long afterwards the Ukraine fell to the Bolsheviks and then Austria began to subside into revolution. 'Now is the time to get out of here,' Sergei told her.[1]

With no time to lose, they boarded a train for Switzerland. After some difficulty at the border, they crossed the frontier as the Austrian revolution broke out behind them.

Princess Catherine Yourievsky, a tsar's daughter, was safe at last.

* * *

When Admiral Kolchak's White Army entered Alapayevsk on 28 September 1918 the search began for Grand Duke Sergei Michaelovich, his secretary Feodor Remez, Grand Duchess Ella, her companion Sister Barbara, Princes Ioann, Constantine and Igor Constantinovich and Prince Vladimir Paley. All had disappeared, believed killed, on 17/18 July. Excavations centred on the abandoned mineshaft at Sinyachikha. Between 21 and 24 October all eight bodies were discovered and brought to the surface. A post mortem established that all (except Sergei, who was shot) died as a result of severe head injuries and the effects of the fall into the pit.

The bodies were washed, clad in wax-coated shrouds, placed in coffins and taken to the cemetery chapel. On 31 October an all-night vigil took place and the following day the coffins were moved to Holy Trinity Cathedral. Enormous crowds of weeping townspeople came to pay their respects at the funeral service. As the coffins were taken to the crypt a White army band played the Imperial Anthem and the cathedral bells solemnly tolled.

It was intended that this crypt should be the Romanovs' last resting place – but that did not turn out to be the case.

* * *

Princess Helen of Serbia was still imprisoned in Perm with no idea of her husband's fate or any news of her family. Hearing about the murders in Alapayevsk, her father King Peter went into mourning thinking his daughter was dead.

Meanwhile, European diplomats were trying to find out what had happened to Helen. The Serbian Minister Miroslav Spalaikovich obtained permission from Lenin to continue the search for his country's princess. It was known that she had been moved from Ekaterinburg as a hostage and Thomas Preston suggested to the Foreign Office that one of the neutral powers could perhaps guarantee her safety.

By the autumn of 1918, as one country after another closed its diplomatic mission in Moscow, Norway found itself looking after the interests of a host of different states in Soviet Russia, where many refugees were stranded. The Norwegians had heard about the plight of the Serbian princess. Thomas Christiansen, the Norwegian Minister, sent an envoy to search for 'the Queen of Serbia'. Despite a report that reached the Foreign Office in London saying that Princess Helen had been reported killed by the Bolsheviks in Perm on 17 November, the envoy succeeded in finding her. On 27 November Niels Ihlen, the Foreign Minister, informed King Haakon that they were doing what they could to 'get her out.'[2]

In November Helen was told she was being moved to the Norwegian Consulate in Moscow, where a diplomatic passport would be arranged for her. In temperatures well below zero, wearing a summer dress and worn out shoes, she was escorted by thirty Red Guards to Moscow where she was taken, not to the Consul Mr Christiansen, but to the Loubianka prison and a notoriously cruel officer named Peters.

Strangely, he was kind to Helen. He confirmed the story about the imperial family's death in Ekaterinburg and managed to find out from Petrograd that her children had reached Sweden safely with their grandmother. Peters also said that he was obliged to keep her under guard but rather than confine her to prison he had arranged for her to have rooms in the Kremlin's Great Palace. He gave her a roast dinner which, after months of prison food Helen was unable to eat. She gave it to one of the guards who had once served her father-in-law Grand Duke Constantine Constantinovich. In return he heated her bath water.

Her three-room apartment was near St Catherine's Hall but despite the kindness of Peters, Helen spent sleepless nights haunted by memories of the past. The librarian sent her books and she was allowed to walk outdoors. When she told Peters she had no coat he offered her a choice from the empress's wardrobe. Helen felt unable to accept, so he bought her an astrakhan coat and left the shop label on it so that she could see where it had come from. Her former governess was allowed to visit and the women went for walks every day, accompanied by a guard with a fixed bayonet.

Thanks to the efforts of Thomas Christiansen, Helen was due to be released on 2 December into the hands of the Norwegians. Peters told her that she would then have forty-eight hours to leave the country. It is probable that she was to be used as a pawn in exchange for a prominent political prisoner.

A message arrived from Mr Christiansen confirming she was to go to the legation, which Helen did, leaving her astrakhan coat behind so that she would not be indebted to a Bolshevik. The Norwegian Mission was being wound up a few days later, so she was given Norwegian papers that would allow her to leave for Finland via Petrograd with the departing Christiansens.

As they sat in the train waiting to depart a soldier arrived – not to arrest Helen this time, but to present her with a bouquet and Peters's apologies that he could not see her off in person. They reached Petrograd the next day and then set off towards the frontier at Belo Ostrov. Here the bridge had been destroyed and they all had to walk to the Finnish side of the border where a train was waiting. They were almost there when a guard stopped them, saying he could not allow the princess to leave Russia. Helen panicked but a hefty bribe from Mr Christiansen secured the soldier's agreement to let her pass.

Finland was now an independent country and once over the border she was free. On 28 December 1918, the United States Consul in Ekaterinburg reported that the princess had reached Stockholm.[3]

Helen was reunited with her mother-in-law and children at the spa town of Saltsjöbaden on the Baltic, where they were now living. At this point it appears that neither Helen nor Mavra knew for certain what had happened at Alapayevsk.

'No news from the sons!' Mavra wrote in despair on 28 January 1919. She was desperate for news of her family. Continuing her letter to Mr Denison in London, who she had asked about schools in England for her son George, she said '...I shall ask Miss Edgly to buy a little white costume for Easter for Veruchka [Vera], to go to church...' As the Swedish crown princess was about to go to London, Mavra said that Daisy '... could bring the dress when she comes back after her sister's wedding.' She continued: 'The climate is as bad as possible this year. Foggy and damp. But I like Sweden. Everybody is most kind to us. The king the first. I passed a day with him at Drottningholm [palace], a lovely place, last week'[4]

It must have been soon after this that they heard that Ioann had been murdered with other members of the family at Alapayevsk. Unwilling to believe this news Helen telephoned King George V for confirmation.

Reeling from shock, she took the children to Paris where they were met by her brother the Prince Regent Alexander of Serbia. Brother and sister then went to their father King Peter in Belgrade but Helen found the similarities with Russia too painful. When King Peter died in 1921 Alexander became King of the Serbs, Croats and Slovenes (later Yugoslavia) and he purchased the Villa Trianon at St Jean Cap Ferrat in the South of France to give Helen a home.

* * *

In Russia the civil war was at its height. As the Bolsheviks advanced on Alapayevsk in July 1919 Father Seraphim, superior of the monastery of St Seraphim of Sarov (and formerly Ella's confessor), obtained permission from the Supreme Commander of the White army Alexander Kolchak, and General Michael Diterikhs, who was supervising the White investigation into the imperial family's murder, to move the Romanovs' coffins to a safer place. On 14 July, helped by two novices, he put the eight coffins on a freight train to the Far East.

It was a gruelling journey along the Trans-Siberian railway. The line was often blocked by troop trains and it took ten days to reach Tyumen. Father Seraphim had no travel documents; to show authorization would have resulted in seizure of the remains by the Bolsheviks. In Omsk he had a lucky escape when the freight car was not searched.

On 29 August they arrived in Chita. The next day, with the co-operation of Ataman Grigory Semenov, a powerful Cossack warlord, Russian and Japanese officers delivered the coffins to the Holy Protection Convent. There they were opened and Ella's grave clothes were exchanged for a nun's habit. The officers dug a large shallow hole in the floor of one of the cells and covered the coffins with earth to conceal them from Bolshevik spies. Father Seraphim lived in the cell, guarding the coffins. Memorial services were held and icon lamps burned continuously.

As the Whites receded and the Bolsheviks closed in, General Diterikhs decided the bodies should be taken to China. Kolchak's authority came to an end at the Russian border – where was the money to come from? Finally, Maria Semenova-Glebov (either the divorced wife or discarded mistress of Semenov) offered the gold ingots Semenov had given her when he left. The journey was therefore financed with Ataman gold.

In February 1920 Father Seraphim loaded the coffins onto the Chinese Eastern Railway and travelled with them towards Harbin. He reached Hajlar without incident but there the Bolsheviks were in control. Near the Chinese border the train was attacked by the communists and Prince Ioann's coffin was taken off and opened. Luckily the Chinese border guards fought off the attackers and restored the coffin to the train. From that point onwards Father Seraphim and his cargo travelled under the protection of the Chinese and Japanese military authorities.

At the beginning of March they arrived in Harbin and were met by Metropolitan Nestor. The coffins were placed in the Russian Church and the last Imperial Ambassador to China, Prince Nicolai Kudashev, was asked to identify the remains. They left Harbin on 8 April, arriving in Mukden five days later. A telegram from Prince Kudashev ordered the freight car to be detained there, as there was a fine chapel and it would be easier to transport the coffins to Europe or another safe place. Nevertheless, later that day Father Seraphim left as planned.

On 16 April they reached Peking (now Beijing) where they were met at the station by Archbishop Innocent, head of the Russian Spiritual Mission.There were no representatives from the Russian Embassy there to meet them, nor any of the city's Russian residents. Even some of the ecclesiastics from the Mission had to be compelled to attend. The Imperial Russian Embassy refused to have anything to do with the remains. It was forbidden to bring dead bodies into the city so they could not be taken to the Russian Spiritual Mission, which was within the city wall. Quickly the dirty wooden coffins were taken in a religious procession to one of the crypts of the Russian Spiritual Mission cemetery outside the city's north gate (Andingmen Gate). Meanwhile '...work began on a new crypt within the church dedicated to St Seraphim of Sarov,'[5] located in the centre of this cemetery.

When the crypt was completed the remains were transferred, enclosed in new zinc coffins. The keys to the crypt, and supervision of it, were handed to Archbishop Innocent. It was hoped that under more favourable conditions the remains could be returned to Russia.

Romania, an Unlikely Saviour

'It was only from them that we met with real sympathy and understanding.'

Another unlikely candidate to help the Romanovs was Romania, where the tsar's cousin was queen. 'Missy,' as Queen Marie was known in the family, was the eldest daughter of Prince Alfred, Duke of Edinburgh, and his autocratic Russian wife, Grand Duchess Maria Alexandrovna. As the granddaughter of Queen Victoria *and* Tsar Alexander II of Russia, Missy was a first cousin of both Nicholas *and* Alexandra. She grew up in Britain and Malta, where her father commanded the Mediterranean Fleet. She was a great beauty and should have made a brilliant marriage. The future King George V, ten years her senior, fell in love with her when he stayed with the Edinburghs at the San Antonio Palace in Malta but Missy's mother was opposed to the marriage. She dictated her daughter's letter of refusal and looked for a bridegroom outside Queen Victoria's orbit. Her eye fell on Romania.

Missy's marriage to Crown Prince Ferdinand in 1893 caused shock and surprise. The Romanian throne was only founded in 1866, when Prince Karl of Hohenzollern-Sigmaringen (from the Catholic branch of the Hohenzollern family) was invited to become ruling prince. In 1878 he wrested independence from Turkey and became King Carol I of an autonomous Romania. The unprepossessing Ferdinand was his nephew and heir.

In Romania Missy's romantic illusions were quickly dispelled. The palace was gloomy, her apartments sombre and depressing. She and

Ferdinand had little in common apart from an interest in botany. Cut off from her favourite sister Victoria Melita ('Ducky'), who in 1894 married her cousin Grand Duke Ernest Ludwig of Hesse and By Rhine, Missy became homesick and depressed.

When the First World War broke out, Romania's Crown Council declared neutrality. This disappointment hastened the end of King Carol, a German at heart, who died on 10 October 1914.

Two years later Romania finally entered the war alongside Britain, France and Russia. Queen Marie threw herself into war work, enrolling as a nurse and travelling miles visiting the wounded in isolated villages. The war went badly for Romania and the Central Powers were soon at the gates of Bucharest. Missy wrote to her cousin the tsar begging him 'send us the help we ask for at once,' but he was in no position to do anything.[1] The royal family and the government were evacuated to Jassy.

Then in March 1917 Missy heard bad news from Russia. Her first thought was for her sister. After the death of Queen Victoria, Ducky had divorced Ernest Ludwig of Hesse and in 1905, without the tsar's permission, she married her Russian cousin Grand Duke Cyril Vladimirovich. His family were next in line to the throne should Tsarevich Alexei and Grand Duke Michael die without legitimate male issue.

'A revolution has broken out in Petersburg [*sic*] ....I hope Ducky is not in danger,' Missy wrote.[2] Cyril had been the first Romanov to break his oath of allegiance to the tsar, marching at the head of his regiment of the *Guarde Equipage* to the Duma to swear loyalty to the Provisional Government. Returning home, he hoisted the red flag on his palace and remained in Petrograd with Ducky, who was pregnant with her third child.

The next thing Missy heard came as a shock. 'Astounding news from Russia that Nicky has abdicated for himself and his son [and] has designated his brother Michael as his successor...' the Queen wrote in her diary on 16 March [NS] 1917. 'I can hardly realise the whole thing, it seems so dreadful.'[3]

King Ferdinand and Queen Marie immediately telegraphed their sympathy. Missy had last seen her cousins in June 1914, when the Russian imperial family visited Constanza in the vain hope that their eldest children, Grand Duchess Olga and Crown Prince Carol, would form an attachment that would lead to marriage.

Missy received a reply in Nicholas's own handwriting. 'I thank you both from the bottom of my heart for your touching message... May God bless you and the Romanian people and grant you the final victory and the fulfilment of all your hopes.'[4]

In her memoirs, published in the 1930s, Missy remained hostile to her cousin Alexandra, who had always made her feel inferior. 'What an hour for that woman,' she wrote, 'who because of her fanaticism has brought about this crisis; she who would listen to no-one except Rasputin, and separated herself little by little from all the members of the family ...' Up to that point Queen Marie was the only member of the family who had dared to criticise Alexandra in print.[5]

* * *

Soon after the revolution Ducky had reached relative safety.

In June 1917 Grand Duke Cyril decided to leave Petrograd. His mother, the widowed Grand Duchess Vladimir, and his brother, Grand Duke Andrei, were in the Caucasus, where they had been exiled by the tsar shortly before the revolution. They were later joined by the grand duchess's other son Grand Duke Boris.

Cyril applied to Kerensky for permission to go to Finland, which was still nominally part of the Russian empire, so that Ducky's child would be born on Russian soil. It also had the advantage that the border was only 25 miles from Petrograd. If the tide turned in Russia it would be easy for them to return.

The stories of the grand duke carrying his pregnant wife across the frozen Gulf of Finland have no basis in fact. They left in comfort by train with their daughters Maria and Kira. They were not permitted to take with them anything of value, only the clothes they could carry and any jewellery that they could conceal in their clothes.

Arriving in Borgo, just east of Helsingfors, they soon settled with friends at Haaiko Manor, from where Ducky was able to send a reassuring letter to Missy in Bucharest. Ducky's son Vladimir was born on 30 August.

In December 1917 Finland declared independence and during the early months of 1918 civil war broke out between the Reds (backed by Soviet Russia) and the Whites (backed by Germany). Finland dissolved into chaos and the family were subjected to house searches by Finnish Reds looking for arms. In February 1918 Cyril refused an offer from King Gustav V to bring him and his family to Sweden. He thought it would look like desertion and, like many others, he and Ducky did not expect the Bolshevik regime to last for long. 'He still hoped for an early collapse of Bolshevism and a return to glory.' The White Guards eventually triumphed and in April 1918 Finland became a German protectorate. Author William Clarke uncovered traces of Cyril having 'engaged in financial discussions with the Germans following the revolution' but when officers close to the grand duke were approached by the Germans about possible military collaboration, the idea was rejected.[6]

* * *

The events in Russia now affected Romania's situation. When the Bolsheviks seized power in the autumn of 1917 the increasingly unreliable help from Russia evaporated, along with any chance of a Romanian victory, as Lenin signed an armistice with Germany. With the Germans occupying most of Romania, resistance seemed useless. Missy fought back her tears. A telegram arrived from King George V telling Missy that she and her children were welcome in England at any time. She suddenly realised that the British knew Romania's position was hopeless.

At the end of January 1918 the Bolsheviks declared war on Romania and seized all their treasure, including Missy's jewels which had been sent to Moscow for safekeeping. A few days later Ukraine declared independence and signed peace. By February Romania was encircled by the enemy. There was now no choice but to make peace or face annihilation.

A preliminary peace was signed on 8 March. Two months later the Treaty of Bucharest was concluded and Romania's war was over. A pro-German government was formed but Queen Marie and her family remained at Jassy.

Then on 22 July came news of the tsar's murder. There was no mention of the fate of his family. Missy was horrified. 'I had always been afraid it would end like this,' she wrote, 'but had hoped against hope that in some way they could have been saved.'[7] Against the wishes of both the government and officialdom Missy insisted on holding a requiem for Nicholas in the small village church at Jassy.

'Poor Nicky!...' she wrote, 'if you had died on the throne what a fuss they would have made, what pompous ceremonies there would have been in every church in every country! But today because you are fallen from power, an exile, they try to ignore you.'[8]

A few days later fifty-one-year old Colonel Joseph Whiteside Boyle arrived.

Joe Boyle, 'the King of the Klondike,' was a very colourful character. Born in Ontario in 1867, he had been a sailor and a prize fighter before making his fortune in the Klondike Gold Rush. When Canada entered the war he raised a machine gun detachment at his own expense and offered his services to the Allies in London. He organised the Russian railway system although he did not speak the language and then went to Romania to arrange relief for the food crisis. While there he became a close friend of Queen Marie. Over 6 feet tall, powerfully built and absolutely fearless, he was attached to the British Military Mission and soon became involved in British Military Intelligence in Russia and Romania. His partner and interpreter, Captain George A. Hill of the British Secret Service, described him as 'a man whose equal I have encountered neither before nor since.'[9] In 1918 he was involved in 'intelligence operations against both the Bolsheviks and the Austro-German forces occupying Romania and South Russia.'[10] At the moment he was convalescing, having suffered a heart attack at the beginning of July while flying in Bessarabia.

Then Count Ugarov arrived in Jassy from Russia bringing Missy news that her 'Aunt Minny', the Dowager Empress Marie Feodorovna, was badly off in the Crimea. Cut off in Romania under German occupation, Missy became concerned for her Russian relatives, for whom the Bolshevik revolution spelt danger.

Ducky was still in Finland, where the Germans were now triumphant, but by July 1918 they were suffering from chronic food shortages. Ducky wrote to the crown princess of Sweden, herself the mother of five children, begging her to send some baby food for Vladimir. '... they can get nothing to give him,' Daisy wrote to Lady Egerton, 'doesn't it sound rather awful. I shall do my best to help her of course.'[11]

But Queen Marie had other relations trapped *inside* Russia. To free them she enlisted Boyle's help.

* * *

Queen Marie's cousin Grand Duchess Marie Pavlovna and her second husband, Prince Sergei Putiatin, had been caught up in the revolution when they went to Moscow to try to retrieve her jewels from the bank. Five days earlier, unknown to them, the Bolsheviks had seized power in Petrograd.

Finding the bank locked and bolted, they had no idea what to do. Suddenly they were carried forward by a crowd rushing down the street from the main boulevard, the Tverskaya. Terrified they would become separated Marie's husband gripped her arm until they stopped in a parallel street. Trucks rushed by full of armed soldiers shooting indiscriminately and bullets whizzed past, shattering window panes behind them. Making their way through side streets, they reached Theatre Square where the Bolshoi Theatre stood. With shooting on all sides, they remained trapped in a small side street with a crowd of people and no way out.

Then a column of soldiers marched in from the square, stopped and aimed their rifles. Instinctively the people behind Marie flattened themselves against a wall and, as the soldiers took aim, they all quickly prostrated themselves. Only Marie remained standing. A bullet hit the wall above her head, followed by two more.

After that she recalled only impressions – people running, falling, cries and moans ringing out, the smell of powder in the air – until they finally reached the home of Sergei's parents late in the afternoon. Shortly afterwards Marie and her husband returned to Petrograd. Her jewels were later retrieved from the bank by her parents-in-law. As the situation in Russia deteriorated they decided to leave for German-occupied Ukraine in the hope of returning in better times.

It was at this point that Marie's status as a former member of the Swedish royal family came in useful. She had been receiving food parcels from them, probably via her former sister-in-law Daisy, the crown princess, but now she asked them to safeguard her jewels.

Some of Marie's jewels had been sold in order to provide money on which to live. The remainder were now hidden. Some of the diamonds were concealed in a jacket that Marie's mother-in-law wore under her dress, while tiaras were secreted under the crown of her hats. To hide the rest required ingenuity, as the Bolsheviks were well aware of the usual places of concealment used by the aristocracy.

Marie therefore emptied a huge bottle of office ink. Inside the empty bottle she put the diamond rays of a tiara unstrung from its wire, poured paraffin over the diamonds and then replaced the ink. A large label all round the bottle obscured its contents and it stood in plain sight on her desk. Other jewels were hidden in home-made paperweights, while used empty cocoa tins were dipped in wax and provided with a wick to simulate a candle. Sometimes these were lit in front of the icons to deceive the servants, who had no idea that priceless jewels were concealed inside.

Before leaving Russia, Marie sent this concealed jewellery to the Swedish Legation for safekeeping. She also took the precaution of asking them for a document that would identify her to the Germans as a princess of the Swedish royal house. She concealed this piece of paper in a bar of soap.

On 2 August she and her husband went to say goodbye to Marie's father.

In March 1918 Grand Duke Paul had moved out of his own palace and was living quietly at Tsarskoe Selo in a small cottage on the estate of his nephew Grand Duke Boris Vladimirovich. In order to live, Paul and his wife were reduced to selling pictures and works of art from their own large palace, which was now impossible to heat. Earlier that year the French diplomat Louis de Robien had reported that although the grand duke remained loyal to the Allies, he was unable to conceal his delight at the German advance which for him and his family meant deliverance from the Bolshevik menace.

When all male members of the Romanov family were ordered to register at the Cheka headquarters, this included Paul's son Prince Vladimir Paley. His only crime had been the refusal to sign a paper renouncing his father. A few days later a Bolshevik doctor arrived at the cottage to examine the grand duke. He was declared too ill to travel and for the time being was allowed to remain at the cottage. All the cars had been requisitioned and the chauffeur had defected, so when Paul wanted to visit Marie and Sergei Putiatin, who were living nearby in a country house at Pavlovsk, he went by carriage, with his wife Olga and their daughters riding alongside on bicycles.

The birth of Marie's son Roman in July 1918 brought a brief ray of happiness into Paul's life. Unbeknown to Marie and her family, Roman's baptism took place on the very day her half-brother Vladimir and other members of the family were killed at Alapayevsk. When Marie said goodbye to her father at the beginning of August she had no idea that she would never see him again.

Marie decided to leave baby Roman with her parents-in-law. Then, accompanied by Sergei's brother Aleck and with no identity documents, they took a train to Orsha, the town forming the frontier between Soviet Russia and the region currently under German occupation. Crossing the frontier proved impossible. They had no permit from the Orsha Soviet and no Ukrainian visa. All Sergei possessed was an indistinct document issued by the Petrograd Soviet which boasted a profusion of impressive looking seals. After much persuasion, the guards finally allowed Marie and Sergei through the Soviet frontier into no man's land. Aleck was left behind with the luggage.

Now they had to cross into German-held territory. Going close to the fence, Marie sliced open the bar of soap with her husband's penknife, called to one of the guards and pushed the paper from the Swedish Legation through to him. He read it and immediately ordered the gates to be opened.

Still their troubles were not over. The local German commander refused to let them across the frontier without a visa from the Ukrainian commissar. They had no option but to trudge back to the frontier and return to Orsha.

On the way, they met the guard who had let them through into German territory. He immediately took them to the Ukrainian commissar, who gave Sergei a pass. He then provided a visa for Aleck and sent two soldiers with Sergei to find his brother and collect the luggage.

After spending the night in the Ukrainian commissar's railway carriage, they all left by train for Kiev the next day. It soon became apparent that it was not safe to remain there, so they decided to go south to Odessa where some friends had a house. Odessa was nearer to the sea and the frontier. They arrived there early in August. Aleck remained in Kiev.

* * *

As Grand Duchess Marie began to recover from her ordeal she suffered from constant anxiety over the fate of her father. It was not possible for her to travel any further, so she wrote to her former father-in-law King Gustav of Sweden, her cousin Queen Marie of Romania and King Alfonso XIII of Spain, begging them to help.

Paul had already refused an offer to leave Russia. Harald Scavenius had suggested that he go with Princess Paley's daughter Marianne Derfelden to the Austrian Embassy, where he would put on an Austrian uniform and be taken to Vienna with a convoy of returning prisoners-of-war. With rumours circulating that both the tsar and his brother Michael had been executed by the Bolsheviks, Marianne was anxious for her step-father to escape. The grand duke refused to wear an enemy uniform and he was afraid of reprisals against other members of the family if he fled.

Marie knew nothing of all this in Odessa. By the end of October the town was cut off when the ammunition stores caught fire. As large shells exploded, panic filled the city. For the moment she was trapped.

* * *

In September a report reached Copenhagen from Waldemar Spare, a Finnish officer who had visited the dowager empress at Harax on 7 September. He reported that she was well, living in relative freedom, guarded by Germans and complaining of a shortage of butter and coffee. At the end of October he returned to Harax, bringing a case of provisions from Empress Marie's Danish relatives.

On 10 October she wrote to Harald Scavenius. 'I hope that you and your gracious wife have not suffered too badly as a result of the terrible state of affairs in Petersburg [*sic*] and that you are both well. At present, we live in some peace and freedom, always hoping for better times and trusting in the grace and compassion of Our Lord. I would be very pleased if you would write to me at your leisure and tell me what is happening and how you live. It is a very long time since I heard from home…'[12]

In response to this letter, Ingeborg Larsen, sister of an employee of the Transatlantic Company of Copenhagen, arrived at Harax in November with letters from the Danish royal family. The Transatlantic Company now offered to act as couriers between the empress and her family in Denmark.

Missy had been in touch with her aunt in September to express her condolences on the death of the tsar. It was clear from Empress Marie's reply, sent from Harax soon afterwards, that she did not believe her son was dead. 'Since my poor Nicky has been taken from Tobolsk I have never heard from him nor from Misha-dear [Grand Duke Michael], so you can understand what anguish I go through. All my hope is in God. He alone can save them and help us to bear our miseries.'[13]

In November, with the situation becoming worse, Missy had talks with Joe Boyle and the Russian Minister Poklevski about getting the dowager empress safely out of the Crimea. 'Boyle is ready to undertake this, he is just the man for a daring job of this kind,' she wrote. 'I promised to help in every way, to obtain a Romanian ship etc, also to get things ready for Aunt Minny and any other members of the family, if they can be induced to leave Russia.' Boyle agreed to start as soon as possible.[14]

As the Bolsheviks approached the Crimea from the north, and with still no news of the fate of the tsar's wife and children, Missy sent several letters by courier to her cousin Grand Duchess Xenia. 'The thought of Nicky [the tsar] fills me with boundless indignation and grief,' she wrote, 'and what has happened to that unfortunate mistaken Alix? who was in *so* many ways the cause of all your misfortunes! And is little Alexei still alive? How and where are all the girls? It's all so fantastic that sometimes one thinks one must be able to wake up out of it all to get back to the old days of happiness. ... Xenia dear ... Please answer if anybody offers to take a letter. I have a safe friend helping.'[15]

'It was a joy to hear from you,' Xenia replied on 25 September. 'It is so awful to hear so little, or even nothing from one's own relations and friends... We can't and don't believe that Nicky has been taken away from us and that this ghastly crime could have happened. We know nothing, but there are kind souls who seem to be quite sure that he is safe and who keep on letting us know that they are well and in safety.' She reiterated what her mother had said; they had heard nothing from Nicholas since he left Tobolsk and nothing from Michael since January.[16]

On 10 November Nicolai Kasnakov arrived in the Crimea bearing a letter from Queen Marie to the dowager empress asking her to leave Russia while there was still time. Xenia was with her mother when the messenger arrived. 'He left Jassy on Monday with a letter to Mama... from Missy... and Colonel Boyle – some Canadian who did some big favours to Missy and the king during difficult times and is a very good man...' the grand duchess wrote in her diary. The plan was to send a transport ship to take the family to Romania and then, possibly, on to England.[17]

The dowager empress dismissed the idea. 'Naturally I am very moved over Kasnakov's good intentions and Missy's interest,' she wrote in her diary, 'but now it is not necessary at the time when the armistice stands before the door and certainly much will change.'[18]

On 11 November 1918 the First World War came to an end when the armistice was signed. The Germans now had to withdraw from the Crimea. King Ferdinand and Queen Marie had received information that a Bolshevik uprising would be timed to coincide with the German withdrawal. The Romanovs would then be killed. Boyle had received similar information from Anglo-French intelligence networks. He went to see the queen.

Missy immediately sent a courier to the dowager empress conveying the king and queen's proposals to send a ship to bring their relatives to safety. Missy also sent a dramatic plea to Xenia to leave before the Bolsheviks arrived. She was sending Colonel Boyle, 'a remarkable man, one in ten thousand,' and begged the family to trust him entirely. '... his methods may be somewhat surprising,' she ended, 'but they are always to the point.'[19]

With allied ships now in the Crimea the dowager empress felt reassured. She refused her niece's offer. Undeterred, Missy wrote again later that month. '... we are anxious for you all because there may be a very dangerous moment when the Germans leave and before the allies arrive... You must trust [Boyle] and listen to him – and if he persuades you to leave please leave and come to us and from there if possible we shall have all arranged so that you can go to England ... Trust Col. Boyle utterly, you will never regret it, he is one of those strong men as one seldom meets...'[20]

Boyle set sail in the *Regele Carol* on 19 November with Commander Basil Pantazzi, a Romanian naval officer. They took with them an armed force of 200 soldiers, a hand-picked crew, guns, provisions and a car to convey the dowager empress to the ship.

They arrived in the Crimea on 24 November, two days before the departure of the Germans. After foiling a local Bolshevik uprising by spreading false reports about the armed strength of their vessel, Boyle drove to Harax accompanied by a Russian guide.

The empress had written to Queen Alexandra to tell her how Missy 'wrote to me a couple of weeks ago and invited me urgently to come to her, as she had heard we lived here in great danger...'[21]

By this time the dowager empress had already refused a similar offer from King George V. Having failed to rescue the tsar, the king was now being urged by his mother to save her sister.

* * *

On 1 November the Commander-in-Chief Mediterranean, Vice Admiral the Honourable Sir Somerset Gough-Calthorpe, received a telegram from London marked 'very secret'. 'His Majesty the King is very anxious that steps should be taken to protect the dowager empress of Russia and family in the event of the German guards being withdrawn. It is believed that they have so far been protecting the person of Her Majesty. The latest information the king has is that they are in the Crimea domiciled in a house close to Livadia or Yalta overlooking the sea. Endeavours are being made to obtain definite information as to their whereabouts.'[22]

A few days later the Admiralty wired Calthorpe again to tell him that it had been established that the empress was at Harax, a red house with red tiles lying behind a local landmark called the Swallow's Nest. It was in reality a Gothic pavilion but it looked like a fairy-tale castle. 'The house called Swallow's Nest is a small white building near Ai-Todor built on a point of rock where the cliff falls into the sea...' the wire continued helpfully.[23]

On 16 November Admiral Calthorpe was told to consider sending a warship to rescue the imperial party. 'The matter is to be arranged with the greatest care and tact,' his orders continued. 'No force is to be used or armed party, and anything approaching a conflict with any guards there may be on the house is to be absolutely avoided.'[24]

The mission was entrusted to Commander C. E. Turle and Lieutenant Commander Korostovzoff, a White Russian officer. They set out with two destroyers, reaching the Crimea on the evening of 20 November. The following day they reached Harax and had an audience with the dowager empress. They brought a letter from Admiral Calthorpe, outlining the king's concern and his offer to take her by ship to Constantinople.

Turle reported the result to the Commander-in-Chief of HMS *Superb*. 'Her Majesty was disinclined to leave the Crimea and is undoubtedly very optimistic concerning the whole situation; as an instance, she still believes that the late Tsar Nicholas is still alive.'[25] That *sang-froid* was not shared by her entourage.

In the face of the empress's refusal to leave, there was nothing Turle could do. He stationed some British cruisers nearby and ordered them to make periodic visits to Yalta and Ai-Todor to ensure all was well.

Marie Feodorovna, however, had been delighted to see the British officer and she took the opportunity to give him some letters, including a note to King George V and a jubilant telegram to be transmitted to Queen Alexandra. 'Hurrah. Delighted at last to wire. Delighted to see one of your captains and hear his kind proposal. Hope that more ships will come openly and soon. Love to you all. Sister Dagmar.'[26] (Dagmar was the Empress's Danish name.)

A few days later Turle returned with Captain Royds bringing newspapers, cigarettes and an offer of hospitality from King Victor Emmanuel III of Italy, who offered to send his yacht *Trinacria* to bring her to safety. The king's wife, Queen Elena, was a sister of Grand Duchesses Militsa and Anastasia, who were also in the Crimea. The empress still refused to leave and as long as she remained, nobody else could leave either.

***

This was the situation when Boyle arrived with a letter from Queen Marie, which he asked the dowager empress to read first before speaking to him. Once again, Missy begged her aunt to pack her things and leave with Boyle.

Diplomatically, the empress told Boyle that, although she was grateful for her niece's concern, she could not abandon all the people who had sacrificed so much for her family. Nor would she go until she knew where her sons were and if they needed her help.

'You can imagine what I felt about it,' she later wrote to Queen Alexandra. 'I was basically furious over the way they wanted to force me [to leave] by sending a ship, but it is of course such a kind and good thought, so I pressed it all down and expressed only my thanks to him and how moved I was...'[27]

Although King Ferdinand had offered to place his palace of Sinaia at her disposal, one of the British officers later reported that the dowager empress told him that '*Nothing* would induce her to go to Romania in that little ship.'[28]

Boyle left Harax with letters for Queen Alexandra in Britain and King Ferdinand in Romania. After visiting the British ships at Sevastopol, he returned to Romania.

* * *

Meanwhile Grand Duchess Marie Pavlovna and Prince Sergei Putiatin were still in Odessa, which was occupied by Austrian troops whose commander shared power with the Russian military governor. Then towards the end of October rumours circulated that there was revolution in Austro-Hungary and Germany. As soon as this news was confirmed, the Austrian troops began to leave. No Allied troops took their place and the situation was becoming dangerous for Marie and Sergei, who feared the Bolsheviks would soon arrive.

Marie decided to write to Missy in Romania. After telling her cousin what she had heard about her father's ordeal in a Bolshevik prison, Marie continued: 'My husband and I succeeded in getting away from Petersburg [*sic*] just at the most dangerous moment about three months ago. We could only take very few things with us and now I have got hardly anything to put on. We hope very much that the English ships may come soon as it is beginning to be disagreeable here again and if it gets worse I simply don't know what will become of us.'[29]

An epidemic of Spanish flu was raging through Odessa, killing many people. Both Marie and Sergei went down with it. While they were still bedridden, a Russian officer arrived from Bessarabia in Romania to see Marie. He was sent by Colonel Boyle, who had been asked by the queen to track her cousin down. Boyle had been informed of Marie's whereabouts and sent a message that he was ready to help. Without any great faith in either Boyle or his messenger, Marie said she would be fit enough to leave in about a week.

The following week the officer returned bearing a letter from Missy offering her cousin a home in Romania. A Romanian officer accompanied him and everything was ready for their departure to Kishinev (now Chisinau).

They travelled in a special railway carriage accompanied by Marie's elderly maid. In Kishinev, Marie and Sergei spent the night in the governor's residence. The next day they left for the provincial town of Jassy, where a message awaited them from the king and queen. As soon as Bucharest was liberated from the Germans the sovereigns would return to their capital and welcome Marie and Sergei as their guests.

* * *

By late 1918 Bucharest had been freed from German occupation. On 1 December the streets were decked with flags and lined with cheering crowds as King Ferdinand and Queen Marie re-entered the city in triumph with their children.

Grand Duchess Marie and her husband had meanwhile arrived in Bucharest and booked into a local hotel. In keeping with her promise, Missy gave them apartments in Cotroceni Palace where they remained as guests of the king and queen. 'Of all the royal families still in possession of their thrones, and all more or less related to us, it was only from them that we met with real sympathy and understanding,' the grand duchess wrote in her memoirs.[30]

Missy was delighted to have her cousin staying with her. The grand duchess was now stateless and also remained penniless until her jewels could be retrieved from Sweden. All she had were 'one or two worn-out dresses made over from my pre-war wardrobe ... thick cotton underwear, no silk stockings and a few miscellaneous articles such as handkerchiefs, the initials of which had been cut out with scissors,' all kept in a worn-out suitcase containing the old toilet articles she had used when nursing during the war.[31]

The queen gave her some clothes and took the younger woman on excursions to visit the destitute people living in villages outside Bucharest. Due to poor roads, long distances and the winter weather, the women were often held up in snow storms or their open car was stuck in mud. It was after dark when they returned home, the grand duchess recalled, 'cold and wet.'[32]

Although Marie and her husband were safe, there was one cloud on the horizon. She may have heard that her brother Dmitri had reached England but she still had no news of her father, who was a prisoner of the Bolsheviks in Petrograd.

The Doomed Grand Dukes

'He was the only one who helped them…'

By the autumn of 1918 the situation of Grand Dukes George and Nicholas Michaelovich, Dmitri Constantinovich and Paul Alexandrovich was desperate. All were prisoners of the Bolsheviks.

In the summer of 1917 Grand Duke George Michaelovich had moved to a rented villa in Retiervi, Finland. Denied permission to go to England by the British government, he hoped that when the Provisional Government allowed him to go abroad he would be able to easily reach Norway or Sweden. The Bolshevik revolution in October changed all that.

By the winter of 1917, with permission to leave Russia unlikely to come, the grand duke moved to a small hotel in Helsingfors (Helsinki). Among the residents were some British officers, including General Poole who attempted to take George with him as part of the departing British Mission. The plan was frustrated by Sir Francis Lindley, the nominal head.

The new year of 1918 began badly. There was fighting in the streets of Helsingfors and one night the grand duke's hotel door was broken open by sailors searching for arms. Despite pleas from his friends, who assured him that Finland would soon be independent from Russia and he would automatically then be abroad, George was determined to obtain a new passport so that he could leave for Europe.

On making enquiries he was told to present himself to the Central Committee. The president of the committee looked at his papers, told George they were not sufficient and said he was to come back and get others. Permission to go abroad would depend on the government in Petrograd.

Early in April George was arrested and thrown into prison. Shortly afterwards, under an escort of Red Guards, he was taken to Petrograd, where he lived in the house of his secretary (his own palace having been taken over by the Bolsheviks).

The following day the grand duke had to present himself before Commissar Uritsky at the Cheka, who would decide his place of exile. During an interview of an hour-and-a-half he was offered a choice of Vologda, Viatka or Perm. He chose Vologda, one of Russia's most ancient towns, famous for its old churches.

'Thank God you are not in this country which was once called Russia and now does not exist any more,' he wrote to his wife in England.[1]

***

Arriving in Vologda with his servant Matorov, Grand Duke George Michaelovich was billeted in a two-storey wooden house on the right bank of the river belonging to a local merchant. His brother Nicholas (known as Bimbo in the family) had arrived on 31 March, and his cousin Grand Duke Dmitri Constantinovich, the brother of Queen Olga of Greece, was also on the river's right bank.

Grand Duke Nicholas Michaelovich had renounced his appanage (the income granted to members of the imperial family from millions of acres of crown lands) after the revolution and had tried to persuade his brothers to do the same. He was now living in 'two rooms on the first floor of a wooden house at one end of a courtyard', on the left bank of the river, accompanied by his ADC General Constantine Brunner and his cook. In April he was visited by Louis de Robien, Third Secretary at the French Embassy, who had known him in better times. De Robien recalled the modestly furnished room with its shabby furnishings, all a far cry from his Petrograd palace on Palace Embankment filled with works of art (from which he had been forced to move to a furnished apartment on the Moika Canal when the palace was taken over by the Bolsheviks). It was even reported that the grand duke had gone two days without bread. The men discussed the situation and, in the event of a restoration, who should be tsar. The grand duke dismissed all the male members of the family as 'incompetent', and was especially sarcastic about his cousin Grand Duke Paul. He felt particularly bitter because Paul was still living at Tsarskoe Selo, thanks partly to the energetic efforts of his wife Princess Paley who, he said, was 'very proud of the fact that her son Vladimir has been included in the banishment with the real grand dukes.' Although Grand Duke Nicholas and his brother George were more or less left in peace by the Bolsheviks, he admitted being afraid for the future.[2]

Grand Duke Dmitri Constantinovich and his adjutant Colonel Korochentzov were living in a room of a local merchant's house. In another room in the same house lived Dmitri's widowed niece Princess Tatiana (elder daughter of Grand Duchess Elisabeth Mavrikievna), whose husband Prince Constantine Bagration had been killed in 1915 leaving her with two young children, Prince Teymuraz, born in 1912, and Princess Natalia, born in 1914. Dmitri looked after Tatiana, and in return she helped him with the problems caused by his failing eyesight. In mid-May another of Dmitri's adjutants, Colonel Alexander von Leiming, arrived with news that a safe passage had been obtained for the grand duke to leave for Finland. Dmitri refused to go, afraid of reprisals against other members of the family.

Apart from a stipulation that they report once a week to the Cheka, the three grand dukes could wander around town and go where they pleased. All the foreign embassies were in town. George Michaelovich befriended the British Consul, who even came up with a plan to smuggle him out of Russia. The grand duke refused, knowing that his relatives would suffer if he escaped. On 23 May Nicholas Michaelovich called at the French Embassy to talk with the Ambassador Joseph Noulens and was able to give him news of the whereabouts of other members of the imperial family.

The grand dukes' exile, which they had been told would last about a month, stretched into three and the damp heat of the summer was exhausting. A rumour that the tsar had been murdered reached Vologda on 3 June. It proved to be false. George and his brother met daily, sometimes joined by Dmitri. It was while the brothers were having lunch at Nicholas's house on 1 July that they were arrested and incarcerated in the district prison about 40 miles from town. The order for their arrest came from Moisei Uritsky in Petrograd. A few hours later Dmitri joined them. They were the only prisoners in the building and after the first day were allowed to have their own camp beds, clothes, pens, ink, paper and cigarettes.

Through the French consul in Moscow, the French ambassador protested about the imprisonment of Grand Duke Nicholas, who 'as a member of the French Institute is our protégé'. He also asked Harald Scavenius, whose legation was looking after French interests, to intervene in Petrograd.[3]

The grand dukes were reported to be fairly well treated. The prison had a small garden where they were allowed to take exercise and they were permitted to see each other. 'They each have a room and can have their meals brought in,' de Robien recorded. The prison governor seemed to be a reasonable man and 'shuts his eyes as much as he can to visits from outside.' Grand Duke Nicholas was reported to be in good spirits and his only complaint was 'the smell of the WCs.'[4]

News that the tsar had been executed in Ekaterinburg reached Vologda on 20 July. The following day the three grand dukes were transferred to Petrograd under guard.

Before their train left, Louis de Robien managed to see them and shake grand duke Nicholas's hand. De Robien found him 'greatly aged and he looked very tired.' The diplomat told them that the French ambassador would do all in his power for them. Nicholas asked him to inform his friend the author and member of the *Académie française* Frederic Masson in Paris. News of the tsar's murder had left the grand duke greatly shocked and he had few illusions as to his own eventual fate. Both Grand Duke Dmitri and Grand Duke Nicholas were unmarried but Grand Duke George, wearing 'a grey suit and a travelling cap', asked de Robien to break the news of his transfer to his wife in London.[5]

Dmitri Constantinovich still maintained a majestic bearing, despite his shabby cap and suit made of soldiers' cloth. His niece Princess Tatiana and her two small children were also at the station, and at the last minute she was permitted to travel to Petrograd with the grand dukes and their servants.

They arrived in Petrograd on 21 July. By the end of that month Grand Dukes Nicholas, Dmitri and George were in the notorious Shpalernaia prison, where a few days later they were joined by Grand Duke Paul Alexandrovich.

* * *

Paul had been arrested at 3.00am on the night of 12 August. As his young daughters Irene and Natalie huddled together barefoot in their nightdresses, the villa was ransacked by armed soldiers. Diaries and correspondence were seized and tea, sugar, Madeira and vodka were confiscated by the gleeful men. When the search was finished the soldiers were ordered to take the grand duke to the local Soviet, which was housed in the Tsarskoe Selo palace of Paul's late brother Grand Duke Vladimir. Irene and Natalie clung pitifully to their father, shaking with sobs as he said goodbye but Princess Paley was permitted to accompany her husband.

Paul was taken to the Cheka headquarters in Petrograd and from there transferred to Shpalernaia prison. Princess Paley went to stay with Marianne Derfelden, her daughter from her first marriage. She was permitted to visit Paul in prison on Tuesdays and Fridays and take food for him every second day. The interviews were held in the presence of a commissar and she was informed beforehand 'what she could talk to him about and what subjects were prohibited.'[6]

Shortly after Paul's arrest Prince Gabriel Constantinovich, a nephew of Grand Duke Dmitri, was also sent to Shpalernaia prison. The prince and his wife had unwisely returned from Finland just after Christmas, failing to listen to friends who told them that the Grand Duchy would soon be independent from Russia. Illness had prevented Gabriel from being sent to Vyatka in March with his brothers Ioann, Constantine and Igor but on 15 August, despite his ill-health, he was arrested and incarcerated in an adjoining prison cell to the grand dukes. He was shocked at their gaunt appearance.

* * *

In Denmark King Christian and Queen Alexandrine were by now thoroughly concerned about the safety of her Romanov uncles, two of whom she had now heard were under arrest.

Queen Alexandrine's mother Grand Duchess Anastasia Michaelovna of Russia was a cousin of Nicholas II's father, Tsar Alexander III. Anastasia had four brothers in Russia – Grand Duke Alexander Michaelovich (Sandro) who was at Ai-Todor with his family in an area which was currently under German occupation; Grand Duke Sergei Michaelovich who had been reportedly killed at Alapayevsk; and Grand Dukes Nicholas and George Michaelovich who were in prison in Petrograd. Only Grand Duke Michael Michaelovich was safe in England, where he had lived for many years.

On 6 August 1918 King Christian telegraphed from his summer home at Marselisborg in Jutland to Erik Scavenius at the Foreign Ministry. Grand Duchess George in London had forwarded an alarming message she had just received from Grand Duke Cyril's wife in Finland. It concerned Grand Duke George. The king forwarded the message to Copenhagen. 'Very anxious for your husband's life[,] have now discovered him to be in dreadful prison in Petrograd with some other relations barely fed. Unless immediate help very little hope for them. Situation for whole family desperate.' Confirmation had arrived that the queen's uncles were in a Bolshevik prison and the king wondered if anything could be done.[7]

A further telegram then arrived from the queen's brother in Germany, Grand Duke Frederick Franz IV of Mecklenburg-Schwerin, saying that their mother urgently requested Alexandrine's help to free their uncles. This information was immediately relayed to Harald Scavenius in Petrograd with instructions to visit the grand dukes in prison.

Grand Duke Frederick Franz also sent a similar telegram to King Haakon of Norway on 10 September, asking him to do all he could 'to save all the imprisoned grand dukes.' Grand Duke George was married to Haakon and Maud's cousin Marie of Greece, and Grand Duke Paul had once been married to Marie's sister Alexandra.

King Haakon had felt like answering that since Germany had brought Lenin back to Russia, *they* should save the victims from the Bolsheviks' claws. He nevertheless asked Ihlen to telegraph the Norwegian Legation and instruct them to do anything possible.[8]

Following an appeal from the British minister, Harald Scavenius was also instructed to help Grand Duke Dmitri Constantinovich and keep the Danish Foreign Ministry informed of developments.

At the urgent request of the Allied representatives in Petrograd (and without waiting for instructions from Copenhagen), Harald Scavenius had already seen the Bolsheviks to demand the safety and decent treatment of the grand dukes. He now visited the prison to see for himself that they were all physically well.

Scavenius met the grand dukes in the prison inspector's office. The four men, who were all in their fifties, each had their own cell,

7 feet by 3 feet. They rose at 7 every morning and were taken out to the courtyard, separately, for about half-an-hour every day before lunch. Occasionally they were able to exchange a few words. Apart from that they had no exercise and the food was bad, usually consisting of 'dirty hot water with a few fish bones floating in it' and black bread.[9] They begged Scavenius to secure their freedom.

He sent them food, bought with money deposited at the Danish Legation by their friends, and hid jewellery and documents belonging to Princess Paley, first in the Austro-Hungarian Legation and then in the Danish Legation. In this, and many other such underground activities, Scavenius collaborated with Peter Dournovo, the former Minister of the Interior.

Scavenius made frequent representations to Commissar Uritsky but was assured that the grand dukes were in prison for their own safety, because otherwise they would be killed by the people. 'That is naturally false,' Scavenius commented in a telegram to the Foreign Ministry.[10] Uritsky visited the prison and told the grand dukes the same story, adding that they would be freed when the German government released Karl Liebknecht and Victor Adler, two Socialist leaders. They were, effectively, hostages.

After a while the grand dukes were allowed to meet and walk in the courtyard twice a day and to use the prison library. Prince Gabriel's wife, the former ballerina Antonia Nestorovskaya, brought food to him and his uncle Dmitri (who was also receiving food brought in by Colonel von Leiming), as well as books to while away the long hours of solitude. She was allowed visits twice a week and was meanwhile making repeated attempts to have her husband freed. Princess Paley obtained a permit to take provisions to supplement Paul's meagre diet. A doctor also visited Paul and Gabriel, who were both ill. Dmitri tried to raise his nephew Gabriel's flagging spirits by telling him jokes.

Letters from Grand Duke George to his wife in London were smuggled in and out of the prison by members of the Danish Legation. In one of them George enclosed a drawing of his prison cell. The grand duchess later said that the Danish royal family and legation did more to help them than any other royal family.

'Yesterday it was my fifty-fifth birthday and strangely enough my fifty-fifth day in prison,' Grand Duke George wrote to his wife on 25 August. 'Imagine my joy when the dear kind nurse of this prison brought me a whole packet of letters from you and the children. It has warmed my heart and given me new courage in my miserable plight and loneliness. Alas, they will again be taken away from me as it is dangerous if they discover that I get letters.' He added that one of the most 'horrible sensations' was the nightly removal of prisoners, without knowing their fate. Usually they were shot.[11]

From London George's wife continued to lobby Queen Mary, King Alfonso and even Cardinal Bourne, the Archbishop of Westminster, to see if the pope could get her husband released. At the end of September the cardinal replied that 'the Germans were trying to persuade the Bolsheviks to send the four grand dukes to the Crimea.'[12] The Russian government denied that Grand Duke George was a hostage and accused the pope of interfering in Russia's internal affairs.

King Alfonso was trying to help. *The Times* reported on 8 August that the monarch 'continues his efforts on behalf of the relatives of the late tsar... Urgent telegrams have informed him of the desperate situation of the Grand Duke George, who is said to be in prison in Petrograd ill and without subsistence or medical aid.' The king was anxious that other monarchs publicly express their approval so that his hand would be strengthened in this humanitarian effort.

Throughout the autumn of 1918 Harald Scavenius and his wife Anna Sofie visited the grand dukes regularly, remaining in constant contact and bringing provisions to supplement the prison rations. George's stomach suffered from constantly eating cold food and eventually the kindly prison nurse brought him a small spirit lamp so he could warm his meals. His servant Matorov continued to bring food to him three times a week.

Scavenius also conducted a secret correspondence with Nicholas Michaelovich, in which the grand duke said he favoured a common *Scandinavian* initiative to obtain their freedom. If that was not possible, it should be a purely *Danish* affair. He seemed to be under the mistaken impression that King Christian controlled Danish foreign policy and that some of the leading Bolsheviks, particularly Lenin, were in favour of the grand dukes leaving Russia.

This optimism was misplaced. On 12 September 1918 Uritsky was murdered. This murder, along with an unsuccessful attempt on Lenin's life, sparked the Red Terror and ended Gabriel and Antonia's hopes of his release.

Scavenius now reported that hundreds of innocent hostages were shot daily and Bolshevik newspapers were crying out that the grand dukes should be executed. There was no protection even for diplomats, who were no longer respected. The British Embassy was stormed and Captain Cromie, a naval attaché, killed. It was Scavenius who, after finding Cromie's 'half-decapitated body thrown into a cellar', took it to the British church where it was buried wrapped in the only flag available – the Dannebrog.[13]

In London Grand Duchess George again became alarmed and Henrik Greben-Castenskiold, the Danish Minister, asked his government on her behalf whether anything could be done for her husband. Once again, the request was forwarded to Harald Scavenius in Petrograd.

The grand duchess also approached her cousin Queen Maud of Norway but the Norwegian government was so radical that Maud saw little hope of them requesting the release of any grand dukes.

An appeal was then made to King Gustav V of Sweden by Princess Paley. The Swedish King asked his representative, Count Koskull, to visit Grand Duke Paul. The count promised to intercede with the Bolsheviks but there was no result.

By the second half of September a joint German-Spanish approach on behalf of the four grand dukes was foundering, and the Germans were on the brink of passing responsibility to Spain.

Scavenius felt that the only realistic hope of obtaining their freedom would come from an approach to the kaiser. When Grand Duke George was advised to seek assistance from the German consul he refused, saying he would not ask a favour from a Hun. By this time Germany's allies were collapsing, defeat was imminent and the kaiser could do little more than instruct his consul in Petrograd, Hans Karl Breiter, to take the grand dukes under his protection.

Grand Duke Paul then asked Scavenius to enquire whether an intervention from the Danish king would be possible. This request was forwarded to the Foreign Ministry, together with the latest reports on the grand dukes. Erik Scavenius, however, did not inform King Christian about Paul's appeal, nor about the Danish government's assessment of the kaiser's lack of influence. Professor Bent Jensen has said that it is 'absolutely unheard of, that a minister withheld from the monarch a private approach from a relative in distress.'[14]

After much persistence from Antonia, who knew Maxim Gorky's wife Maria Andreievna, Commissar for Theatres, after about a month in prison Prince Gabriel was released into a private clinic. Before leaving Shpalernaia prison he went to Dmitri's cell to bid farewell to the favourite uncle of his youth and receive his blessing. Soon afterwards Gorky took Gabriel and Antonia into his own apartment and they were finally given permission to make their way out of Russia.

'Did I tell you or Miss E that I saw twice Gabriel's wife after he was arrested?' Grand Duchess Elisabeth Mavrikievna wrote to a friend in London in January 1919. 'Now they are in Finland.'[15]

* * *

The Bolsheviks now began to make things even more unpleasant for the imprisoned grand dukes by removing the kindly nurse, although the director of the prison managed to keep her there a little longer. Soon afterwards, the Danish king and queen received another appeal for help from the four men. Christian immediately informed Erik Scavenius that the royal family would take care of them if their release and journey to Denmark could be negotiated. This implied that they would foot the bill for the men's support themselves and not ask the Treasury to pay. Erik again approached Harald and this offer reached the grand dukes in prison.

The British government, impressed by Harald Scavenius's humanitarian efforts, had also instructed their ambassador in Copenhagen, Sir Ralph Spencer Paget, to ask if Denmark would take care of the four men. Since the storming of the British Embassy they had been unable to obtain direct information from Petrograd.

On 5 October Grand Duke Nicholas wrote to Harald, optimistically outlining how he would leave Petrograd on a Swedish ship, travel from Stockholm to Malmø and then across to Denmark. He had received a letter from his niece Queen Alexandrine, from which he was delighted to learn that the Dowager Empress Marie Feodorovna was now able to correspond freely with her Danish relatives but was worried about his brother George, whose health was suffering from the lack of warm food, despite the help of the spirit lamp.

Harald had made several attempts during the autumn to obtain the men's release but he had to report on 12 October that it was 'absolutely impossible at the moment.'[16]

He and Anna Sofie continued to take food to the prison. Through the legation, they also sent money and valuables belonging to the grand dukes to safety in Denmark.

On 13 October Harald received another letter from Grand Duke Nicholas. He was disappointed that a proposed approach for their release from Hetman Skoropadsky in Kiev had come to nothing. Skoropadsky was to have instructed his Foreign Ministry to telegraph Adolph Joffe in Berlin. Nicholas was annoyed that nothing positive had come of this initiative and vented his anger on the German government. He was convinced that only a signal from Berlin would persuade the Bolsheviks to release them – but the signal would not come because the Germans preferred the Romanovs to be in prison so they could not 'betray to the world the shameless things the German government had done with the Bolsheviks,'[17] by which he presumably meant helping them get back into Russia.

Although Harald Scavenius informed King Christian, whether the Foreign Ministry brought this letter to the attention of the king and queen is unknown. In any case, Germany's defeat and the collapse of the monarchy in November 1918 ended any hopes of assistance from that quarter.

Rumours circulated that the grand dukes would be set free on the first anniversary of the Bolshevik takeover, or, as Grand Duke George called it, 'Lenin's accession to the throne'.[18] Then the men were informed that they could purchase their freedom – but they had no money. Soon afterwards, the prison director and the nurse were removed for being too kind.

From Switzerland on 2 December Queen Olga of Greece made a desperate appeal to King George V on behalf of her brother Grand Duke Dmitri and her son-in-law Grand Duke George: 'I write to you in the anguish of my heart! You know that my brother – the last one I have ... is in prison with Minny's [Grand Duchess George's] husband George, his brother Nicholas and Paul since this summer, they are kept as hostages ... your ships and troops are already at Odessa and as I hope, poor darling Aunt Minny [the Dowager Empress Marie] is under their protection... Do what you can, my darling Sunbeam....'[19]

On 6 December Paul, who was by now very ill, was transferred to the prison hospital on the island of Golodai. Before he left he was allowed to say goodbye to his young daughters Irene and Natalie. They never saw their father again.

Princess Paley was still permitted to visit Paul twice a week. Three times a week she also carried two heavy baskets of food and linen to the prison hospital. Paul again refused all offers of escape to Finland, as he feared reprisals against other members of the family. His wife tried to have him transferred to the private hospital of Dr Orshansky, to no avail. Her last visit was on Christmas Day. After that, although the princess continued to bring food she was no longer allowed to see her husband.

The other grand dukes remained in Shpalernaia prison. George's last letter to his wife was dated 27 November. It was becoming more and more difficult to smuggle letters in and out but he nevertheless continued to write, as he found it comforting to pour out his feelings on paper.

On 8 December Nicholas smuggled out a final letter to Harald Scavenius, hidden in the soup tureen which the grand duke's faithful servant brought in. He had no news, other than that Dmitri was completely shrunken and suffered from his heart and George complained of his stomach. There were no more matches to light the spirit lamp. He himself was in 'high spirits' (he wrote this in English) and was now convinced that he would *never* be freed. He asked Harald to forward the letter to Queen Alexandrine so that she would know her uncles were still alive.[20]

Harald immediately telegraphed the Foreign Ministry asking them to tell the queen. She was also informed that her uncles had received the parcel of warm clothes which she had sent, via the legation, from Grand Duchess George in England. (Things sent through the British Mission had been returned to the grand duchess.) Nicholas's letter was not forwarded because, at this point, under pressure mainly from the French, the Danish government closed the legation and recalled Harald Scavenius. He would leave Petrograd on 15 December.

Harald protested against leaving the people who needed his help, especially as their lives could depend on him remaining in Russia. It was 'more than painful', he told the Foreign Ministry, in an attempt to obtain leave to remain. His pleas fell on deaf ears and he had no choice but to obey orders.[21] Before he left, Harald made one last-ditch attempt to obtain the grand dukes' release. 'I think

I ought to add,' he telegraphed on 6 December after reporting the worsening conditions in the prison, 'that I can probably free the three grand dukes in Petrograd [Paul was still in hospital], provided I can have the disposal of 500,000 roubles' – the equivalent of £50,000 sterling, or one million Danish kroner. It appears this was a bribe to one of the guards in the prison.[22]

Although Erik Scavenius had deliberately kept much information from the king and queen this last appeal from Harald was brought to their attention. At the same time they were informed of Harald's imminent recall. Henrik Greben-Castenskiold, the minister in London, was also told and on 10 December he contacted Grand Duchess George. Time was running short.

The grand duchess did not have such a large sum of money at her disposal but, by chance, a director of the Landmandsbank of Copenhagen was in London. Emil Glückstadt now offered to lend the money if the grand duchess deposited her jewels as security. He would then arrange for the 500,000 rouble ransom to be sent to Harald Scavenius in Petrograd.

Grand Duchess George had taken only a few of her jewels when she left Russia in July 1914 on what was supposed to be a short holiday. Now, at a brief meeting with Greben-Castenskiold and Glückstadt, she handed them over. It seems that they were not valuable enough because they were returned to her shortly afterwards. Greben-Castenskiold now had to find another solution.

On 11 December he informed Glückstadt that the king and queen of Denmark had stood as surety for the loan. Shortly afterwards, an order was sent to the representative of the Russian Trading Company in Petrograd, asking him to pay the money to the Danish Minister.

Erik Scavenius then told Harald that 'the royal persons in question' (the king and queen) authorised him to dispose of it as agreed. If the payment did not arrive in time, the minister must obtain the money by other means. Erik stressed that it was assumed that the operation could be carried out without damaging Danish interests. Rescuing the grand dukes was not of course, 'in Danish interests'.[23]

The plan was never realised. By 14 December the Foreign Ministry were of the opinion that they probably could do nothing to free the grand dukes because of Harald Scavenius's imminent journey.

The following day he left Petrograd, taking with him Grand Duke Nicholas's letter of 8 December. The money had not arrived. On 21 December the Foreign Ministry informed Greben-Castenskiold that 'nothing could be undertaken' because of Harald Scavenius's recall.[24]

Before he left Petrograd, Scavenius left extra provisions at the prison for the grand dukes. He also arranged for a number of trunks belonging to Grand Duke Michael Alexandrovich (of whom nothing definite had been heard since June) and the dowager empress's seal, which had been deposited in the legation, to be sent to Denmark. 'I am so angry that the good Scavenius is no longer in St Petersburg,' [sic] the dowager empress wrote to Queen Alexandra in London when she heard of his recall, '... he was the only one who helped them...'[25]

In London Grand Duchess George now had no idea how she could get provisions to her husband or, indeed, how he could be freed. She approached the American President Woodrow Wilson, who was staying at Buckingham Palace that December. The president's staff said he was too busy to see her, so she gave a letter for him to Queen Mary. It went unanswered.

Early in 1919 Queen Alexandrine asked the Danish Foreign Ministry to obtain information about the grand dukes. Learning they were still in prison, towards the end of January she sent a letter to them with a Danish businessman who was travelling to Petrograd.

On 28 January Princess Paley arrived at the hospital as usual with her husband's food. Later that day he was returned to Shpalernaia prison.

It is not clear whether Queen Alexandrine's letter reached her uncles. Maxim Gorky went to Moscow and interceded with Lenin for their lives. Gorky succeeded, and jumped on a train the next day with the signed liberation orders. By the time he arrived in Petrograd, it was too late. Early in the morning of 30 January 1919, Grand Dukes George and Nicholas Michaelovich, Dmitri Constantinovich and Paul Alexandrovich were taken to the SS Peter and Paul Fortress. Here they were marched out to a trench near the Trubetskoy Bastion and executed by firing squad. Their bodies were thrown into a common grave.

'... those fiends came to tell them in that prison that they would be free next day,' Grand Duchess George told her sister-in-law Grand Duchess Xenia. '... instead of which they were driven to the Peter & Paul Fortress and shot... Such irony, to be buried two steps from the place they had a right to be buried... The truth came out only a few days after when a man was boasting in the streets that he had a pair of boots on belonging to a Romanov he had shot the day before. To think that people like that can exist!'[26]

Dmitri's body was taken away the next day by his former adjutant and buried in the garden of a private house, where it still remains.[27]

'Why did they kill my beloved brother?' lamented Queen Olga of Greece from her exile in Switzerland. '... Now I am the last one remaining in our family ... [I have] no brother, no home ... but I need to endure, endure and endure.'[28] The only thing that kept her going was her strong religious faith.

Although an unmarked mass grave has been found in the grounds of the fortress, the remains of the other grand dukes have not been positively identified.

King George's Embarrassment

'You are here only by accident.'

The British government's refusal to grant asylum to the Romanov men had so far kept them out but at the end of 1918 a new embarrassment arose for King George. Unexpectedly, a Russian grand duke appeared in London.

Grand Duke Dmitri Pavlovich was the son of Grand Duke Paul by his first marriage to Princess Alexandra of Greece (the elder daughter of King George I and Queen Olga), who had died at his birth in 1891. Banished to the Persian front at the end of 1916 for his part in the murder of Rasputin, Dmitri had refused to return to Petrograd after the tsar's abdication. Although the Provisional Government had offered him a pardon, the grand duke had no wish to live in Russia under a republic. The tsar's punishment undoubtedly saved his life.

After the revolution he travelled to Tehran where he became a liaison officer with the British Mission and lived with the British Minister Sir Charles Marling. When Marling was recalled to London, he and his wife Lucia took Dmitri with them. Reaching Marseilles, they found that anti-Russian feeling in France was strong. It was only upon the insistence of the British Ambassador Lord Derby that Dmitri was allowed to cross France by train to Paris. He made his way to London with the Marlings, arriving on 17 December 1918. With no other rooms available, the grand duke booked into the Burlington Hotel in Cork Street.

There was some difficulty about Dmitri's presence in England because he had slipped into the country with the returning diplomatic mission. Lady Marling therefore went to see the king's assistant private secretary Lord Cromer to inform him of the grand duke's arrival. Dmitri was quickly visited by a Foreign Office representative who asked him to leave Britain, suggesting he go to Malta. He refused unless the order came directly from King George V. The matter was dropped.

The news of the grand duke's arrival can only have been awkward for King George – not only because he had failed to save Dmitri's cousin the tsar but also because, unknown to the grand duke, his father Grand Duke Paul was still languishing in a Bolshevik prison hospital.

* * *

By now the First World War had ended in an armistice and the fall of more European thrones. 'How are the mighty fallen,' King George wrote in his diary when he heard news of the kaiser's abdication.[1]

William had refused calls to abdicate in favour of the crown prince's eldest son, a move that could perhaps have been acceptable to the Allies and preserved the monarchy. By early November 1918 a naval mutiny at Kiel had spread to agitators and social democrats in Berlin, the troops were deserting and the kaiser was told that the German army no longer existed. On 9 November, as the old order fell apart, the German Chancellor Prince Max of Baden announced the abdication of the kaiser and Crown Prince William.

A republic was proclaimed and as mutinous troops marched towards his headquarters at Spa in Belgium, the kaiser agreed to go to Holland. William's arrival at the border town of Eijsden was totally unexpected. His request for asylum was referred to The Hague and, after lengthy telephone negotiations, Queen Wilhelmina of the Netherlands granted him sanctuary. When William crossed the Dutch border on 11 November, the day the armistice ended the war, the first thing he asked for was a cup of really good English tea.

He was offered accommodation at Amerongen Castle, Utrecht. Later William bought Huis Doorn, a charming manor house with outbuildings and a park, 5 miles west of Amerongen. It was owned by Baroness Wilhelmina van Heemstra, the great-grandmother of the actress Audrey Hepburn. Here the kaiser lived the remainder of his life in exile.

Although King George had done nothing to help the Romanovs, within days of the armistice in 1918 he made covert contact with his cousin Ernie, the Grand Duke of Hesse, through a British officer. The king and queen wanted the grand duke to know that the war had not spoilt their feelings for Hesse and that they were pleased to be in touch with him again. Grand Duke Ernest Ludwig later said that 'George V always remained the same towards him, the most family-orientated human being.' When he wrote his memoirs Ernie, who died in 1937, probably did not know that it was the king, and not his prime minister, who denied asylum to his sister Empress Alexandra.[2]

The Austro-Hungarian throne had also fallen.

Early in 1919 King George received a plea for help on behalf of Emperor Carl and Empress Zita of Austria-Hungary (to whom the king was not even distantly related). In the wake of revolution in Vienna, they had fled to their shooting lodge at Eckartsau, near the border with Slovakia and Hungary. Prince Sixtus of Bourbon-Parma, Zita's brother, later said that he had been received by King George and Queen Mary and stressed the perilous condition the imperial couple were in, as Austria now had a Socialist government. The king, afraid of another Ekaterinburg situation, despatched Lieutenant Colonel Edward Lisle Strutt to Eckhartsau to take the royal family to safety in Switzerland.

King George's failure to help the Romanovs must have been on his conscience.

* * *

In the late afternoon of 17 December Dmitri called on his aunt Grand Duchess George of Russia, who was living in a small house in Regent's Park. It was only while talking to her that Dmitri learned about his father's true situation. 'Poor papa was imprisoned at the end of July and released only three or four weeks ago to go into the hospital, because his health went downhill,' he confided to his diary.[3]

The grand duchess was worried about her husband, who was also still in Shpalernaia prison, and now that Harald Scavenius had been recalled she had no way of getting further news. Her own situation in London was also desperate, as she lacked funds.

The news of Dmitri's sister was brighter. Marie had given birth to a son and was believed to have reached Odessa with her husband.

Although pleased to hear about Marie, Dmitri endured torment on his father's behalf. His equilibrium collapsed and he confided to his diary that he found it hard to maintain any kind of sanity.

The following day Dmitri arrived for lunch with his aunt and was told that Queen Alexandra 'wanted very much to see me.' The grand duchess had disposed of her car for financial reasons, so she and her daughters Nina and Xenia accompanied Dmitri by public transport. 'I laughingly remarked that the Romanovs abroad had come to such a pass that they had to take a bus to the palace [*sic*],' he wrote in his diary.[4]

At Marlborough House they were met by the king's unmarried sister Princess Victoria. Queen Alexandra and Queen Maud of Norway, who had just arrived in England after four years' separation due to the war, then joined them for lunch. Dmitri thought Queen Alexandra 'has aged terribly and grown thin, and she is so deaf that it is awfully difficult to speak to her.' She was only interested in obtaining the lurid details of Rasputin's assassination. 'And did you really kill Rasputin! But how beautiful,' she exclaimed.[5] After lunch Dmitri had a long conversation with Princess Victoria, during which he began to speak his mind. She promised to speak to King George, to whom she remained close.

Dmitri had now heard all the horrible rumours flying around about the remainder of the imperial family. His Aunt Ella, half-brother Vladimir Paley and the other Romanovs held at Alapayevsk had, he confided to his diary, been thrown down a well; the tsar was either dead or in hiding (Dmitri feared the former was more likely true) and the Americans were saying that the tsarina and the children were living somewhere safely. He also learned that the King of Italy had offered to send a ship to take the dowager empress and her family to Italy. But, he wondered, who would help his own father?

Thanks to the efforts of Sir Charles Marling, who informed the Foreign Office that Dmitri would undoubtedly be the next emperor of Russia, the grand duke obtained an honorary commission in the British army. The British government were so worried about the grand duke's presence in the country that the Foreign Office sent someone to ask him how he would feel 'about being sent to join the English troops in Salonika.' Dmitri replied that he would rather leave the army altogether, as once there he would not be able to return to London.

'I saw something in his face that told me clearly that he had something else in mind,' the grand duke's diary continued, 'and therefore I asked him a very direct question. I asked him is it my commission in the army or my presence in England that is so disturbing for everybody?' The man frankly admitted that it was both. They decided to leave the matter open until Dmitri had seen the king, whose decision on the matter Dmitri would respect. However, Dmitri was afraid that King George, influenced by his entourage, would tell him that at the moment things were too difficult and it would be better if he left the country. 'And I will then, of course, be obliged to leave England and seek refuge somewhere else. Naturally that would be frightfully difficult and disheartening.'[6]

On 22 December Dmitri was invited to Buckingham Palace for tea with King George and Queen Mary. He recorded his impressions in his diary. 'It was very strange to be in a palace again. The long, wide corridor reminded me a bit of Gatchina, but this one was not as full of various things. But the style was the same, or rather the absence of style (corresponding to the middle of the last century), the silk and the heavy damask, the walls covered with yellow paper. There were huge pictures of the various kings at their coronations. I was finally led to a room where a footman stood and opened the door, pronouncing my name in a loud voice.'

The king, a short man in civilian clothes, stood in the centre of the large drawing room beside the somewhat grand Queen Mary, who had 'a stern and unwelcoming expression'. Although Dmitri's late mother Princess Alexandra of Greece had been George's cousin, he still found the situation rather awkward.

To break the ice Dmitri thanked George for granting him a commission in the British army and also remarked on his likeness to the late tsar. The king and queen spoke sympathetically about Russian affairs and, during tea, continued discussing Russia and Dmitri's role in the murder of Rasputin.

The king said he hoped that the Allies would now intervene in Russia, as there could be no peace 'while the Bolshevik menace remains.' Only President Woodrow Wilson, he thought, was in a position to 'make a loud and definitive declaration about the menace of Bolshevism.'

King George was clearly still worried and frightened by the thought of unrest in Britain. 'We would so like to help poor Aunt Minny [the dowager empress] and daughters,' he said, 'but of course the grand dukes could not come to England, the times here are much too difficult.' Dmitri thought that he seemed tormented by his inability to help his relatives and could hardly bear the fact that the Russian national anthem was not sung any more. There was a nervous twitch around George's mouth at the beginning of their conversation and Dmitri left the palace with the feeling that the king had been scared into inactivity by his entourage.[7]

A few days later Dmitri found out that the man from the Foreign Office did indeed have an ulterior motive. 'It seems he meant to suggest that I should take off my uniform and put myself into mufti. Thereafter I found out that the king was supposed to tell me the same thing, but didn't. Consequently that matter is still up in the air.'[8]

Over the next few days Dmitri called on other relatives, including the king's uncle the Duke of Connaught and aunt, Princess Beatrice. With the princess at her home in Kensington Palace were her son the Marquess of Carisbrooke, and the king's children twenty-one-year-old Princess Mary, eighteen-year-old Prince Henry and sixteen-year-old Prince George, who listened with 'great attentiveness' to Dmitri's stories of events in Russia.[9] A few weeks later news reached the dowager empress in the Crimea that Dmitri was in London and it was being said that he would be betrothed to the king's daughter Princess Mary.

'Generally speaking,' Dmitri wrote, 'the English family treat me very kindly, except the king and Queen Alexandra, whom I have only seen once. As for Queen Alexandra, it surprises me that she didn't want to see me again.'[10]

By this time Dmitri had moved to the more congenial Ritz Hotel. On 7 January 1919 Dmitri and Lady Marling lunched with the Danish Ambassador to London, Henrik Greben-Castenskiold. Among the guests were Harald and Anna Sofie Scavenius who had arrived from Petrograd ten days earlier. If Dmitri hoped to hear more about his father and the conditions in which he was kept he was disappointed. Anna Sofie told him that she had seen Grand Duke Paul in prison and, Dmitri, noted, 'he didn't look too bad. Unfortunately, they are both awfully terse, so I didn't succeed in learning much.'[11]

Dmitri was extremely worried about his father and even thought of going to Petrograd in disguise to snatch him out of the claws of the Bolsheviks. The contrast between his father's circumstances and his own life at the Ritz was almost unbearable. Probably through his aunt Grand Duchess George, Dmitri had learnt about the unsuccessful attempt at ransoming the three grand dukes held in Shpalernaia prison. He then heard that his sister Marie and her husband Sergei Putiatin were going to Paris and were 'obsessed with the idea of saving papa.' They seemed to think that because the French and English generals were sympathetic towards them in Odessa, they would be able to obtain funds to pay a ransom for Grand Duke Paul either in Paris or London ('I wish,' wrote Dmitri). 'Marie is forgetting that such funding would have to be approved by the *Chambre des Deputies* or the House of Commons, and naturally such approval will not be obtained,' he wrote despondently.[12]

In early February rumours began to circulate that the four grand dukes had been shot by the Bolsheviks. Dmitri immediately went to see Grand Duchess George to see what she knew. He found her in tears and terribly upset. She had already spoken to the Danish ambassador, who had telegraphed Copenhagen to see whether they could confirm the dreadful news. It was not the first time that such rumours had been published. With no *official* news about his father's fate the grand duke could only hope that the reports were not entirely true. It was too horrible for him to contemplate. He was totally dazed. This time, however, the news proved to be correct.

The king sent Harry Stonor, the Deputy Master of the Royal Household, to see Dmitri. Thinking it was a visit of condolence from the monarch, the grand duke was surprised when Stonor informed him that he had been sent to express His Majesty's pleasure that Dmitri had become an honorary member of the Marlborough Club.

Once again, Dmitri was invited to tea with the king and queen at Buckingham Palace. This somewhat awkward meeting took place at five o'clock on 13 February. Dmitri recorded it in his diary, this time writing in English. 'Of course when I came into the room, they both said how awfully sorry they were about the death of papa. But immediately after that they started to say what an awful mess it was now in Russia and that he [the king] does not know what to do. It's a hopeless show altogether and that perhaps it's the best thing to leave Russia to settle her troubles as best she can and without the help of other nations.'

This time the king made a poor impression on Dmitri, because he 'thinks of giving up the show as a hopeless one. And that of course is very bad from our Russian point of view. His Majesty was apparently very ill at ease and didn't know what to say to me.' Dmitri recorded that the king only made one definite statement, speaking up very suddenly and apropos of nothing. 'I am sure that in time to come everybody will say that England did not help the Russian grand dukes when she ought to do so. But what can I do when one does not even listen to me and when I tried to say something about the tsar and the Russian family they tell me that I uphold absolutism. The grand dukes are not wanted here in England. You are here only by accident.' The meeting left Dmitri feeling uncomfortable and he departed with the impression that George was a 'cowed and terrified man'.[13]

By March Dmitri had the strong impression that King George did not wish him to remain in British uniform any longer.

* * *

Dmitri's sister was staying with her cousin Missy at Cotroceni Palace in Romania when a telegram from Dmitri told her of their father's death at the hands of a Bolshevik firing squad. Like her brother, Marie was totally shattered by this news. 'You will understand what a nightmare it is for me,' she wrote to Grand Duchess Xenia. 'Everything, everything disappears into the past, everything which is good, everything which is bright and the only thing that's left is the terrible reality...'[14] Shortly afterwards she heard that her aunt Grand Duchess Ella and her step-brother Prince Vladimir Paley had also been killed, with other members of the family.

After her parents-in-law arrived safely in Bucharest with her baby son Roman, Marie was anxious to get to London to see Dmitri. They had not met since his exile after Rasputin's murder in December 1916.

On 1 March Queen Marie of Romania left for Paris to attend the peace conference. She had wanted to take her cousin with her, but the Romanian government denied this request on hearing that the grand duchess would not be welcome at the British court. After spending ten days in Paris, Missy arrived in London. At Buckingham Palace she was shocked at the way her cousin the king 'was obliged, because of public opinion, to treat his own relations: no grand duke was welcome, and the sovereign, being strictly constitutional, never even tried to impose his own will, or to allow his personal sympathies to colour his actions,' Missy wrote.[15] She was saddened not to be able to have taken Marie with her, just because by birth she was a Russian grand duchess.

George was no more helpful about the money of Missy's mother the Duchess of Coburg, who was by birth Grand Duchess Maria Alexandrovna of Russia. After she returned home, Missy wrote to tell King George that her mother's funds had been left in the imperial treasury in Moscow. This considerable sum of money was part of her marriage treaty, signed in 1874. Her Russian income was therefore in communist hands and she was living in poverty in Switzerland. George replied that Britain had not recognised the Bolshevik government (and did not do so until 1924), so nothing could be done.

There was one respect in which they could help though. While in London, an old letter reached Missy from her sister Ducky in Finland. She and Cyril were trapped in Borgo and Missy enlisted Queen Mary's help to send some provisions to the family. Much later, she heard that the parcel had arrived safely and brightened Ducky's exile.

Meanwhile, unable to go to England with Missy, Marie and Sergei Putiatin each applied for a French visa. Marie's took a long time to arrive and at the age of twenty-eight the reality of life outside of the gilded cage of the Romanovs now began to dawn upon her. '... we had outlived our epoch and were doomed,' she wrote.[16]

Marie travelled to Paris and then on to London as an ordinary tourist, to be reunited with Dmitri.

* * *

On 9 May 1919 brother and sister were at Victoria Station to witness the arrival of their aunt the Dowager Empress Marie Feodorovna and members of her family, who had been rescued from the Bolsheviks at the eleventh hour. This was one Romanov rescue that the king *had* been able to achieve.

By April 1919 the situation in the Crimea had changed. The French had evacuated the peninsula, the Bolsheviks were closing in and the Romanovs were now in grave danger. Some members of the family had already left the area. In December 1918 Xenia's husband Grand Duke Alexander Michaelovich, their eldest son Prince Andrew and his pregnant wife Elsa sailed for France on HMS *Forsythe*. The empress' younger daughter had also left.

Olga and her husband Nicolai Kulikovsky were determined to remain in Russia. On 23 December [OS] 1918 the empress recorded in her diary, 'Xenia and Olga came to lunch [and] when Olga went, Xenia told me that just after Christmas Olga would go away, which has upset [she wrote this word in English] me completely, as I did not expect it.' She had a headache for the rest of the day and blamed Nicolai Kulikovsky for her daughter's decision.[17]

Olga's departure was delayed for several days. Finally, on 1/14 January 1919 Olga, Nicolai and their son Tihon left Yalta for the Caucasus on the steamship *Konstantin*. Among their small party were the Empress Marie's Cossack bodyguard Timofei Yashik and two officers, Bulygin and Gramotin who, at the dowager empress's request, would travel on to Siberia to see what they could discover about the fate of the tsar. Olga and her party landed in Novorossisk and travelled by train to Rostov-on-Don where General Denikin was in command. He advised them to move on. General Kutiepov offered the loan of his private railway carriage so that they could continue their journey by train. The offer was gratefully accepted and the following day they travelled to the small Cossack village of Novominskaya, about 74 miles south-west of Rostov, where Yashik's family lived. After living briefly with Yashik's family, they rented a small house with four rooms and a kitchen, with an orchard running down to the river.

'It is so far away,' Empress Marie lamented, 'and I can not even get telegrams or letters from her except on occasions, which are so few ... I was not very friendly towards her husband, who has given me this great sorrow...'[18] Olga's letters were usually carried by friends or loyal officers; some of the replies arrived by post. Since then the situation in the Crimea had become critical.

With the Bolsheviks closing in, on 6 April the Rear Admiral of the Black Sea Fleet was warned to expect imminent orders. 'In view of the present situation in Crimea you should be prepared to remove the dowager empress and her suite in one of His Majesty's ships if she desires to leave,' the Admiralty wired.

This was followed by a telegram, expressing the king's concern for the family's safety. 'The Admiralty considers the situation is now such that they should be embarked whatever may be their personal desires and moved to a place of safety as soon as preparations can be made,' the telegram read. 'Their eventual destination will be communicated later. Report what action you are taking.'[19]

The imperial family were gathered at Harax when Captain Charles Johnson of HMS *Marlborough* arrived. He stressed the seriousness of the situation and produced instructions to evacuate the family that very evening. He also brought the empress an offer of asylum from King George V and a letter from Queen Alexandra, begging her sister to leave while there was still time. After much persuasion she consented to go – but only on condition that all the family, the retainers and scores of refugees who were in danger from the Bolsheviks would be evacuated with her. She may have been jolted into action by the fate of other members of the family. On 3 March [NS] the dowager empress recorded in her diary: 'I read in the English newspapers about the disgusting, horrific murder of poor beloved Paul, Mitia, Nicolai and Georgi [in the SS Peter and Paul Fortress]. It's so bad, I don't want to believe it.'[20] Finally the Empress realised what could happen to any of the Romanovs who fell into Bolshevik hands.

As they hastily started packing, Xenia was told that they would board at five o'clock 'and everyone should be there. What grief and desperation,' she added sadly.[21] What to take with them was a question that exercised everyone. As jewels, silver, paintings and Fabergé trinkets were hastily put into cases the total treasure on board the *Marlborough* must have been equivalent to many millions of pounds. With this were the more mundane things; one of Xenia's young sons took his pet canary.

The empress had asked to embark at secluded Koreiz cove. A hastily improvised jetty was constructed by the ship's carpenter as marines and sailors arrived to defend the cove from the approaching Red Army. Secrecy was vital. Any move that betrayed the evacuation to the Bolsheviks could be fatal. A few minutes later the family made their way down to the beach. As they walked across the shaky jetty Captain Johnson changed his mind and ordered them to be ferried aboard. The dowager empress, accompanied by her dogs, took her last steps on Russian soil and boarded a pinnace.

The ship had been hastily rearranged to accommodate all the extra passengers. The empress was given the captain's quarters and, as spare bedding was brought in from the imperial estates, the older people occupied the officers' cabins and the young people crammed themselves in where and how they could.

After dark they sailed for Yalta, where the ship's guns covered the port as the evacuation continued for another three days.

With still no definite information as to the empress's final destination, HMS *Marlborough* weighed anchor on 11 April 1919. The ship would go first to Constantinople, where Grand Dukes Nicholas and Peter and their party would board HMS *Nelson* bound for Genoa.

As the imperial estates vanished from sight the Empress Marie recorded the final moments in her diary. 'It was heartrending to see the beautiful coast disappear little by little behind a thick fog that hid it from our eyes for the last time.'[22]

* * *

On 12 April a cablegram was sent from Lord Milner, Secretary of State for the Colonies in London to Lord Methuen, the Governor of Malta. 'HMS *Marlborough* due at Constantinople today is proceeding to Malta arriving probably on Tuesday...' After listing the people on board he continued, 'Please receive them with as little ceremony as possible and unofficially, and you had better not meet them yourself. They will arrive practically destitute without clothes or money. Pending decision as to where they are to go, temporary accommodation will be required, but it is not considered desirable to house them where the Governor is in residence. His Majesty suggests San Antonio Palace may be available. Do not allow arrival or any reference to it to appear in the local papers. All proper expenses of maintenance and clothing will be refunded to you.' These instructions were later changed and at 4.55pm on 20 April the Empress Marie was received in Malta with all the honours due to the king's aunt.[23]

The dowager empress spent eight days at the San Antonio Palace in Malta, the very place where King George had fallen in love with Missy, before leaving for England on HMS *Lord Nelson*.

On 6 May the Naval Secretary at the Admiralty in London cabled more instructions to the commanding officer of the ship. 'Owing to stringent orders about dogs, I request you will inform the owners that their dogs cannot be landed and taken to London but that they will have to undergo quarantine. No exceptions will be made.'[24]

The dowager empress arrived at Portsmouth on 9 May and was greeted by Queen Alexandra. They had not met since the summer of 1914. A special train took them to London but even this reception was muted. 'The king wishes that there should be no ceremony of any kind, no salute, no guards of honour, no press reporters and no photographers present,' a telegram from the Naval Secretary to the Commander in Chief Portsmouth explained. 'He wishes you to meet the empress ... and if you think fit, the admiral superintendant should also accompany you; he does not wish the military to be represented.'[25]

The British government, who had recognised the Provisional Government a week after the tsar's abdication, could not be seen welcoming members of the imperial family with open arms. After the withdrawal of the asylum offer, the presence of the tsar's mother – the king's aunt – could only have been an embarrassment to everyone concerned.

* * *

Notwithstanding Dmitri's previous rather unsatisfactory encounters with King George other invitations followed. In the summer of 1919 he was invited to Royal Ascot, then to a Buckingham Palace garden party, but he had no significant contact with the king and queen although they were 'very courteous.'[26] Although he had tea with the king's sister Queen Maud of Norway, Dmitri disliked the Prince of Wales and was not part of his set. At royal functions, to his disgust, he was often paired up with the king's daughter Princess Mary, about whose looks he had nothing good to say. Dmitri made several unkind references in his diary to the fact that Princess Mary looked like a housemaid.

Dmitri had one further meeting with King George during his time in London. By this time Marie and Sergei Putiatin had been in England for almost a year. Marie's jewels had arrived from Sweden, still concealed in ink pots, fake candles and paperweights, and for a while at least she had some financial reserves. She and Sergei rented a small house in Kensington and Dmitri was persuaded to leave the Ritz and move in with them.

In March 1920 they were all invited to lunch at Buckingham Palace. The king's sisters Princess Victoria and Princess Louise, Duchess of Fife (the Princess Royal), her unmarried daughter Princess Maud, and Princess Mary were the only others present.

The king immediately got off to a bad start with Dmitri by saying that 'affairs in Russia are perfectly hopeless and that Lenin is an idealist!' Things then went from bad to worse as George continued to speak about Russia. 'Our men were so awfully disappointed when they knew that Arkhangelsk is [*sic*] taken by the Bolsheviks [this was in February 1920]. To think that all their efforts are now lost for nothing and the town gave itself up to the Reds!' Dmitri, of course, had no sympathy for the British troops.

Finally, as his diary entry recorded, 'at the end of lunch, His Majesty was graciously pleased to say: "You don't know what our feelings were after the Russian revolution, as we saw that the Germans were sending all their divisions from the Eastern Front to the Western. We all thought that we could not hold out, but thanks to the Americans – the position was saved!" That was the moment when all the blood rushed to my head,' Dmitri continued in a rage. '*Who* had sent a congratulatory telegram to Kerensky? *Who* had pretended that the [February] Russian revolution would lead to victory? *Who* did not lift a finger to save Nicky and his family? He is a scoundrel! This wretch George will not, please God, be forgiven by Russians even far into the future! Marie was trembling all over with indignation when we left, and it's not surprising.'[27]

Dmitri left the palace in anger.

In April Marie went to visit her step-mother Princess Olga Paley in Paris and decided to leave England and make her home there. She returned to London to make arrangements but, soon after her arrival, received a letter telling her that baby Roman had died in Bucharest on 29 July after a short illness. She was tormented 'with self-accusations and feelings of guilt,' which she confided to her brother.[28] Marie moved to Paris in the summer of 1920. Dmitri followed.

* * *

The departure of the Dowager Empress Marie to her native Denmark in 1919, followed by Marie and Dmitri the following year, was not the end of King George's involvement with the Romanovs. Grand Duchess Xenia remained in England, where the king granted her a grace-and-favour home at Frogmore, near Windsor Castle.

In 1919 HMS *Kent* transported twenty-nine cases of the imperial family's belongings out of Russia. 'The king hopes that the officer in command of HMS *Kent* will be instructed to keep these cases in safe custody as they may contain property of the utmost value to the imperial family,' Lord Stamfordham wrote.[29]

When the cases (believed to be only twenty) arrived in London they had to be fumigated before being opened in the presence of the king, queen, Queen Alexandra and Xenia. They were found to contain nothing but rubbish and were soon forgotten. A few months later Xenia received a letter from Baroness Buxhoeveden asking whether she had found Empress Alexandra's jewels, which were concealed in a roll of cloth in one of the boxes. Armed with the exact location, Xenia went back to the boxes and found them.

At least three caches of jewels were left behind. One was given to a nun, who hid some jewels in a well and concealed others in a belfry and graves in the cemetery at the Ivanovsky Convent in Tobolsk. When the convent was closed in 1923 an elderly nun was going to throw them in the river but was persuaded instead to give them to a local fish merchant. He hid 154 items of jewellery in the basement of his house in two glass jars placed inside a wooden case. These were discovered by Stalin's secret police in 1933 after the nun was arrested and interrogated. Today these items would be worth in excess of seven million pounds.

Two more caches are still missing, including a suitcase given to the priest Alexei Vassiliev, which is said to contain diamonds and 'crowns' belonging to the empress and her daughters. The priest died in 1930 and the treasure is believed to be hidden in Tobolsk or Omsk. Another casket, given to Claudia Bittner by her husband Colonel Kobylinsky (to whom it had been given by the tsar), was later given to Constantine Pechekos. When interrogated in 1934, he said it was hidden in his brother's house at Omsk, which turned out to be untrue. He then attempted suicide and, again, the treasure was never found. Other jewels, and even a stash of tsarist gold, are believed to still remain hidden in the area.

Curiously, the tsarina's valet Volkov recounts in his memoirs a plan by Colonel Kobylinsky to move the imperial family to a house being built in the grounds of the Ivanovsky Convent. Volkov says he was asked to go there, make arrangements for the purchase and assign the rooms. The plan was foiled by the arrival of Commissar Pankratov.[30]

* * *

In 1921, Thomas Preston, former British Consul at Ekaterinburg, arrived in London and had an audience with the king at Buckingham Palace. 'Saw Mr Preston, our consul at Ekaterinburg, who was there when dear Nicky and Alicky and their family were murdered,' George recorded on 19 February, 'he told me many interesting things.'[31] One of the interesting things the king and Preston discussed was the alleged remains of the family found at the Four Brothers' Mine.

The final White investigator Nicholas Sokolov (who replaced Sergeyev in February 1919) had concluded that the imperial family and their servants were shot in the basement of the Ipatiev House and their bodies taken on trucks into the woods. There, he said, they were undressed, chopped up with knives and destroyed by sulphuric acid, or on bonfires with the aid of petrol. The Bolsheviks also burned the family's clothes, but some remnants of the jewels secreted in them were left lying on the ground. These, and the charred remains of bones, had been discovered by the Whites at the Four Brothers Mine.

A small box containing these remains was said to have been brought to Europe by the French General Janin after the British refused to take them. Lady Violet Kirkpatrick, who worked at the Foreign Office in London, recalled that in 1920 they were in the possession of Miles Lampson, a British diplomat recently returned from Peking, who said he was going to deliver the box to Queen Alexandra at Marlborough House. The king told Preston 'that they were in such a state that they had to be fumigated before they were touched.'[32]

In 1976 the royal archivist said that he 'was unable to confirm the handover' but it is believed that that box was taken to Marlborough House to be passed on to the dowager empress in Denmark. Olga and Xenia 'wept over the little box before it went to France,'[33] but its present whereabouts are something of an enigma.

For George V it was a 'great embarrassment' to have the box in England,[34] and the remains were certainly not welcome at Buckingham Palace. At the urgent insistence of his mother George had rescued the dowager empress but, even in death, he was unwilling to give sanctuary to the tsar and his family.

* * *

In 1938 Queen Mary was visited by the kaiser's grandson Prince Friedrich Georg of Prussia, known as Fritzi, who had recently stayed with his grandfather at Huis Doorn in Holland. After the visit, that inveterate diarist 'Chips' Channon met Fritzi and recorded a juicy piece of royal gossip about the tsar.

William had expressed regret at how things turned out. 'The kaiser told Fritzi only last week that he is still haunted by the fate which befell the tsar and his family. He had sent the tsar a telegram offering him a free and protected passage through Germany, had he wished to escape by sea. (This was at the moment when the tsar had tried to get to England.)'

Continuing with the diary entry, Channon then went on to blame Lloyd George, 'who spoilt and stopped everything, and the late king [George V] had been weak with him, not understanding the danger.'

And then comes the most telling part of all. 'Their responsibility in the matter has ever been a millstone to both Queen Mary and King George, and their failure to help their poor Russian relatives in the hour of danger is the one blot on their lives. Of late, Fritzi tells me, Queen Mary has been sorely conscience stricken.'[35]

Maybe the king and queen did feel some remorse after all.

Postscript

It would be another seventy years before the world knew what had happened to Nicholas II and his family. While rumour and counter-rumour flourished and pretenders came forward one by one purporting to be one of the children, there was no trace of the family and no bodies.

The story of the Romanovs' murder is well-known. The seven members of the Russian imperial family and their four servants were ushered into the cellar of the Ipatiev House and shot by their Bolshevik captors. Those who did not die immediately were finished off with bayonets. The murder was savage in its brutality and notable for the Bolsheviks' lack of organisation and co-ordination. The assassins were further unnerved when the tsar's daughters refused to die quickly. When they were stripped for burial it was discovered that the girls were protected by corsets, into which several pounds of jewellery had been sewn.

Investigations by the White Russian Nicholas Sokolov, whose book was published in 1924, concluded that the bodies had been burnt, doused with acid and thrown into a pit. 'The world will never know what we did with them,' boasted a Bolshevik commissar.

Then in 1989 it was announced that the grave of the tsar and his family had been found. Its location had in fact always been known to local people, while Soviet officials would have had access to details of the site since 1920 when Yurovsky's Note describing the murders was deposited in the Kremlin Archives. It now appears that there had been Soviet involvement in the search to find the grave, a search that was conducted 'secretly' in Koptyaki Forest by Andrei Avdonin and Gely Ryabov in 1979.[1]

After unearthing the grave they removed three skulls, which were afterwards returned to the site. They said that at the time it was too dangerous to make the story public. Yet it is clear that the burial site was secretly opened some time between 1980 and the official exhumation in 1991, as a small metal icon the men had placed there in a plastic bag was found rusted and broken – with bits contained in *several* plastic bags.

In April 1989 the *Moscow News* reported the grave's discovery. That same month President Mikhail Gorbachev was received in London by the queen. Technically the way was now open for the monarch to visit Russia – but there was the little matter of the fate of her relatives, the tsar and his family, to clarify first.

So it was perhaps no coincidence that in 1991 after the breakup of the Soviet Union the grave was officially excavated. The order was given by Boris Yeltsin (the same man who as Regional First Secretary had ordered the demolition of the Ipatiev House in 1977). When the grave was opened, the remains of only nine bodies were found. Two bodies were missing. They turned out to be those of Alexei and one of his sisters. The news caused a media sensation and reignited stories of the escape of one of the tsar's daughters.

Many people had been buried in the woods around Koptyaki at the time of the revolution, so in 1992, to authenticate the remains, they were examined by a forensic team from the University of Florida led by Dr William Maples.

Then, in what at the time was a new scientific breakthrough, some bone samples were flown to England for DNA testing by Dr Peter Gill at the Forensic Science Service at Aldermaston. Using DNA from the tsarina's great-nephew the Duke of Edinburgh, plus DNA from other close relatives, the tests determined that there was a probability of 98.5% that the bones were those of the imperial family. Still, there were thousands of missing bones, a complete absence of teeth and nothing that corresponded to Alexei and one of his sisters.

Which sister? Even this caused controversy. The Russians insisted it was nineteen-year-old Maria, while American experts believed that Anastasia was unaccounted for, as the bones were too mature for a seventeen-year-old. Nevertheless, the Russians insisted it was Anastasia, probably to prove that the numerous pretenders (most notably Anna Anderson) had been impostors and that Anastasia had died with her family. According to the Note left by Yurovsky, two bodies were burnt and buried separately in the forest. The searches continued.

The first modern account of the murders was published by Russian playwright and author Edvard Radzinsky in 1993. Working from Yurovsky's Note in the State Archives, he established that after being massacred in a hail of bullets in the basement of the Ipatiev House, the Romanovs' bodies were taken to the Four Brothers Mine outside the town, where they were stripped and thrown down an old mineshaft. The family's clothes were then burnt and, according to Yurovsky, hand grenades were thrown into the mine in an attempt to destroy the bodies. (The remains discovered in the forest however showed no trace of damage from such a blast.)

By the morning, accounts of the disposal of the bodies and the location were circulating round Ekaterinburg. With the White Army about to take the city, Yurovsky had to think quickly. That night he and his men returned to the mine, hoisted up the naked bodies and took them deeper into the woods, first on carts, then in a lorry. By the early morning of 19 July, the lorry was stuck firm and could go no further. A decision was therefore made to bury the bodies where they were, at Porosenkov Log (Pig's Meadow) near the Koptyaki Road. They dug a common grave 6 foot by 8 foot and 2 feet deep, put in all but two of the bodies and doused the faces with sulphuric acid. Then they filled in the hole and laid railway sleepers on top. But what of the other two bodies?

According to Radzinsky, the jewels concealed in the grand duchess' corsets deflected the bullets, meaning that they didn't die in the first hail of fire. Olga and Tatiana were shot in the head; Maria and Anastasia sat up screaming and were said to have been finished off with bayonet thrusts and rifle butts. Radzinsky's theory is that the haemophiliac Alexei was also wearing a jewelled corset and that he and one of his sisters left the murder room alive. Sympathetic guards secretly pulled them off the lorry when it became stuck near level crossing no. 184, after which they may have died in the woods, or they may have been rescued.

When Radzinsky wrote his book the rescue theory was still perfectly feasible as there were two bodies still unaccounted for, as well as numerous stories of survivors surfacing all over the globe.

Yurovsky, Radzinsky said, now had to cover up the fact that two bodies were missing, so he invented the story that two bodies were burnt (despite the fact that it would have been impossible in a forest under those conditions) and the remains buried nearby.

This became the accepted version of the end of the imperial family.

* * *

On 24 July 1920 photographs of the coffins of the Alapayevsk victims were published in *The Sphere* in London. 'It was recently reported in the Chinese vernacular press ... that the bodies of the former imperial Russian family had been brought to Peking, were taken outside the North Gate (Andingmen), and buried in the little Russian cemetery there,' said the account. 'It was understood that the bodies had received interment, but when your correspondent visited he discovered the coffins laid out in the little chapel, where they were evidently the objects of daily or weekly attention. The lead-lined and lead encased coffins are 7 feet in length. Each bears a brass plate with an inscription.'

The *Sphere's* report was brought to the notice of Grand Duchess Ella's brother Grand Duke Ernest Ludwig of Hesse and her sisters the Marchioness of Milford Haven and Princess Irene of Prussia. In 1921 they arranged for the bodies of Ella and Sister Barbara to be taken to Jerusalem, accompanied by the faithful Father Seraphim, for burial in the Russian Orthodox Church of St Mary Magdalene on the Mount of Olives. In 1888 Ella and her husband Grand Duke Sergei Alexandrovich had assisted at the consecration of the church, which was dedicated to the Grand Duke's mother Empress Marie Alexandrovna. Grand Duchess Elisabeth Feodorovna was later canonised by the Russian Orthodox Church and her statue now stands above the West Door of Westminster Abbey.

The coffins of the other victims of Alapayevsk remained at St Seraphim's until 1937, when the Japanese occupied China. Then they were moved to the All Holy Martyrs Church on the Mission territory inside the city wall.

After the Second World War, amid fears that the Soviet army would arrive, Archbishop Victor was asked to hide the coffins of Grand Duke Sergei Michaelovich and the Constantinovichi princes.

Those of Vladimir Paley and Remez (probably considered the least important) were left in their places. Preceded by a priest carrying a candle, the others were carried in procession and lowered into three underground cells. The operation was conducted during the night in the greatest secrecy with the help of some Russian officers.

There are two versions of what happened next. Either Archbishop Victor was ordered by the Soviet authorities to transport the coffins back to the territory of the Mission cemetery in 1947 and place them in St Seraphim Chapel's crypt beyond the city wall; or the coffins were buried in the little chapel dedicated to the Apostle Simon the Zealot underneath the main church of All Holy Martyrs. Both versions agree that copper plates with the name of the deceased were placed on the coffins, which were then covered with sand and cemented in. No visible signs of the burial remained; everything was done quietly and without publicity under the pretext of repairs to the building.

In 1949 the Chinese communists took power and the territory of the Russian Mission was handed over to the Soviet Union. The secret of the burial place was faithfully kept.

The Mission was closed in 1954. Three years later, by order of the Soviet ambassador, the Church of All Holy Martyrs was destroyed to make way for the new Russian Embassy. The Mission cemetery was destroyed in 1987. It is said that 'on orders from Moscow' the Romanov remains, 'which had been in the Russian Spiritual Mission [All Holy Martyrs] ... were buried in the Orthodox cemetery near the city's Andingmen Gate,' where St Seraphim's stood.

St Seraphim's functioned until 1962. It was then used as a warehouse before being destroyed in 1986. The cemetery was destroyed in 1988. The unoccupied spaces around it were cleared to make way for Qingnianhu Park and the site of the cemetery became a golf course.[2]

The only certain thing is that all the Russian cemeteries and churches were destroyed and neither the Chinese nor the Russians have any records relating to the Romanov remains. Latest research indicates that the Romanovs' final resting place is probably underneath the golf course.

***

Although the tsar's brother Michael was also killed, his widow Natasha did reach safety. After Michael disappeared from Perm in June 1918 Natasha stormed into the Petrograd Cheka and demanded to see Uritsky. A fierce argument ensued when she could get no news of her husband's whereabouts. Uritsky then lost his temper, accused her of engineering Michael's escape and threw her into the women's prison Gorokhovaya No. 2 where he said she would remain until she told him the truth.

Natasha spent ten weeks as a prisoner of the Bolsheviks. After feigning illness for some time, a sympathetic doctor diagnosed 'tuberculosis' and she was moved to a nursing home at the end of August. One night she calmly walked out of the building and hid with friends until a false passport could be obtained.

The Germans believed the Bolshevik stories that Michael had escaped and, determined to win him over to their side, they decided to use Natasha as bait. They were quite happy to provide false documents and ensure that Natasha crossed safely from Russia into German-occupied territory, where they assumed that the grand duke would join her.

Wearing the disguise of a Sister of Mercy and bearing the passport of Frau Tania Klenow Natasha left by train, passed through the frontier without problems and boarded another train for Kiev where she was to meet her daughter. Tata, who had also suffered a spell in prison, had managed to take with her quite a bit of her mother's jewellery. There was a scary moment at the frontier in Orsha when she found that luggage was being searched – a problem that was solved when her companion Princess Wiasemsky discovered that the Bolshevik guards were susceptible to bribery. Reunited, mother and daughter arrived at the house of the Davidoffs, the friends with whom Natasha had arranged to stay. Natasha was then taken ill. Pleurisy was diagnosed and she spent some weeks in bed.

The news of Natasha's escape reached the dowager empress, at that time still in the Crimea, who had no idea that her son Michael was dead. 'The wife [Natasha] was also in prison in Petersburg [*sic*] ... and is now in Kiev, and one says she will now get to Denmark to her son. Poor Misha!' the dowager empress wrote to Queen Alexandra on 27 October.[3]

King Christian had already telegraphed an invitation to Natasha to join her son George in Denmark. The Germans now saw 'a suitable way to place the monarchic circles under an obligation' to them by helping her get there. They made it a condition that once in Copenhagen, Natasha was not to influence the court against the Germans.[4] Natasha would travel with Tata and three other people. King Christian later commented 'that he had invited [her] ...alone, and did not expect that she would appear with so many companions,'[5] but the necessary papers for the journey were provided, she posed for a new passport photograph and everything was arranged.

Before she could leave, the armistice was signed and the journey became impossible. Natasha had to escape before the Bolsheviks took power in Kiev. She and her companions fled to Odessa. The only overland route from there was through Romania but the frontier was closed. They could only hope that an Allied ship would arrive soon.

They were saved by the arrival of the British, who finally evacuated Natasha and her party on board HMS *Neride*. She travelled via Constantinople, then on board the *Agamemnon* to Malta, from there to France and finally to England where she arrived in March 1919 anxious to be reunited with her son.

During his time in Denmark George had clearly won the king's heart. 'Georgie left together with Miss Neame for England to live with his mother – after having been here in this house since 7 May 1918, and will therefore be missed,' King Christian wrote in his dairy on 11 April 1919. The king kept a photograph of 'Georgie' in his study, and he wrote the date of the little boy's arrival on the back. George had spent eleven months in Denmark but from the tone of an undated note it seems he had been hoping to join Natasha much earlier. 'Shall we go to England, or to you? ...' he wrote to her. 'This garden is very small, and the park too is small. I congratulate you on your birthday. From Georgie.'[6] Her birthday was in June, so perhaps he had meant to write Name Day, which is more important to Russians than a birthday.

With no news of Michael's fate George and Natasha made their own life, first in England and later in France. George was killed in a car crash in the South of France in 1931; Natasha died in Paris in 1952. The redoubtable Miss Neame was living with her brother John in Bexhill by 1939 and died at Southwood Nursing Home, Torquay, in 1941.

* * *

The Dowager Empress Marie Feodorovna made her home in Denmark, maintaining a court in exile at Hvidøre, the villa she owned jointly with Queen Alexandra. She died there in 1928, never believing that her sons Nicholas and Michael were dead.[7] In 2006 her remains were brought from Roskilde Cathedral in Denmark and reburied in the SS Peter and Paul Cathedral in St Petersburg.

Grand Duchess Xenia settled in England, living in grace and favour houses provided by the British royal family, first at Frogmore then at Wilderness House, Hampton Court. She died in 1960. Her estranged husband Grand Duke Alexander Michaelovich was refused entry to Britain. He lived in France until his death in 1933.[8]

Xenia's sister Grand Duchess Olga spent two years living in the Caucasus, staying one step ahead of the Bolsheviks. During this time she gave birth to her second son, Guri. The family eventually reached Denmark but moved to Canada after the Second World War. Olga died there in 1960.

Harald Scavenius, the Danish Minister who did so much to help the Romanovs, went on to become Foreign Minister from 1920–1922; then Danish Minister at the Legations in Rome, Berne and The Hague. He died in The Hague in 1939.

Princess Helen of Serbia divided her life between the South of France and England, where her children were at school. She never remarried and after the Second World War settled in Nice, where she died in 1962.

Princess Catherine Yourievsky and Prince Sergei Obolensky moved to London in 1919. She became a successful singer but heart trouble and asthma ended her career. The couple divorced in 1923 and Catherine bought a bungalow on Hayling Island, an area on the south coast reputedly beneficial for asthma, which she shared with her younger companion Nana Hammersley. The ladies were often seen driving around in a small car, calling at a local shop to buy produce. Catherine never forgot she was a tsar's daughter, insisting on being addressed as Your Serene Highness. In 1936 she sold The Haven at a profit and purchased two almshouses on the Havant Road. These were converted into a bungalow called 'Naini', which she claimed was the Indian word for princess. She had no regular income. Sergei and other friends helped her out and there was a quarterly cheque from a member of the British royal family. Catherine said it was from Princess Marina, granddaughter of her half-brother Grand Duke Vladimir. In 1934 Catherine attended Marina's marriage to the Duke of Kent, bringing back some wedding cake to share with local schoolchildren. Around the time of Queen Mary's death in 1953 Catherine's quarterly allowance stopped. She now took the bus to the hairdresser's salon instead of a taxi and was mocked by children for her eccentric dress sense. A weekly standing order at the off-licence had used up most of her money and there were rows over unpaid bills. Some people, remembering her royal blood, were more lenient about payment and gave her food. Nevertheless, she had to sell her jewels. Her last brooch was reputedly sold for £40.00 and a bottle of gin. Finally, after years of faded grandeur, she moved to Wray House Nursing Home. A brief, unassuming announcement in a local newspaper recorded her death there on 22 December 1959. She is buried in the churchyard of St Peter's Church, Northney.

Queen Olga of Greece moved to London and then Rome, where she lived at the villa owned by her son Prince Christopher. She died there in 1926. The Greek royal family was once more in exile and she was buried in Florence alongside her son King Constantine. His wife Queen Sophie, who died in 1932, was laid to rest beside them. After the restoration of the monarchy the three bodies were brought back to Greece in 1936 for burial at Tatoi. Olga, who had always hoped to return to Greece, achieved her wish in death. Prince Philip, the Duke of Edinburgh, is her grandson.

After the execution of Grand Duke Dmitri Constantinovich in the SS Peter and Paul Fortress his niece Princess Tatiana Bagration escaped from Russia. She and her children were helped by Dmitri's ADC Colonel Alexander Korotchenzov, who acquired Georgian passports for the family. They fled to Kiev and eventually left Russia with the help of Queen Marie of Romania. In 1921 Tatiana was encouraged to make a marriage of convenience with Korotchenzov but he died from influenza three months later, leaving her widowed for the second time. After her children had grown up she took the veil as Mother Tamara and became Abbess of the Mount of Olives Convent in Jerusalem. She died in 1979.

Grand Duchess Vladimir, whose jewels were smuggled out of Petrograd by Bertie Stopford, left the Caucasus on an Italian liner in 1920 and died later that year. All her sons survived the revolution.

Her niece the younger Grand Duchess Marie Pavlovna started a successful embroidery business, Kitmir, in Paris, where her clients included Coco Chanel. Later, her marriage having failed, she moved to New York and worked at the Bergdorf Goodman department store. She later wrote her memoirs and became a photojournalist, before moving to Argentina. Finally she returned to Europe and became a frequent visitor to Mainau in Germany, the island home of Count Lennart Bernadotte, her son by Prince William of Sweden. She died in Germany in 1958 and is buried at Mainau.

Her brother Grand Duke Dmitri Pavlovich lived for a while in Paris. After several affairs (including one with Coco Chanel), in 1926 he married morganatically American heiress Audrey Emery and they had one son, Paul Ilyinsky, before the marriage disintegrated. During the 1920s Dmitri's health, which had never been strong, worsened and finally tuberculosis was diagnosed. Advised that his only hope was treatment in a sanatorium he went to Davos in Switzerland, where he died in 1942. He was buried in the local cemetery, with a simple wooden cross placed over his grave. There he remained until his body was disinterred almost two decades later, cremated and sent to Mainau, where it was deposited in the Bernadotte crypt alongside the remains of the recently deceased Marie Pavlovna. Brother and sister, so close in life, now lie together in death.

Their step-mother Princess Paley and half-sisters Irene and Natalie also reached Europe. In mid-December 1918, with Grand Duke Paul in a Bolshevik prison hospital and Vladimir Paley killed, it was decided that fifteen-year-old Irene and thirteen-year-old Natalie should leave Russia as soon as possible.

Peter Dournovo, the former Minister of the Interior who was now involved in underground activities, approached Princess Paley with a plan. Captain Sergei Herschelman had arrived from Finland where he would be returning that evening disguised as a Red Guard. Dournovo proposed that Irene and Natalie accompany him using passports in the name of the princess's laundress Petroff and posing as her daughters. The full plan of escape was then explained and after much hesitation the princess agreed.

That afternoon Irene and Natalie went with their half-sister Marianne Derfelden and the laundress to a flat in the capital where they met Captain Herschelman and received their false passports.

Taking leave of Marianne, they all boarded a tram to Ochta station and from there took a train to the small station of Waskélévo, arriving at ten o'clock that night. There they boarded a cattle truck filled with Finnish peasants. Half an hour later the cattle truck stopped. Tired and hungry, the girls and their escorts had to jump out with their bags into deep snow and follow a track to a small *isba* (house). Here they were given three horse drawn sledges. The first was occupied by an English lady and a Swedish man, the second by Irene and the captain, with Natalie and Mme Petroff following in the third.

At three in the morning they arrived at another *isba* where Captain Herschelman asked for fresh horses. The man there refused. The snow was melting, so he could not drive them and anyway, he claimed, there was less than 2 miles to walk. Irene and Natalie set off again with the men carrying their bags, this time on foot with the melting snow clinging to their felt boots and almost collapsing from exhaustion, drinking the snow thirstily to keep going. Only the thought of what might happen to their father if they were caught trying to escape spurred them on.

After a lot more than 2 miles they came to a rivulet where the ice was already cracking. Somehow they had to get across. The Swede, a hardened sportsman, came to the rescue, lying down to make a bridge out of his body across which the four women were able to walk.

Further on they reached a house, where they snatched two hours' sleep on a wooden bench before getting into sledges again. Finally, thirty-two hours after leaving Petrograd, they reached the Finnish frontier at Terijoki.

Safely over the border, the girls were taken to the Rauha Sanatorium near the Imatra Falls, where they were well looked after by friends of Dournovo and Captain Herschelman until they could be reunited with their parents. Only after the death of Grand Duke Paul did Princess Paley join her daughters. She was among a party who crossed the frozen Gulf of Finland by sledge, wearing white clothes to camouflage them from the Bolshevik searchlights.

The grief-stricken widow and daughters made their home in France.

* * *

On 17 July 1998, eighty years to the day after their murder, the remains of Nicholas II, Empress Alexandra, Olga, Tatiana, Anastasia and their four servants were finally laid to rest in a side chapel of the SS Peter and Paul Cathedral.

After a requiem in the Cathedral of the Annunciation in Ekaterinburg, the coffins arrived at St Petersburg's Pulkova Airport on 16 July and were driven in procession to the fortress. The flags of Russia and St Petersburg, with black mourning ribbons, hung from lamp posts and the route was lined with troops. At the Winter Palace, where the cortège briefly slowed down, the Russian flag flew at half mast and there were garlands of fir branches where the imperial garden had formerly stood. Many Russians mingled with the tourists to see the hearses pass. At the Fortress the coffins were carried in by soldiers, escorted by pipers from the Royal Scots Dragoon Guards (formerly the Scots Greys, of whom Nicholas had been colonel-in-chief).

Yet the Orthodox Church remained sceptical. Neither Patriarch Alexei II nor the Metropolitan of St Petersburg attended the burial and it was left to Archpriest Boris Glebov to conduct a service for 'Christian victims of the revolution', during which the names of the deceased were not even mentioned. It became more the government's desperate quest for legitimacy as successors to the Romanovs than a public recognition of this terrible crime.

After the service, attended by more than fifty members of the Romanov family as well as President Boris Yeltsin, the tiny child-sized coffins of Caucasian oak were carried to St Catherine's Chapel where they were buried in the same vault. The imperial standard draped the coffins of Nicholas and Alexandra; the tsar's also had a sword, crossed with its scabbard. As Nicholas's coffin was lowered last of all a nineteen-gun salute was fired from the banks of the Neva.

In 2000 the Russian Orthodox Church canonised Nicholas II and his whole family as passion bearers, saying they had undergone suffering with gentleness, patience and humility. The Orthodox Church Outside Russia canonised the family in 1981.

In July 2007 members of the Military Historical Club in Ekaterinburg discovered forty-four partial bone fragments buried in a small hollow, about 50 feet from where the Romanov remains were found in Koptyaki Forest. The bone fragments were very damaged and had apparently been covered in acid and burnt, then thoroughly smashed with spades before being tossed into the smaller pit. Initial tests indicated that they are the bones of Alexei and his sister.

As tests and arguments continue, at the time of writing Alexei and Maria remain unburied.

* * *

Yet not everyone has accepted the familiar version of the time and place of the imperial family's deaths. In their book *The Fall of the Romanovs* historian Professor Mark Steinberg and the historian-archivist at the State Archives of the Russian Federation Vladimir Khrustalev mention the 'baffling counterevidence' in contemporary accounts of many of the witnesses, including guards at the Ipatiev House. Citing stories of a train going to Perm and sightings of a battered, escaped girl who some believed to be Anastasia, they say that 'the evidence that the whole family was killed is itself problematic.'[9]

Early White investigators concluded that only Nicholas and Alexei had been killed.

Sir Charles Eliot, the erudite High Commissioner in Siberia, filed a report about an aeroplane flying over the Ipatiev House and a train with its blinds drawn heading towards Perm. He believed that the surviving members of the family were on board. Others think that the train was evacuating gold and platinum from Ekaterinburg. Did Eliot fall foul of Bolshevik disinformation?

On 16 September 1918, in an official report sent to Mr Alston in Vladivostok, Thomas Preston also said surviving members had been moved. He stated that after the tsar's murder, 'the rest of the members of the imperial family were taken away to an unknown destination … there is still [the] possibility of them having been taken north by the Bolsheviks in their retreat to Verhoutry [sic].'[10]

Robert Ingham, the young ADC who looked after the dowager empress and her family in Malta in 1919, also knew something. When interviewed, he was unable to talk about it. He had signed the Official Secrets Act.

Then there was Major William Peer Groves, a liaison officer with the Air Ministry in Japan, who told both his son and daughter, independently, that not all the family had died at Ekaterinburg but were rescued with the help of the British. His son later said in an interview that in 1918 his father 'was in Southern Russia ... on one of two expeditions which ... went north from Odessa, and one of which reached ... Kiev.' At that point he separated from the rest of the mission and returned to Odessa some time later. He brought back two pieces of jewellery, which were believed to be tokens that the family was still alive. One was given to the dowager empress while she was staying in Malta in 1919; the other was given to an unidentified member of the family in France.[11] The dowager empress certainly believed that the tsar and his family were alive – but how then to explain the fact that she never heard from them again?

The widow of Sir Thomas Preston later said that the Japanese wanted to help rescue the imperial family but were too late. Perhaps significantly, another visitor to the dowager empress in Malta was the Imperial Japanese Consul, which brings us back to the mysterious telegram sent just after Christmas 1918 mentioning the word 'family' seven times. According to Shay McNeal, a further telegram from the Department of State says that 'family' was used to cover a reference to Japan.[12]

When interviewed in the 1970s Thomas Preston (by now Sir Thomas) said that relevant documents were being withheld. Then, in an interview conducted in 1987 after Preston's death, his widow and sister-in-law suddenly stated that he had been summoned to the Ipatiev House early on the morning of 17 July as an official eyewitness to view the family's corpses. However, the bodies of two of the tsar's daughters were not there – Anastasia and, he thought, Tatiana.[13] Some authors have tried to tie this in with Richard Meinertzhagen's account of a rescue attempt prompted by King George V, with 'one child being literally thrown into the plane at Ekaterinburg.' Senior Intelligence Officers, including Stephen Alley, were later quoted as saying that one or more of the Romanovs had been saved.

Yet this flies in the fact of all the evidence, as the indisputable fact is that after July 1918 there were no *positive* sightings of the imperial family, only rumours and hearsay. People believed they were alive because they *wanted* to believe.

In stark contrast to stories of apparent survival there are the remains of the bodies and the seemingly incontrovertible DNA evidence, although whether DNA from the lock of the dowager empress's hair, kept by the tsar's grandmother Queen Louise of Denmark, has been tested, remains doubtful.[14]

So it seems that most of the family were buried together – is it possible that they didn't all die together at the time and place stated by the history books?

Patriarch Kirill has recently questioned why the Soviet authorities did not destroy the burial site if it really is genuine. Some have made the point that the Ekaterinburg remains were discovered by Gely Ryabov, a former Soviet policeman with the CID; others have pointed out that the timing of the find, reported in April 1989, came just days after the queen had accepted an invitation from President Gorbachev to visit Russia. Timely indeed.[15]

But if the Romanov women were alive in the autumn of 1918 (as many of Europe's royal families believed), perhaps in Perm, and then killed later, why would the Bolsheviks bring the bodies back to Ekaterinburg to be buried there? Russia was in the middle of a civil war. Surely they would be left where they died.

Recently Russian historian Veniamin Alekseyev has also cast doubt on the 'official' version. He hopes that documents regarding secret diplomatic contacts between Germany and Lenin's Russia and a possible exchange of the Romanov women will throw new light on what really happened. These are due to be released in 2018. Forensic tests have also been ordered on the so-called Yurovsky Note, as there are now doubts that Yurovsky was indeed the author.[16]

Maybe the answer lies not in the murder of the family, but in what happened beforehand – possibly in the embarrassing failure of some negotiations.

Perhaps the future will provide more answers – and maybe even yield up the rest of that tantalizing Romanov treasure.

Notes

LRA = Leeds Russian Archive
TNA = The National Archives, Kew, London.
F.O. = Foreign Office.
Xenia archive. Copies of Grand Duchess Xenia's papers in the author's possession.

Introduction
1. *The Sunday Times,* 23 October 1994.
2. *The Daily Mail,* 28 April 2000.
3. Grand Duke Alexander, *Once,* p 296.
4. Marie of Roumania, p 37.

Chapter 1
1. Vorres, p 130.
2. Gilliard, p 48.
3. Douglas Smith, p 293.
4. Douglas Smith, p 378.
5. Quoted in Massie, p 315.
6. See Douglas Smith, pp 631–2, for a discussion of this point.
7. See Clarke, *Romanoff Gold*, pp 302 & 402.
8. Dehn, p 148.
9. See Rappaport, *Four Sisters,* p 435 note 10. The letter is in the archives of the Royal Navy Submarine Museum, Gosport (A 1917/16/002). The icon was donated to the chapel of HMS *Dolphin* by Frank Best's widow in 1962.
10. 'Gunshot on the Moika' by Archpriest Vladimir Tsypin. Translated by Dr William Lee. In *Sovereign* No. 3, p 105. Nicholasha wanted the tsar to abdicate but others did not. Grand Duke Nicholas Michaelovich and Grand Duchess Elisabeth Mavrikievna were also at

the Duma that day apparently trying to save the tsar's throne. I am
indebted to Marlene Eilers Koenig for this information.
11. Bykov, pp 25–6; Pares, p 467.
12. Quoted in Massie, p 397.

Chapter 2
1. Paley, p 53.
2. Van der Kiste & Hall, p 101. Diary 28 February–3 March 1917.
3. Zeepvat. 'The Only Lady Admiral in the World.' *Royalty Digest*, Jan. 2002. p 211.
4. Zeepvat, *Romanov Autumn,* p 221.
5. Stopford, p 311.
6. Kudrina, p 89.
7. Alexander, *Once,* p 319.
8. Kudrina, p 89.
9. Kudrina, p 89.
10. Vorres, pp 151–2.
11, Kudrina, p 89.
12. Kudrina, p 89.
13. Alexander, *Once,* pp 320–1.
14. Ulstrup, p 446.
15. Battiscombe, p 29.
16. Prince Christopher, p 78.
17. de Stoeckl, p 115.
18. Zeepvat, *The Only Lady Admiral.*
19. Van der Kiste & Hall, p 116.
20. Dehn, p 165.
21. Botkin, p 140.
22. Quoted in King & Wilson, p 57.

Chapter 3
1. Rose, p 209.
2. Rose, p 208.
3. Clay, p 302.
4. Grand Duchess George, p 178; Pope-Hennessy, p 507.
5. Maylunas & Mironenko, p 546.
6. TNA. FO800/205. 19 March 1917.
7. TNA. FO371/2998. 19 March 1917.
8. Massie, p 484.
9. *The Martha and Mary Convent,* p 49.
10. Mountbatten Papers, Southampton University. MS 62 MB1/T90. 6 May 1917. Quoted in Hall, *Princesses on the Wards,* p 106.
11. Miller, p 153.
12. Nicolson, p 393.
13. Waters, p 245.
14. Bokhanov p 531; Service, p 50.

15. TNA. FO371/2998.
16. Maylunas & Mironenko, p 559; Steinberg & Khrustalev, p 119.
17. TNA. FO371/2998 & 371/3008.
18. Bokhanov, p 531.
19. Clarke, *Romanoff Gold,* p 42.
20. TNA. FO371/2998.
21. Clarke, *Romanoff Gold,* p 37; Gilliard, p 167.
22. TNA. FO800/205/63. 30 March 1917.
23. TNA. FO/800/205/65. 2 April 1917.
24. Quoted in Maylunas & Mironenko, p 567.
25. TNA. FO/800/205. 6 April 1917.
26. Quoted in Rose, p 213.
27. Maylunus & Mironenko, p 561.
28. TNA. FO 800/205. 6 April 1917.
29. TNA/Cab 23/2, War Cabinet 118. Quoted in Summers & Mangold, p 244.
30. TNA. FO 800/205. 15 April 1917.
31. Quoted in Summers & Mangold, p 244.
32. Quoted in Summers & Mangold, p 245.
33. Clark, *Romanoff Gold,* p 41; Quoted in Summers & Mangold, p 245.
34. Grand Duchess George, pp 184–5.
35. Grand Duchess George, p 187.
36. Grand Duchess George, p 187.
37. TNA. FO 800/205. 4 April 1917.
38. Quoted in Rose, p 212.
39. TNA. FO 800/205. 18 April 1917.
40. TNA. FO 800/205. 11 May 1917.
41. TNA. FO800/205. 23 April 1917.
42. *Evening Standard,* 4 July 1932; Bokhanov, p 546.
43. Buchanan II, p 106.
44. Quoted in Clay, p 341.
45. FO 370/273 & 1003/50/405 Quoted in Summers & Mangold, p 246.
46. Maylunas & Mirenenko, p 561.
47. Trevelyan, pp 277–8.
48. Princess Olga Romanoff, pp 8–9.
49. Carter, p 472.
50. Morrow, pp 220–1.

Chapter 4

1. Bomann-Larsen, p 128.
2. Bomann-Larsen, p 430 note 11.
3. Bomann-Larsen, pp 124, & 431 note 14.
4. Buxhoeveden, *Life & Tragedy,* p 276; Bomann-Larsen, pp 132–3; Maylunus & Mironenko, p 560.

5. Wig, p 52.
6. Bomann-Larsen, p 135.
7. Lerche & Mandal, p 102; Buchwaldt, p 38.
8. Lerche & Mandal, p 104.
9. Van der Kiste, *Northern Crowns*, p 61.
10. Ponsonby, p 188.
11. Jensen, pp 106–07.
12. TNA. FO800/205. 24 & 27 March 1917.
13. Preben-Hansen, p 20.
14. Waters, p 255.
15. Tjernald, p 59.
16. Tjernald, p137.
17. Van der Kiste, *Crowns*, p 131.
18. Hall, *Little Mother*, p 294.
19. Mengden, p 115.
20. Jensen, p 34.

Chapter 5

1. Quoted in Rose, p 216.
2. Rose, p 174.
3. Rose, p 174.
4. Mountbatten Papers, Southampton University. MS 62 MB1/T90, 6 June 1917. Quoted in Hall, *Princesses on the Wards*, p 107.
5. Quoted in Miller, p 154.
6. Gilliard, p 72.
7. Rappaport, *Ekaterinburg*, p 120.
8. Bokhanov, pp 549–50.
9. TNA. FO 800/205. 8 August 1917.
10. Pakula, p 223.
11. Alexandrov, plate 16.
12. Quoted in Crawford, p 326.
13. Quoted in Crawford, p 332.
14. Crawford, p 331.
15. Pipes, p 748.
16. Nicholas's diary in GARF. Quoted in Radzinsky, p 26.
17. Greg King & Penny Wilson, *Atlantis*. 'Fate of the Romanovs' issue, p 22.
18. de Robien, p 115.
19. Perry & Pleshnakov, p 178.
20. Xenia archive, Grand Duchess Cyril to Grand Duchess Xenia; Van der Kiste & Hall, p 140.
21. Kudrina, in *Kejserinde Dagmar*, p 48.
22. Jensen, pp 43–4.
23. Jensen, pp 44–5; Hall, *Little Mother*, p 298.
24. de Robien, p 116.

Chapter 6

1. Putiatin, 'Last Days... '
2. *Kejserinde Dagmar,* p 222.
3. de Robien, p 213.
4. Hall, *Little Mother,* p 301.
5. Gilliard, p 243.
6. Trewin, p 90.
7. Broadlands Archives. Victoria Milford Haven to Nona Kerr.
8. www.ancestry.co.uk – England and Wales National Probate Calendar.
9. Princess Eugenie, pp 222–6 has many similar entries.
10. Gilliard, p 263.
11. Sotheby's auction catalogue, p 52.
12. Gilliard, p 256.
13. Almedingen, pp 115–6.
14. Almedingen, pp 116–8.
15. Jensen, p 49. Ree returned to Petrograd in December 1918.
16. Jensen pp 49 & 52; Kudrina, in *Kejserinde Dagmar,* p 48.
17. Jensen, pp 52–3.
18. German F.O. document AS 1356, quoted in Summers & Mangold, p 272.
19. Kudrina, in *Kejserinde Dagmar,* p 48.
20. Majolier, p 122.
21. Majolier, p 88.
22. LRA MS1363/114. No longer on deposit at LRA.
23. Quoted in Crawford, p 345.
24. Crawford, p 345.
25. Bruun Rasmussen auctioneers, Copenhagen. Russian auction, 6 June 2016.
26. Bomann-Larsen, p 436, note 3.
27. Bomann-Larsen, p 436 note 3.
28. LRA MS1363/116. No longer on deposit at LRA.
29. LRA MS1363/117. No longer on deposit at LRA.
30. Ulstrup, p 419.
31. LRA MS 1363/119. No longer on deposit at LRA. His birthday was 24 July/6 August.

Chapter 7

1. Service, pp 141–2.
2. Urbach, pp 129–30.
3. O'Connor, p 229, quoting Diterikhs.
4. Rose, p 216.
5. Bulygin, p 202.
6. King & Wilson, p 213.
7. Warwick, p 54.

8. Almedingen, pp 110–12.
9. Urbach, p 100.
10. Urbach, pp 142 & 230.
11. Urbach, pp 100–01.
12. Service, pp 223–4.
13. Summers & Mangold, p 274.
14. King & Wilson, pp 77–8.
15. Gilliard, p 257.
16. Service, pp 225–6; Waters, pp 254–5.
17. Service, pp 226–7.
18. German F.O. documents, quoted in Summers & Mangold, p 273.
19. Service, p 223; King & Wilson, p 214.

Chapter 8
1. McNeal, pp 46 & 80.
2. Summers & Mangold, pp 250/51; Cook, p 137.
3. Cook, *Romanovs* p 137; Summers & Mangold, p 251.
4. Summers & Mangold, p 252.
5. Summers & Mangold, p 394, note 32.
6. Summers & Mangold, pp 250–1.
7. McNeal, pp 46 & 44.
8. Summers & Mangold, pp 253–4.
9. Windsor, p 130.
10. Clarke, *Romanoff Gold,* p 130.
11. Clarke, *Romanoff Gold,* pp 130–1.
12. FO371/3329; Summers & Mangold, p 395, note 34.
13. See Summers & Mangold, p 261.
14. King & Wilson, p 91.
15. King & Wilson, p 96; Summers & Mangold, p 259.
16. King & Wilson, pp 96–7.
17. Kozlov & Khrustalev, *Last Diary,* p 116.
18. Quoted in Massie, p 477.
19. Jensen, pp 72–3.
20. Massie, p 490.
21. Eugenie, p 290.
22. Hall, *Little Mother,* p 305.
23. Kudrina, in *Kejserinde Dagmar,* p 48.
24. Van der Kiste & Hall, p 130.
25. Kudrina, in *Kejserinde Dagmar,* p 48.

Chapter 9
1. Jensen, p 71.
2. Jensen, p 67.
3. Crawford, p 358.

4. Crawford, p 360.
5. Crawford, p 361.
6. Massie, *Pavlovsk*, p 140.
7. TNA. FO370/3328.
8. Gerlardi, *Splendour*, p 360.
9. 'Fragments of Memories', in Royal Russia No 7, p 113.
10. Paley, p 206.
11. Quoted in Zeepvat, *Romanov Autumn*, p 224.
12. Sotheby's auction catalogue, p 115.
13. Sotheby's auction catalogue, p 98.
14. King & Wilson, p 220.
15. Preston, p 81.
16. Zeepvat, p 225.
17. See King and Wilson, pp 260–1.
18. Sotheby's auction catalogue, p 84.
19. Sotheby's auction catalogue, p 84.
20. Sáenz, pp 83/84; Maylunus & Mironenko, p 676.
21. Miller, p 160.
22. Zeepvat, p 227.

Chapter 10

1. O'Connor, p 248. See also pp 234 & 246.
2. King & Wilson, p 195.
3. King & Wilson, p 214.
4. See King & Wilson, pp 225–7.
5. Rappaport, *Ekaterinburg*, p 68.
6. Mossolov, pp 260/1; information from Anthony Summers.
7. Urbach, p 335.
8. See Summers & Mangold, pp 276 & 278.
9. Pipes, p 640.
10. Quoted in Summers & Mangold, p 46.
11. King & Wilson, p 233; Bykov, p 77.
12. Quoted in King & Wilson, p 221. For a full discussion of the Officer letters see King & Wilson pp 221–67, and *Atlantis, Special Fate of the Romanovs Issue,* pp 73–86.
13. Quoted in King & Wilson, p 223.
14. Quoted in Massie, p 488.
15. For the ages of the guards see King & Wilson, p 21, and for the incident with the grand duchess see pp 243–5 & 247.
16. Quoted in King & Wilson, pp 231–2.
17. Quoted in King & Wilson, p 267.
18. Quoted in Summers & Mangold, p 310.
19. 'Prince Michael Bids to Clear George V's Name Over Tsar's Death,' by Richard Palmer. *Daily Express* online, 2 February 2010. Fellowes

was an uncle of Julian Fellowes (Baron Fellowes of West Stafford), the creator of *Downton Abbey*.

20. www.rafweb.org/Biographies/Fellowes
21. www.burkes-peerage.net.articles/page13idec.aspz
22. 'Prince Michael Bids to Clear George V's Name Over Tsar's Death,' by Richard Palmer. *Daily Express* online, 2 February 2010.
23. Private information.
24. TNA FO371/3977 & FO371/3335; Summers & Mangold, p 85.
25. www.wartimememoriesproject.com/greatwar/thosewhoserved
26. Rodney, p 214.
27. Sotheby's auction catalogue, p 88.
28. Ackerman, p 100.
29 Michael Smith, p 187.
30. Michael Smith, p 197; Cook, *Romanovs,* pp 153/4; John Crossland, 'British Spies in Plot to Save the Tsar.' *Sunday Times,* 15 October 2006.
31. Cook, *Romanovs,* p 154.
32. Cook, *Romanovs,* p 155.
33. Cook, *Romanovs,* p 156; Cook, *Rasputin,* p 276; John Crossland, 'British Spies in Plot to Save the Tsar.' *Sunday Times,* 15 October 2006.
34. Preston, p 110.
35. McNeal, pp 142 & 114; Occleshaw *Conspiracies,* p 137.
36. Occleshaw, *Conspiracies,* pp 94–5.
37. Occleshaw, *Conspiracies,* p 99.
38. Summers & Mangold, 2002 revised edition, p 367.
39. Kozlov & Khrustalev, p 198.
40. Kozlov & Khrustalev, p 198.

Chapter 11

1. Occleshaw, *Conspiracies,* p 26.
2. Rappaport, *Ekaterinburg,* p 200.
3. Carter, p 132.
4. Rappaport, *Ekaterinburg,* p 210.
5. TNA FO 800/205/307.
6. German official documents quoted by Sokolov. O'Connor, p 160.
7. Quoted in Summers & Mangold, p 291.
8. German F.O. documents, quoted in O'Connor, p 161.
9. German Foreign Ministry Document A30764. Summers & Mangold, p 291. See also O'Connor, pp 161 & 257.
10. Quoted in Ferro, p 270.
11. German Foreign Office Document quoted in Summers & Mangold, p 266.
12. TNA. FO 800/205.
13. TNA. FO 800/205.
14. Carter, p 481.
15. TNA. FO/800/304.

16. RA QM/PRIV/QMD/1918: 24 July
17. RA QM/PRIV/QMD/1918: 25 July; Rose, p 216.
18. 'Half a Century of Royal Letters.' *Royalty Digest Quarterly* No 4, 2016, p 57. Queen Ena to Queen Marie of Romania. 1 June 1917.
19. Kudrina, in *Kejserinde Dagmar*, p 50.
20. *The Times*, 3 August 1918; Occleshaw, p 64.
21. Jonathan Iglesias, 'King Alfonso XIII and his attempts to save the Imperial Family of Russia.' www.theorthodoxchurchinfo/blog/news/
22. TNA. FO800/205.
23. TNA. FO800/205.
24. TNA. FO 800/327.
25. Jonathan Iglesias, 'King Alfonso XIII and his attempts to save the Imperial Family of Russia.' www.theorthodoxchurchinfo/blog/news/
26. Kudrina, in *Kejserinde Dagmar*, p 50.
27. TNA. FO800/205.
28. Clarke, *Romanoff Gold*, pp 131–2.
29. Miller, p 155.
30. Miller, p 156.
31. Miller, p 156.
32. Occleshaw, *Conspiracies*, p 73.
33. Cortes Cavanillas, p 265.
34. Quoted in Summers & Mangold, p 362.
35. Jonathan Iglesias, 'King Alfonso XIII and his attempts to save the Imperial Family of Russia.' www.theorthodoxchurchinfo/blog/news/
36. Jonathan Iglesias, 'King Alfonso XIII and his attempts to save the Imperial Family of Russia.' www.theorthodoxchurchinfo/blog/news/
37. Summers & Mangold, p 363.
38. Occleshaw, *Conspiracies*, p 65.
39. Van Tuyll, p 180; Oudendijk, p 258.
40. Ferro, p 270.
41. Occleshaw, *Conspiracies*, pp 63–4.
42. Ferro, p 270.
43. TNA FO371/3977; TNA FO371 3325.
44. Summers & Mangold, p 295.
45. Bomann-Larsen, p 214.
46. Hough, p 326.
47. Broadlands Archives. Summers & Mangold, pp 81 & 266.
48. Frankland, p 363.
49. TNA. FO 800/205.
50. Hough, p 327; Miller, pp 157 & 160.
51. The Royal Archives, Madrid.
52. Miller, p 158.
53. Michael Thornton. 'Anastasia Mystery Remains Unsolved.' *Sunday Express*, 17 May 1992
54. Broadlands Archives, quoted in Summers & Mangold, p 294.

55. Ferro, p 271.
56. Ferro, p 271.
57. Summers & Mangold, *El Expediente Sobre El Zar.* Postscript.
58. Page telegram quoted in Summers & Mangold, pp 92 & 364; for 'family seven times' see McNeal, pp 137–8 & 255–9.
59. Hall, *Little Mother,* p 314; *Deuxieme Bureau* report Berne to Paris, 18 Aug. 1918. Collection of Anthony Summers.
60. de Robien, p 294.
61. Hough, p 327.
62. Xenia archive. Van der Kiste & Hall, pp 158–9.

Chapter 12

1. Obolensky, p 188.
2. Zeepvat, *Romanov Autumn,* p 227; Bomann-Larsen, p 214.
3. Cook, *Romanovs* p 236.
4. Collection of Ian Shapiro.
5. Lubov Millar, p 227. For the journey of the Alapayevsk coffins see Hall, Coryne. 'The Romanov Graves in Beijing.' *Royalty Digest Quarterly,* Vol 2, 2007.

Chapter 13

1. Marie of Roumania, Vol. III, p 66.
2. Marie of Roumania, Vol. III, p 150.
3. Marie of Roumania, Vol. III, p 151.
4. Marie of Roumania, Vol. III p 153.
5. Marie of Roumania, Vol. III, p 151–2; Urbach, p 100.
6. Perry & Pleshnakov, p 226, Clarke, *Romanoff Gold,* p xiii; for Grand Duchess Vladimir and her sons' time in the Caucasus see Hall, *Imperial Dancer,* pp 188/203.
7. Marie of Roumania, Vol. III, p 394.
8. Marie of Roumania, Vol. III, pp 246–8.
9. Quoted in Pakula, p 242.
10. Rodney, p 191.
11. Van der Kiste, *Victoria Melita,* pp 134–5.
12. Hall, *Little Mother,* p 314.
13. *Royalty Digest Quarterly,* Vol 1, 2017, p 57.
14. Marie of Roumania, Vol. III, p 427.
15. Xenia archive. Van der Kiste & Hall, p 137.
16. *Royalty Digest Quarterly,* Vol. 1, 2017, p 57.
17. Van der Kiste & Hall, pp 138/9. Diary 27 October/9 November 1918.
18. Ulstrup, p 262. 28 October/10 November 1918.
19. Xenia archive. Van der Kiste & Hall, p 139.
20. Xenia archive. Van der Kiste & Hall, p 139.
21. Ulstrup, p 428. 26 November 1918 NS.

22. TNA. Admiralty telegram No. 103Z. 1 November 1918.
23. TNA. ADM 137/952 No. 1512. 5 November 1918.
24. TNA. ADM telegram 240z, 16 November 1918.
25. Occleshaw. *With the Greatest Care & Tact.*
26. TNA. ADM 137/953. No. 747z.
27. Ulstrup, p 428. 26 November NS 1918.
28. Hall, *Little Mother,* p 317; RA GEOVM1344A/55.
29. *Royalty Digest Quarterly,* Vol. 1, 2017 p 56. 19 November 1918.
30. Marie of Russia, *Exile,* p 13.
31. Perry & Plekashnikov, p 257; Marie of Russia, *Exile,* p 29.
32. Quoted in Pakula, p 265.

Chapter 14

1. Grand Duchess George, p 219.
2. de Robien, pp 253–4.
3. de Robien, p 277.
4. de Robien, p 279.
5. de Robien, p 280.
6. Grand Duchess George, p 229.
7. Jensen, pp 106–7.
8. Bomann-Larsen, p 214.
9. Grand Duchess George, p 237.
10. Jensen, p 104.
11. Grand Duchess George, p 230.
12. Grand Duchess George, p 231.
13. Brook-Shepherd, *Iron Maze,* pp 88–9.
14. Jensen, p 113.
15. Collection of Ian Shapiro. Elisabeth Mavrikievna to Mr Denison.
16. Jensen, p. 115.
17. Jensen, p 115.
18. Grand Duchess George, p 236.
19. Quoted in Gerladi *Splendour,* p 349.
20. Jensen, pp 116–7.
21. Jensen, p 118.
22. Jensen, pp 118–9.
23. Jensen, p 119.
24. Jensen, p 120.
25. Ulstrup, p 430.
26. Xenia archive. Van der Kiste & Hall, p 143.
27. Penny Wilson, in *The Other Grand Dukes,* p 132.
28. Gerladi, *Splendour,* p 350.

Chapter 15

1. Quoted in Carter, p 483.
2. Urbach, p 137.

3. Diary. 8 December 1918. Translated by Dr William Lee. All entries in Dmitri's diary are according to the Old Style Russian Calendar.
4. Diary. 5 December 1918. O.S. Translated by Dr William Lee.
5. Diary. 5 December 1918. O.S. Translated by Dr William Lee.
6. Diary. 8 December 1918. O.S. Translated by Dr William Lee.
7. Diary, 9 December 1918. O.S. Translated by Dr William Lee.
8. Diary. 19 December 1918. O.S. Translated by Dr William Lee.
9. Diary. 16 December 1918. O.S. Translated by Dr William Lee.
10. Diary. 30 December 1918. OS. Translated by Dr William Lee.
11. Diary. 25 December 1918. OS. Translated by Dr William Lee.
12. Diary. 12 January 1919. OS. Translated by Dr William Lee.
13. Diary. 31 January 1919. OS. Transcribed by Dr William Lee.
14. Xenia archive. Van der Kiste & Hall, p 143. 19 February 1919.
15. Mandache, p 43.
16. Marie of Russia, *Exile,* p 47.
17. Ulstrup, p 285.
18. Ulstrup, p 291.
19. TNA. ADM 1/8938. No.1407. 819z.
20. Ulstrup, p 315.
21. Van der Kiste & Hall, p 144.
22. Ulstrup, p 342.
23. National Archives of Malta. 12 April 1919.
24. TNA ADM1/8938.
25. TNA. Admiralty files. 5 May 1919.
26. Diary. 27 June 1919. O.S. Translated by Dr William Lee.
27. Diary. 14 March 1920. O.S. Translated by Dr William Lee.
28. Meinert, p 131.
29. TNA. FO 371/3977A.
30. For the full story of the jewels see King & Wilson *Atlantis,* special Fate of the Romanovs issue, pp 44/47; Clarke, *Romanoff Gold,* pp 221/2; Liesowska, 'Fascinating new clues emerge on lost tsarist gold and diamonds worth an untold fortune.' *The Siberian Times,* 20 November 2017; and Will Stewart, 'Is £26 million stash of gold belonging to Russia's last tsar buried by a Siberian railway track?' in *Daily Mail online,* 22 November 2017; for Volkov, see *Memories of Alexei Volkov,* Chapter 16 on the Alexander Palace website. www.alexanderpalace.org/palace/
31. Summers & Mangold, p 268.
32. 'Sir Thomas Preston Recalls Ekaterinburg'. *The Spectator*, 11 March 1972.
33. Summers & Mangold, pp 380–1;Vorres p 171.
34. King & Wilson, p 370.
35. Channon, p 175; Edwards, pp 3812.

Postcript

1. For a full discussion on Soviet involvement and the excavation of the grave, see King & Wilson, pp 381–399.
2. For the movements of the Alapayevsk coffins see Hall, Coryne. 'The Romanov Graves in Beijing'. In *Royalty Digest Quarterly,* Vol 2, 2007.
3. Ulstrup, p 419.
4. Crawford, p 376.
5. Crawford, p 376.
6. Diary, Jespersen p 270. The photograph is still in Christian X's study at Amalienborg Palace. George's letter – LRA. MS1363/188. No longer on deposit at LRA.
7. For Empress Marie's life in exile see Hall, *Little Mother of Russia;* and Hall & Driver, *Hvidøre, A Royal Retreat.*
8. For Xenia's life in exile see Van der Kiste & Hall, *Once a Grand Duchess.*
9. Steinberg & Khrustalev, p 295.
10. Phil Tomaselli, on the Alexander Palace discussion forum. 11 December 2005.
11. Interview transcripts kindly provided by Anthony Summers.
12. Occleshaw, p 131 & 140; Empress Marie in Malta: Hall, *Little Mother,* pp 324–5. For the inconclusive story of the mysterious telegram, see McNeal pp 256–7 & 263.
13. Information from Anthony Summers; Occleshaw, *Conspiracies,* pp 139/40.
14. von Buchwald, p 101. The envelopes of hair kept by Queen Louise were displayed in the exhibition 'From the Royal Attics' at Amalienborg Palace in 2016.
15. Conference, 'The Case of the Murder of the Imperial family. New Examinations and Archival Materials. Discussion'. 27 November 2017. Reported in *Romanov News* no. 116; Anthony Summers & Tom Mangold, letter to *The Times,* 15 April 1989; Dr Helen Szamuely, letter to *The Times,* 28 April 1989.
16. 'Respected historian suggests 'lost' Russian princess Anastasia fled to America.' *The Siberian Times,* 27 February 2014; 'Considerable time needed to complete tests on Yekaterinburg remains', Interfax, Moscow. 27 November 2017.

Select Bibliography

All books are published in London unless otherwise stated.

Books:
Ackerman, Carl W. *Trailing the Bolsheviki.* (New York: Charles Scribner, 1919)

Alexander, Grand Duke of Russia. *Once a Grand Duke.* (Cassell, 1932)

Alexandrov, Victor. *The End of the Romanovs.* (Hutchinson, 1966)

Almedingen, E. M. *An Unbroken Unity.* (The Bodley Head, 1964)

Anon. (Stopford) *The Russian Diary of an Englishman.* (New York: McBride & Co, 1919)

Aronson, Theo. *Crowns in Conflict.* (John Murray, 1986)

Battiscombe, Georgina. *Queen Alexandra.* (Constable, 1969)

Beéche, Arturo (editor). *The Other Grand Dukes.* (California: Eurohistory. com, 2012)

Benagh, Christine. *An Englishman at the Court of the Tsar.* (California: Conciliar Press, 2000)

Bokhanov, Alexander. *Imperator Nikolai II.* (Russia: Russkoe Slovo, 1998)

Bomann-Larsen, Tor. *Makten. Haakon & Maud IV.* (Oslo: Cappelen Damm AS, 2008)

Botkin, Gleb. *The Real Romanovs.* (Putnam, 1932)

Brook-Shepherd, Gordon. *Iron Maze.* (Macmillan, 1998)

Brook-Shepherd, Gordon. *The Last Empress.* (Harper Collins, 1991)

Buchanan, Sir George. *My Mission to Russia.* Volume 2. (Cassell, 1923)

Buchwaldt, Randi. *Kongehusets farmor og oldemor: Dronning Alexandrine.* (Denmark: Hernov, 1998)

Buchwaldt, Randi. *Marselisborg – slot og fristed.* (Denmark: Hernov, 2000)

Buxhoeveden, Baroness Sophie. *Left Behind.* (New York: Longmans Green, 1929)

Buxhoeveden, Baroness Sophie. *The Life & Tragedy of Alexandra Feodorovna.* (New York: Longmans, Green, 1928)

Bykov, Paul. *The Last Days of Tsardom.* (Martin Lawrence, 1934)

Carter, Miranda. *The Three Emperors.* (Fig Tree Publishing, 2009)

Channon, Sir Henry. Chips. *The Diaries of Sir Henry Channon.* Edited by Robert Rhodes James. (Weidenfeld & Nicolson, 1967)

Christopher, Prince of Greece. *Memoirs.* (Hurst & Blackett, 1938)

Clarke, William. *Hidden Treasures of the Romanovs. Saving the Royal Jewels.* (Edinburgh: National Museums of Scotland, 2009)

Clarke, William. *Romanoff Gold.* (Stroud: Sutton Publishing, 2007)

Clarke, William. *The Lost Fortune of the Tsars.* (Weidenfeld & Nicolson, 1994)

Clay, Catrine. *King, Kaiser, Tsar.* (John Murray, 2006)

Cook, Andrew. *The Murder of the Romanovs.* (Stroud: Amberley Publishing, 2011)

Cook, Andrew. *To Kill Rasputin.* (Stroud: Tempus Publishing, 2005)

Crawford, Rosemary & Donald. *Michael and Natasha.* (Weidenfeld & Nicolson, 1997)

de Robien, Louis. *The Diary of a Diplomat in Russia. 1917–1918.* (Michael Joseph, 1969)

de Stoeckl, Baroness. *Not All Vanity.* (John Murray, 1950)

den Hertog, Johan & Kruizinga, Samuel. *Caught in the Middle. Neutrals, Neutrality & the First World War.* (Amsterdam: Amsterdam University Press, 2011)

Dehn, Lili. *The Real Tsaritsa.* (Thornton Butterworth, 1922)

Edwards, Anne. *Matriarch. Queen Mary and the House of Windsor.* (Hodder & Stoughton, 1984)

Eugenie, Princess of Greece. *Le Tsarevich, Enfant martyr.* (Paris: Perrin, 1990)

Ferrand, Jacques. *Le Grand Duc Paul Alexandrovich de Russie.* (Paris, 1993)

Ferro, Marc. Nicholas II. *The Last of the Tsars.* (Viking, 1991)

Frankland, Noble. *Witness of a Century.* (Shepheard-Walwyn, 1993)

Gabriel Constantinovich, Grand Duke. *Memories in the Marble Palace.* (Toronto: Reprinted by Gilbert's Books, Canada. 2009)

H.I. & R.H. Grand Duchess George. *A Romanov Diary.* (New York: Atlantic International Publications, 1988)

Gerladi, Julia. *Born to Rule.* (Headline Press, 2005)

Gerladi, Julia. *From Splendour to Revolution.* (New York: St Martin's Press, 2011)

Gilliard, Pierre. *Thirteen Years at the Russian Court.* (Hutchinson, 1921)

Grey, Pauline. *The Grand Duke's Woman.* (MacDonald and Jane's, 1976)

Hall, Coryne. *Imperial Dancer. Mathilde Kschessinska and the Romanovs.* (Stroud, Sutton Publishing, 2005)

Hall, Coryne. *Little Mother of Russia. A Biography of the Empress Marie Feodorovna, 1847–1928.* (Shepheard-Walwyn, 1999)

Hall, Coryne. *Princesses on the Wards. Royal Women in Nursing Through Wars and Revolutions.* (Stroud: The History Press, 2014)

Hall, Coryne and Driver, Senta. *Hvidøre. A Royal Retreat.* (Sweden: Rosvall Royal Books, 2012)

Hough, Richard. *Louis & Victoria.* (Weidenfeld & Nicolson, 1974)

Jensen, Professor Bent. *Zarmoder blant Zarmordere.* (Copenhagen: Gyldendal, 1997)

Jespersen, Knud J. V. *Rytterkongen. Et portræt af Christian 10.* (Copenhagen, Gyldendal, 2007)

Kejserinde Dagmar. Exhibition Catalogue. (Copenhagen: The Royal Silver Room, 1997)

King, Greg and Wilson, Penny. *The Fate of the Romanovs.* (John Wiley, 2003)

Korneva, Galina & Cheboksarova, Tatiana. *Russia and Europe. Dynastic Ties.* (St Petersburg: Images of Russia, 2012)

Korneva, Galina & Cheboksarova, Tatiana. *Russia and Europe. Dynastic Ties.* (California: Eurohistory, 2013)

Kozlov, Vladimir A, & Khrustalev, Vladimir M (ed), *The Last Diary of Tsaritsa Alexandra.* (Yale: Yale University Press, 1997)

Lerche, Anna & Mandal, Marcus. *A Royal Family.* (Copenhagen: Aschehoug, 2003)

Majolier, Nathalie. *Step-daughter of Imperial Russia.* (Stanley Paul, 1940)

Mandache, Diana. *Later Chapters of My Life.* (Stroud: Sutton Publishing, 2004)

Marie, Grand Duchess of Russia. *Education of a Princess.* (New York: Viking Press, 1930)

Marie, Grand Duchess of Russia. *A Princess in Exile.* (New York: Viking Press, 1932)

Marie, Queen of Roumania. *The Story of My Life. Volume III.* (Cassel, 1935)

Marie Louise, Princess. *My Memories of Six Reigns.* (Evans Brothers, 1956)

Massie, Robert, *Nicholas & Alexandra.* (Victor Gollancz, 1968)

Massie, Suzanne. *Pavlovsk: The Life of a Russian Palace.* (Hodder & Stoughton, 1990)

Maylunas, Andrei; and Mironenko, Sergei. *A Lifelong Passion.* (Weidenfeld & Nicolson, 1996)

Meinert, Dr Marion. *Maria Pavlovna. A Romanov Grand Duchess in Russia and in Exile.* (Mainau: The Lennart-Bernadotte Foundation, 2004)

Mengden, Zenaide. *Grevinde Zinaide Mendens Erindringer.* (Denmark: H. Hagerup, 1943)

Millar, Lubov. *Grand Duchess Elizabeth of Russia. New Martyr of the Communist Yoke.* (California: Nikodemos Orthodox Publication Society, 1991)

Miller, Ilana D. *The Four Graces.* (California: Eurohistory/Kensington House Books, 2011).

Morrow, Ann. *Cousins Divided.* (Stroud: Sutton Publishing, 2006)

Mossolov, A.A. *At the Court of the Last Tsar.* (Methuen, 1935)

Nicolson, Harold. *King George V.* (Constable, 1952)

Norwich, John Julius (ed). *The Duff Cooper Diaries.* (Weidenfeld & Nicolson, 2005)

Obolensky, Prince Serge. *One Man in His Time.* (Hutchinson, 1960)

Occleshaw, Michael. *Armour Against Fate.* (Columbus Books, 1989)

Occleshaw, Michael. *The Romanov Conspiracies.* (Chapmans, 1993)

Oudendijk, William J. *Ways and By-Ways in Diplomacy.* (P Davis, 1939)

Pakula, Hannah. *The Last Romantic. A Biography of Queen Marie of Roumania*. (Weidenfeld paperbacks, 1984)

Paley, Princess. *Memories of Russia, 1916–1919*. (Herbert Jenkins Ltd, 1924)

Pantazzi, Ethel Greening. *Roumania in Light and Shadow*. (The Ryerson Press, 1921)

Perry, John Curtis & Pleshakov, Constantine. *The Flight of the Romanovs*. (New York: Basic Books,1999)

Pares, Bernard. *The Fall of the Russian Monarchy*. (Jonathan Cape, 1939)

Ponsonby, Sir Frederick. *Recollections of Three Reigns*. (Eyre & Spottiswoode, 1951)

Pope-Hennessy, James. *Queen Mary*. (George Allen & Unwin Ltd, 1959)

Preston, Sir Thomas. *Before the Curtain*. (John Murray, 1950)

Putiatine, Princess Nathalie. *Princess Olga, My Mother*. (Valletta: Gulf Publishing, 1982)

Radzinsky, Edvard. *The Last Tsar*. (Doubleday, 1992)

Rappaport, Helen. *Ekaterinburg*. (Hutchinson, 2008)

Rappaport, Helen. *Four Sisters*. (Macmillan, 2014)

Rodney, William. *Joe Boyle, King of the Klondike*. (Toronto: McGraw-Hill Ryerson, 1974)

Romanoff, Princess Olga with Coryne Hall. *Princess Olga. A Wild and Barefoot Romanov*. (Shepheard-Walwyn, 2017)

Rose, Kenneth. *George V*. (Weidenfeld & Nicolson, 1983)

Russlands Skatte – Kejserlige Gaver. (Copenhagen: The Royal Silver Room, Exhibition Catalogue. 2002)

Sáenz, Jorge F. *A Poet Among the Romanovs. Prince Vladimir Paley*. (California: Eurohistory.com, 2004)

Service, Robert. *The Last of the Tsars*. (Macmillan, 2017)

Smith, Douglas. *Rasputin*. (Macmillan, 2016)

Smith, Michael. *Six. A History of Britain's Secret Intelligence Service. Part 1*. (Dialogue, 2010)

Steinberg, Mark D & Khrustalev, Vladimir M. *The Fall of the Romanovs*. (Yale: Yale University Press, 1995)

Summers, Anthony & Mangold, Tom. *El Expediente Sobre El Zar*. (Barcelona: Plaza & Janés, 1978)

Summers, Anthony & Mangold, Tom. *The File on the Tsar*. (Victor Gollancz, 1976, 1987 & 2002)

The Martha-Mary Convent and Rule of St Elizabeth the New Martyr. (Moscow, 1914. Reprinted by Holy Trinity Monastery, Jordanville, 1991)

The Romanovs. Documents & Photographs relating to the Russian Imperial House. (Sotheby's Auction Catalogue, London, 1990)

Trevelyan, Raleigh. *Grand Dukes and Diamonds*. (Martin Secker & Warburg, 1991)

Trewin, J. C. *Tutor to the Tsarevich*. (Macmillan, 1975)

Tjernald, Staffan. *Darling Daisy*. (Sweden, Bonniers, 1981)

Ulstrup, Preben (ed). *Kejserinde Dagmars fangenskab på Krim*. (Copenhagen, Gyldendal, 2005)

Urbach, Karina. *Go Betweens for Hitler.* (Oxford: Oxford University Press, 2015)

Van der Kiste, John. *A Divided Kingdom.* (Stroud: Sutton Publishing, 2007)

Van der Kiste, John. *Crowns in a Changing World.* (Stroud: Alan Sutton, 1993)

Van der Kiste, John. *Edward VII's Children.* (Stroud: Alan Sutton, 1989)

Van der Kiste, John. *Princess Victoria Melita.* (Stroud: Alan Sutton, 1991)

Van der Kiste, John and Hall, Coryne. *Once a Grand Duchess. Xenia, Sister of Nicholas II.* (Stroud: Sutton Publishing, 2002)

Van Tuyll, Hubert P. *The Nethelands and World War I. Espionage, Diplomacy and Survival.* (Brill, 2001)

Volkov, Alexei. *Memories of Alexei Volkov. Personal Valet to Tsarina Alexandra Feodorovna 1910–1918.* (originally published by Payot, Paris, 1928. Translated from French by Robert Moshein for the Alexander Palace Time Machine website, 2004)

Von Buchwald, Elisabeth. *From the Royal Attics.* (Copenhagen: Kongernes Samling, 2016).

Vyrubova, Anna. *Memories of the Russian Court.* (MacMillan, 1923)

Warwick, Christopher. *Ella: Princess, Saint & Martyr.* (John Wiley, 2006)

Waters, General H. H. Wallscourt. *Potsdam and Doorn.* (John Murray, 1935)

Wig, Kjell Arnljot. *Kongen Ser tilbake.* (Norway, Cappelen, 1977)

Windsor, H.R.H. the Duke of, *A King's Story.* (Cassell, 1951)

Wonlar-Larsky, Nadine. *The Russia That I Loved.* (Elsie MacSwinney, 1937)

Zeepvat, Charlotte. *Romanov Autumn.* (Stroud: Sutton Publishing, 2000)

Articles:

Crossland, John. 'British Spies in Plot to Save Tsar.' *Sunday Times,* 15 October 2006.

Hall, Coryne. 'Princess Catherine Yourievsky, The Final Curtain.' *Royalty Digest,* December 2000.

Hall, Coryne. 'The Romanov Graves in Beijing.' *Royalty Digest Quarterly,* Vol 2, 2007.

Horbury, David (ed). 'Half a Century of Royal Letters, collected by John Wimbles from the Romanian National Archives and other sources'. *Royalty Digest Quarterly, Volume 4, 2016; & Volume 1,* 2017.

Konstantinovna, Princess Vera. 'Fragments of Memories, Part 2' (Translated by Irene W. Galaktionova). *Royal Russia No. 7. Winter* 2015.

Kudrina, Julia. 'How Terrible to Think That This is Only the Beginning.' *The Poppy & the Owl. The Journal of the Friends of the Liddle Collection,* November 1998.

Kudrina, Julia. 'Our Beloved Empress.' In Kejserinde Dagmar. Exhibition Catalogue. (Copenhagen: The Royal Silver Room, 1997)

Occleshaw, Michael. 'With the Greatest Care and Tact.' *Royalty Digest,* March 1993.

Poutiatine, Princess Olga 'The Last Days of the Grand Duke Michael.' *The Quarterly Review,* January 1926.

Poutiatine, Princess Olga. 'La Mysterieuse Disparition du Grand-Duc Michel Alexandrovich.' *Revue des Deux Mondes, Paris.* November 1923.

'Sir Thomas Preston Recalls Ekaterinburg.' *The Spectator.* 11 March 1972.

Thornton, Michael. 'Anastasia Mystery Remains Unsolved.' *Sunday Express,* 17 May 1992

Tsypin, Archpriest Vladislav 'Gunshot on the Moika and the End of the Russian Empire.' (Translated by Dr William Lee.) *Sovereign. The Life and Reign of Emperor Nicholas II, No 3.* 2017.

Zeepvat, Charlotte. 'The Only Lady Admiral in the World.' *Royalty Digest,* December 2001 & January 2002.

Documentaries:
The Royal Jewels. Nordisk Film TV, Denmark, 2011.

Newspapers and Journals:
Atlantis.
Atlantis – Special Fate of the Romanovs Issue.
Royal Russia Annual
Royalty Digest Quarterly
Sovereign. The Life and Reign of Emperor Nicholas II.
The European Royal History Journal
The New York Times
The Times

Internet:
Aksel-Hansen, Esther. 'Breve fra Petrograd 1917–1918.' Edited by Bernadette Preben-Hansen. (Copenhagen, 2007). Accessed via www.preben.nl /EAH.pdf

Iglesias, Jonathan. 'King Alfonso XIII and his attempts to save the Imperial Family of Russia.' www.theorthodoxchurchinfo/blog/news/

Liesowska, Anna. 'Fascinating new clues emerge on lost tsarist gold and diamonds worth an untold fortune.' The Siberian Times, 20 November 2017. http://siberiantimes.com/other/others/features/fascinating-new-clues-emerge-on-lost-tsarist-gold-and-diamonds-worth-an-untold-fortune/

Palmer, Richard. 'Prince Michael Bids to Clear George V's Name Over Tsar's Death.' Daily Express online, 2 February 2010. http://webcache.googleusercontent.com/...g-Prince-Michael-bids-to-clear-George-V-s-name-over-Tsar-s-death+&cd=5&hl=en&ct=clnk&gl=uk

Preben-Hansen, Bernadette. 'Harald Scavenius, en dansk diplomat i Europe 1904–39.' (2015) http://www.academia.edu/12744837/Harald_Scavenius_A_Danish_Envoy_in_Europe_1904-1939_2015_

Stewart, Will. 'Is 26 million stash of gold belonging to Russia's last tsar buried by a Siberian railway track?' Mail Online, 22 November 2017. http://www.dailymail.co.uk/news/article-5103369/KGB-file-claims-soldier-hid-26-boxes-Nicholas-II-s-gold.html

The Alexander Palace Time Machine, www.alexanderpalace.org/palace/

Index

Ackerman, Carl 163
Adler, Victor 221
Agueros (Spanish Ambassador in Norway)
177
Ai-Todor, Crimea 8, 40–41, 62, 70, 73, 91,
97, 135–137, 211–212, 219
Aksel-Hansen, Esther 69
Albert, Prince Consort 75
Alekseyev, Veniamin 261
Alexander II, Tsar 21, 191, 200
Alexander III, Tsar 19–20, 61, 66–67, 74, 79,
87, 104–105, 191, 219
Alexander Michaelovich (Sandro), Grand
Duke 36–41, 61–62, 70, 73, 122, 219, 239,
254
Alexander of Battenberg, Prince – see
Carisbrooke
Alexander of Serbia, Prince Regent 197
Alexander of Württemberg, Duke 76
Alexandra Feodorovna, Empress 14, 15,
16, 17, 18, 19, 21, 22–23, 25, 27, 28, 32,
34, 35, 36, 43–47, 49–53, 55, 56, 57, 59,
60, 65–66, 69–73, 79, 81, 84, 100–102,
105–6, 108, 114–115, 117–118, 120,
124, 126–127, 132–134, 143, 147–148,
150, 158, 170–171, 175, 176–183, 185,
187–189, 196, 232–233, 244, 248, 258
Alexandra, Queen 14, 39, 44–45, 49, 55, 64,
70, 74, 113, 174, 176, 179, 185, 211–213,
228, 233, 235, 240, 242, 244–245, 252,
254
Alexandra of Greece, Princess 21, 230, 234
Alexandrine of Denmark, Queen 67–68, 70,
111–113, 141, 189, 219–220, 224, 226–228
Alexei II, Patriarch 258
Alexei, Tsarevich 15, 17, 19, 21–22, 24,
27–28, 29, 32, 38, 47, 64–65, 78,

80–81, 85–86, 88–89, 96, 99–103, 119,
126–127, 133–134, 158, 160–161, 170,
171, 174–175, 178, 185, 188, 201, 209,
248–249, 259
Alexeyev, General Michael 27–28, 48, 120
Alfonso XIII of Spain, King 53, 54 81, 89,
175–182, 186, 188, 207, 222
Alice of Hesse, Grand Duchess 44
Alix of Hesse – see Alexandra Feodorovna,
Empress
Alley, Major Stephen (British Intelligence
agent) 164–165, 260
Alvensleben, Count Werner von (ADC to the
Kaiser) 164
Anastasia Michaelovna, Grand Duchess of
Mecklenburg-Schwerin 67, 219
Anastasia Nicolaievna, Grand Duchess 14–17,
19, 79–80, 127, 131, 174, 184, 218,
248–249, 258–260
Anastasia of Montenegro (Stana), Wife of
Grand Duke Nicholas Nicolaievich 35, 40,
99, 212
Andersen, Hans Niels 68
Anderson, Anna 249
Andrei Vladimirovich, Grand Duke 21, 82,
83, 202
Andrew Alexandrovich, Prince 41, 62, 239
Armitstead, Henry 123–124, 164
Augusta Victoria of Germany, Empress 117,
171
Avdayev, Alexander 131–132, 147, 157–159,
161
Avdonin, Andrei 248
Bagration, Prince Constantine 217
Bagration, Prince Teymuraz 217–218, 255
Bagration, Princess Natalia 217–218, 255
Bagration, Princess Tatiana 217–218, 255

Balfour, Arthur (British Foreign Secretary) 51–53, 56, 59–61, 84, 86, 89, 123, 127–128, 168–169, 173, 176–179
Baltazzi, Mme 35–36, 141
Barbara, Sister 107, 133, 143, 145, 149, 194, 250
Bariatinsky, Prince Alexander 191
Bark, Peter (Tsarist Minister of Finance) 24
Barker, Sir Francis 123–124
Beatrice, Princess 235
Beloborodov, Alexander (Chairman of the Ural Regional Soviet) 130, 144, 146, 159
Benckendorff, Count Paul (Grand Marshall of the Court) 34, 79, 117
Benedict XV, Pope 179–181, 187–189, 222
Bertie, Lord (British Ambassador in Paris) 57
Berzin, Reinhold 153
Bethmann-Hollweg, Theodore von 69
Bezak, Feodor 154
Bittner, Claudia 99, 244
Bonar Law, Andrew (Chancellor of the Exchequer) 49
Boris Vladimirovich, Grand Duke 21, 82–83, 202, 206
Borunov, Peter, 139
Bothmer, Karl von (German Military Attaché) 109
Botkin, Dr Eugene 42, 79, 88, 127, 133
Bourne, Cardinal (Archbishop of Westminster) 222
Boyle, Colonel Joseph Whiteside 162, 204, 209–210, 212–213
Brandström, Edvard (Swedish Ambassador) 142
Brasov, George 66, 109–113, 252–253
Breiter, Hans Karl (German Consul in Petrograd) 223
Brest-Litovsk 103, 111, 116–117, 119, 121, 123, 127, 135, 146, 152, 155, 181
Brockdorff-Rantzau, Graf Ulrich (German Minister in Copenhagen) 137
Browning, Colonel Frederick 123
Brunner, General Constantine 216
Buchanan, Sir George (British Ambassador in Petrograd) 31, 45, 48–50, 56 –72, 74, 84, 86, 91, 95, 122, 174
Bulygin, Captain Paul 239
Burian, Count Stephen (Austro-Hungarian Foreign Minister) 180

Bussche, Baron von dem 182
Buxhoeveden, Baroness Sophie (Isa) 65, 79, 85, 99, 102, 134, 244
Bykov, Paul 157
Calthorpe – see Gough-Calthorpe
Carisbrooke, Alexander Marquess of 53, 77, 235
Carl I of Austria-Hungary, Emperor 180, 232
Carol of Romania, Crown Prince 201
Carol I of Romania, King 200–201
Castenskiold-Benzon, Ludwig Helmuth Frederik Holger 92
Catherine, Sister 107, 133, 143, 145
Catherine of Russia, Princess 35, 90, 105, 140, 142, 196–197
Cecil, Lord Robert 60, 123, 178, 190
Cecilie of Germany, Crown Princess 68, 141
Channon, Sir Henry (Chips) 246
Chelyshev, Vassili 138–139
Chemodurov, Terenty 127, 133–134, 173
Chicherin, Georgi (Soviet Commissar for Foreign Affairs) 153, 170–171, 181–183
Christian IX of Denmark, King 35, 44, 68, 70
Christian X of Denmark, King 64, 67–69, 91, 93, 97, 108–109, 111–113, 132, 135, 137, 171–172, 180–181, 188–189, 219–220, 222–223, 225, 227, 252–253
Christiansen, Thomas (Norwegian Consul in Moscow) 195–196
Christopher of Greece, Prince 255
Chukazev, Sergei 161
Clarke, William 203
Connaught, Prince Arthur Duke of 71–72, 174, 235
Connaught, Louise Margaret Duchess of 72
Constantine Constantinovich, Grand Duke (KR) 35, 105, 142, 195
Constantine Constantinovich, Prince 104–105, 140, 143, 149, 190, 194, 219
Constantine Nicolaievich, Grand Duke 35
Constantine I of Greece, King 55, 140, 255
Contreras, Fernando Gomez (Spanish *Chargé d'affaires* in Petrograd) 182–183
Cramer, Captain Frits 109–110
Crighton, Nona 77

Cromer, Lord 128, 231
Cromie, Captain Francis 125, 223
Cumming, Mansfield, Head of MI1c (now MI6) 123, 163
Cyril, Grand Duchess – see Victoria Melita
Cyril Vladimirovich, Grand Duke 21, 28, 31, 201–203, 220, 238
Dagmar – see Marie Feodorovna
Daisy – see Margaret, Crown Princess
Daisy of Pless, Princess 115
Dato, Eduardo (Minister of Foreign Affairs in Madrid) 175, 180
David – see Edward, Prince of Wales
Davidson, Sir Arthur 55
de Robien, Louis (French diplomat) 97, 119, 189, 206, 216, 218
Dehn, Lili 27, 42, 78
Demidova, Anna 127, 133
Denikin, General Anton 239
Derby, Earl of 230
Derevenko, Andrei (Sailor-nanny to Tsarevich Alexei) 78, 80, 85
Derevenko, Dr Vladimir 79, 88, 134, 146–147, 151–152, 157, 160, 173
Derevenko, Nicholas ('Kolia') 99, 134
Derfelden, Marianne 208, 219, 256
Digby-Jones, Captain Charles Kenelm, (British Intelligence Officer) 165
Diterikhs, General Michael 151, 197–198
Djulber, Crimea 40, 98–99, 135–137
Dmitri Alexandrovich, Prince 41
Dmitri Constantinovich, Grand Duke 15, 104, 215–226, 228, 255
Dmitri Pavlovich, Grand Duke 21, 24, 120, 214, 230–238, 242–243, 256
Dolgorukov, General Prince Alexander 154
Dolgoruky, Prince Sergei (Secretary to the Dowager Empress) 38
Dolgoruky, Prince Vassili (Adjutant) 88, 100, 127–128, 134, 160
Dolgoruky, Princess Catherine (Katia) 191
Dournovo, Peter 221, 256–257
Ducky – see Victoria Melita
Dzerjinsky, Felix 145
Dzhunkovsky, Vladimir 22
Edinburgh, Prince Alfred Duke of 200
Edinburgh, Prince Philip Duke of 14–15, 63, 248, 255
Edward VII, King 14, 44, 49, 64
Edward, Prince of Wales (later Duke of Windsor) 101, 123, 125, 242
Edwards, Middleton (British Consul in Geneva) 154–155
Egerton, Lady 185, 204
Eichhorn, General Herman von 119, 154

Elena of Italy, Queen 188, 212
Eliot, Sir Charles (British High Commissioner & Consul-general to Siberia) 129, 162, 165, 183, 259
Elisabeth Feodorovna (Ella), Grand Duchess 15, 21–22, 46, 106–107, 117–118, 120, 133, 143, 145, 148–148, 171, 178, 189–190, 194, 197–198, 233, 237, 250
Elisabeth Mavrikievna (Mavra), Grand Duchess 35, 41, 90, 105, 140–142, 145, 149, 196–197, 217, 224
Elizabeth II, Queen 14–15, 83
Ella – see Elisabeth Feodorovna
Emery, Audrey 256
Ena – see Victoria Eugenie
Ernest Ludwig, Grand Duke of Hesse 21, 46, 118–120, 184–185, 187, 201, 232, 250
Esher, Lord 116
Fabergé, Carl 18, 84, 240
Federov, Doctor 29
Feodor Alexandrovich, Prince 41, 62
Fellowes, Air Commodore Peregrine Forbes Morant 161–162
Ferdinand I of Romania, King 200–201, 209, 210, 213–214
Fogel, Captain Nicholas 37
Francis, Duke of Teck 76
Frederik VIII of Denmark, King 64, 67
Frederik of Denmark, Crown Prince 67
Frederick Franz III of Mecklenburg-Schwerin, Grand Duke 67
Frederick Franz IV of Mecklenburg-Schwerin, Grand Duke 220
Friedrich Georg of Prussia (Fritzi), Prince 246
Four Brothers Mine 173, 189, 245, 249
Gabriel Constantinovich, Prince 105, 219, 221–222, 224
George, Prince – see Kent
George I of the Hellenes, King 35, 140, 230
George of Greece, Prince 190
George V, King 44–47, 49–53, 55–56, 57, 59–64, 68–70, 75–77, 82, 89, 91, 115, 122–123, 125, 129, 132, 141, 149, 161–162, 166, 173, 176, 177, 185, 187, 190, 197, 200, 203, 211–212, 225, 231–232, 234–238, 240, 242–246, 260
George of Russia, Grand Duchess (born Princess Marie of Greece) 45, 137, 174, 176, 220, 223, 226–229, 232, 236, 238
George Constantinovich, Prince 90, 140, 142–143, 197
George Michaelovich, Grand Duke 45, 57–59, 66, 68, 137, 140, 177, 215–223, 225
Gibbes, Sydney 99–100, 103, 134, 156
Gill, Dr Peter 248

Gilliard, Pierre 51, 79–81, 88, 99, 101, 103, 127, 134, 156
Glebov, Archpriest Boris 258
Glückstadt, Emil 227
Goloshchokin, Philipp 126, 129, 159, 169
Gorbachev, President Mikhail 248, 261
Gordon-Smith, Stephen Bertholt 165

Gorky, Maxim 224, 228
Gough-Calthorpe, Vice Admiral the Hon Sir Somerset 211
Gramotin (Russian officer) 239
Graves, General William 188
Greben-Castenskiold, Henrik (Danish Minister in London) 223, 227–228, 235
Guchkov, Alexander 27, 29, 32, 42
Gustav V of Sweden, King 64, 72, 81, 89, 97, 142, 197, 203, 207, 223
Gustav Adolf of Sweden, Crown Prince 71, 143
Haakon VII of Norway, King 64–68, 89, 97, 112, 172, 195, 220
Haase, Major – see Ernest Ludwig of Hesse
Hall, Sir Reginald 123
Hanbury-Williams, Sir John 39
Hardinge, Sir Arthur (British Ambassador to Madrid) 54
Hardinge, Charles, Lord (Permanent Under Secretary at the Foreign Office) 49, 57–58, 65
Hartmann, Cardinal von, Archbishop of Cologne 187
Helen of Serbia, Princess 34–36, 41, 90, 105–106, 132–133, 140, 143–150, 184, 194–197, 254
Helfferich, Dr Karl (German Ambassador to Moscow) 171
Hendrikova, Anastasia 79, 85, 103, 134, 150
Henry, Prince (son of George V) 235
Henry of Battenberg, Prince 53
Henry of Prussia, Prince 46, 53, 120, 139, 189
Herschelman, Captain Sergei 256–257
Hertling, Georg von (Chancellor of Germany) 180
Hewins, Ralph 124–125
Hill, Captain George A 204
Hill, Lieutenant George Edward 164
Hindenburg, General 116
Hintz, Paul von (Under Secretary at the German Foreign Office) 183
Hitching, Lieutenant John 164
Howard, Sir Esme (British Ambassador to Sweden) 172
Ihlen, Niels Claus (Norwegian Foreign Minister) 112, 195

Ingrid of Denmark, Queen 67
Ioann Constantinovich, Prince 35, 90, 104–105, 140, 142–144, 146, 148–149, 152, 194, 197, 219
Ignatiev, Count 36, 38
Igor Constantinovich, Prince 104–105, 140, 143, 145, 149, 190, 194, 219
Ilyinsky, Prince Paul 256
Ingham, Robert 259
Innocent, Archbishop 198–199
Ipatiev, Nicholas 131
Ipatiev House, Ekaterinburg 131–135, 146–148, 151–152, 157–161, 163–167, 173, 184, 245, 247–249, 259–260
Irene of Prussia, Princess 46, 120, 171, 185–186, 250
Irina Alexandrovna, Princess - See Youssoupov
Isa - See Buxhoeveden
Ivanov, General N. I. 25
Ivanov, Nicholas (lawyer) 31
Jackson, Margaret 100–101
Jaime de Bourbon, Duke of Madrid 180
Janin, General 245
Jensen, Professor Bent 74, 223
Joffe, Adolf (Soviet Ambassador to Germany) 116, 119, 136, 152, 170, 182, 225
Johnson, Captain Charles 240
Johnson, Nicholas 27, 30–32, 59, 86, 107–108, 112, 138–139
Juan, Don, Count of Barcelona 188
Kaiser – see William II
Karakhan, Lev (Deputy Foreign Commissar) 120, 168
Kasnakov, Nicolai 209
Kent, Prince George Duke of 235, 255
Kerensky, Alexander 27, 32–33, 46, 50, 60, 69, 74, 78, 84–88, 91, 93, 95, 101–102, 202, 243
Kharitonov, Ivan 103, 133, 167, 245, 247, 258
Khitrovo, Margarita 86
Khrustalev, Vladimir 259
Kiev 36–39, 55, 70, 137, 139, 153–154, 184, 193, 207, 225, 252–253, 255, 260
Kiknadze, Vladimir 79
King, Greg 129, 153
Kirill, Patriarch 261
Kirkpatrick, Lady Violet 245
Kislitsyn, Major-General Vladimir 119
Kobylinsky, Captain Eugene 81, 88, 99–100, 102–103, 126, 128, 244
Kolchak, Admiral Alexander (Supreme Ruler of the White Government at Omsk) 166, 197
Kolpashchikov, Ivan 138–139

Kornilov, General Lavr 42–43, 91
Korochentzov, Colonel Alexander 217, 255

Korostovzoff, Lieutenant Commander 211

Koskull, Count (Swedish representative in Petrograd) 223
Knollys, Lord 75
Knud of Denmark, Prince 67, 111
Krasnov, General Peter 95
Krebs, Carl Immanuel 135
Krivovna, Alexandra 143–144
Kschessinska, Mathilde 18, 104
Kudashev, Prince Nicolai 198
Kuhlmann, William von (State Secretary) 152
Kulikovsky, Guri 254
Kulikovsky, Nicolai 20, 36, 41, 91, 239, 254
Kulikovsky, Tihon 91, 239, 254
Lampson, Miles (British *chargé d'affaires* in Peking) 245
Lange, Christian (Secretary of the Interparliamentary Union, Norway) 65

Larsen, Ingeborg 208
Leiming, Colonel Alexander von 217, 221
Lenin, Vladimir 20, 93–94, 97, 99, 103–104, 107, 116, 118, 121–122, 126, 153, 155–156, 168, 182–183, 195, 203, 220, 222, 228, 243
Lennart of Sweden, Prince (later Count Lennart Bernadotte) 71, 256
Leuchtenberg, Duke George 153
Leuchtenberg, Duke Nicholas (brother of Duke George) 153–154
Liebknecht, Karl 182, 221
Lied, Jonas 122–124, 164
Lieven, Professor Dominic 63
Lindley, Sir Francis (Counsellor, then *chargé d'affaires* at the British Embassy) 95, 215
Lloyd George, David 45, 47, 49, 52–55, 60–62, 65, 76–77, 125, 175, 186, 232, 246
Locker Lampson, Oliver 80, 83
Lockhart, Robert Bruce (British Consul-General in Moscow) 128, 168
Louis of Battenberg, Prince (later Marquess of Milford Haven) 46, 53, 77
Louise of Battenberg, Princess 47, 77
Louise of Denmark, Queen 44, 68, 261
Louise, Princess Royal & Duchess of Fife 174, 243
Ludendorff, General 116
Lvov, Prince George 26–27, 39, 48, 51, 58, 84

McLaren, Lieutenant Commander Malcolm 164

McNeal, Shay 188, 260
Magener, Adolf 184
Makarov, Pavel 88–89
Malama, Doctor 99
Malinovsky, Captain Dmitri 133, 157, 173
Mamontov, Natasha (Tata) 86, 95, 110, 252–253
Mangold, Tom 124, 129, 155, 166
Mannerheim, General 143
Maples, Dr William 248
Margaret of Hesse-Cassel, Princess 115
Margaret of Sweden, Crown Princess (Daisy) 71–73, 120, 185, 187, 197, 204–205
Maria Alexandrovna, Duchess of Edinburgh & Saxe-Coburg 200, 238
Marie Alexandrovna, Empress 152, 250
Maria Cristina of Spain, Queen 53
Maria Nicolaievna, Grand Duchess 14, 17, 19, 79, 105, 127–128, 159, 173, 174, 189, 248–249, 259
Marie Pavlovna the elder – see Vladimir, Grand Duchess
Marie Pavlovna the younger, Grand Duchess 21, 30, 71, 82, 90, 205–208, 213–214, 232–233, 236–238, 242–243, 256
Marie Feodorovna, Dowager Empress of Russia 14, 17, 22, 23, 25, 26, 29–30, 36–40, 44–45, 55, 64, 68–71, 73–74, 87, 90–93, 97–98, 108, 113, 135–138, 140, 154, 175–176, 178–181, 188–189, 204, 208–213, 224–225, 228, 233, 235, 238–243, 245–246, 252, 254, 259–261
Marie of Greece - See George, Grand Duchess
Marie of Romania (Missy), Queen 16, 175, 200–204, 207–214, 237–238, 241, 255
Marie Louise, Princess (formerly of Schleswig-Holstein) 77, 185
Marina of Greece, Duchess of Kent 254–255
Marina Petrovna, Princess 40, 98
Markov, Andrei 138–139
Markov, Lieutenant Sergei (Monarchist officer) 80, 119, 184
Marling, Lady Lucia 231, 235
Marling, Sir Charles (British Minister in Tehran) 230, 233
Mary, Princess 235, 242–243
Mary, Queen 45–46, 49, 53, 62, 72, 76, 82, 101, 115, 168, 174, 176–177, 188, 222, 228, 232, 234, 236, 242, 246
Mary Adelaide, Duchess of Teck 76
Masson, Frederic 218
Matorov (servant of Grand Duke George Michaelovich) 216, 222
Matveyev, Alexei, Lawyer 32, 86, 96
Maud of Fife, Princess 243

Maud of Norway, Queen 58, 64, 66, 71, 172, 223, 233, 242
Maurice of Battenberg, Prince 53
Mavra – see Elisabeth Mavrikievna
Max of Baden, Prince (Last Chancellor of Imperial Germany) 72, 154, 231
Meinertzhagen, Colonel Richard 124, 166
Mengden, Countess Zenaide (Zina) 38–39
Merry de Val, Alfonso (Spanish Ambassador in London) 89, 175
Methuen, Lord (Governor of Malta) 241
Michael I, Tsar 17–18, 131
Michael Alexandrovich, Grand Duke 20–21, 26–34, 37–38, 48, 57–60, 66–67, 85–86, 90, 85–96, 107–110, 113, 120, 138–139, 145, 153, 169, 201, 208–209, 228, 252, 254
Michael Michaelovich, Grand Duke 61, 68, 123, 220
Michael Nicolaeivich, Grand Duke 41, 61, 104
Michael of Kent, Prince 161
Michelson, Lieutenant Ernest 164
Michich, Major Jarko 147–148
Miechen – see Vladimir, Grand Duchess
Milford Haven, Marchioness of – see Victoria of Battenberg, Princess
Militsa of Montenegro, wife of Grand Duke Peter 35, 40, 98, 188, 212
Milner, Lord 185, 241
Milyukov, Paul 27, 45, 48–50, 57, 84, 119–120
Mirbach, Count William von (German Ambassador to Moscow) 116–118, 120–121, 153, 155
Missy – see Marie of Romania
Mitchell-Thompson, Sir William 123
Moltke, Count Carl (Danish Ambassador in Berlin) 111, 136
Mossolov, Count Alexander 153–154
Mountbatten, Lord Louis (later Earl Mountbatten of Burma) 187
Myasnikov, Gabriel 139
Nadejda Petrovna, Princess 40, 98
Nadolny, Rudolf 182–183
Nagorny, Klementy 78, 80, 134
Nametkin, Alexander (White Russian investigator) 173, 184
Nansen, Fridtjof 64, 124
Naryshkin, Elizaveta 79
Neame, Margaret 86, 95–96, 110–113, 253
Neklioudov (Provisional Government's Ambassador to Madrid) 54
Nestorovskaya, Antonia (Nina) 221, 224
Nicholas II, Tsar 14–29, 31–32, 34–37, 39–40, 41–57, 60–66, 68–70, 72, 78–82, 84–85, 87–90, 93–94, 97, 99–105, 108,

114–122, 124–129, 131–135, 141, 146–147, 151–156, 158–159, 161–163, 167–173, 175, 178, 180, 182, 184–185, 187–189, 191–193, 200, 201–202, 203, 208–209, 211–212, 217–219, 222, 231, 233–234, 237, 239, 244, 246–248, 254, 258–260
Nicholas Constantinovich, Grand Duke 15
Nicholas Michaelovich (Bimbo) Grand Duke 32–44, 61, 68, 85, 104, 215–219, 222, 224–226, 228, 240
Nicholas Nicolaievich (Nicholasha), Grand Duke 23, 28 35, 40, 82, 99, 136–137, 241
Nikita Alexandrovich, Prince 41
Nikolsky, Alexander 89, 102
Nina of Russia, Princess 45, 174, 233
Noulens, Joseph (French Ambassador) 180, 217–218
Obolensky, Prince Sergei 192–194, 254
Olav of Norway, Crown Prince 66
Oleg Constantinovich, Prince 105
Olga Alexandrovna, Grand Duchess 14, 19–20, 36–37, 41, 62, 90–91, 98, 136, 239, 245, 254, 258
Olga Nicolaievna, Grand Duchess 14, 17–19, 23, 27, 72, 79, 85, 86, 102, 120, 128, 131, 158, 173, 174, 184, 187, 189, 201, 249, 261
Olga of Greece, Queen 35, 41, 90, 104, 139–141, 216, 225, 229–230, 255
Oudendijk, William J (Acting Dutch Minister in Petrograd) 182
Pacelli, Archbishop Eugenio (Apostolic Nuncio in Munich) 180–182
Page, Nelson (American Ambassador in Rome) 188
Paget, Sir Ralph (British Ambassador in Denmark) 68, 171, 224
Paley, Prince Vladimir 42, 104, 109, 133, 143, 145, 149, 194, 206, 233, 237, 251, 256
Paley, Princess Irene 42, 206, 219, 226, 256–257
Paley, Princess Natalie 42, 206, 219, 226, 256–257
Paley, Princess Olga 42, 90, 206, 217, 219, 221, 223, 226, 228, 243, 256–257
Pankratov, Vassili 89, 245
Pantazzi, Commander Basil 210
Paul Alexandrovich, Grand Duke 21, 31, 42, 82, 90, 97, 104, 206, 208, 215, 217–221, 223, 225–228, 230–231, 235–236, 240, 256–257
Pechekos, Constantine 244
Peer Groves, Major William 259–260

Perm 107–108, 138–139, 144–145, 150, 156, 160, 170–172, 183–184, 194–195, 216, 252, 259, 261

Peter Nicolaievich, Grand Duke 35, 40, 98, 137, 241

Peter of Serbia, King 34, 194, 197

Peter of Oldenburg, Prince 20

Peters (Bolshevik officer in Moscow) 195–196

Petroff, Mme 256–257

Pickens, Miss 192–193

Poklevski (Russian Minister in Romania) 209

Polo de Bernabé Luis (Spanish Ambassador in Berlin) 176, 181

Ponsonby, Sir Frederick 68

Poole, General 179, 185, 215

Prebensen (Norwegian Minister in Petrograd) 58, 64

Preston, Lady 260

Preston, Thomas (later Sir Thomas), British Consul in Ekaterinburg 145–146, 156–157, 161, 168, 184, 186, 190, 195, 245, 259–260

Princess Royal – see Louise

Putiatin, Prince Aleck 207

Putiatin, Prince Paul 24, 109

Putiatin, Prince Roman 206–207, 237, 243

Putiatin, Prince Sergei 90, 205–206, 213, 236, 238, 242

Putiatin, Princess Olga 24, 27, 30–32, 34, 96, 107

Radek, Karl 120, 170, 182–183

Radzinsky, Edvard 249–250

Rasputin, Gregory 21–23, 35–36, 40, 51, 126, 163, 176, 202, 230, 233–234

Ratibor und Corvey, Prince Maximilian von (German Ambassador in Madrid) 175–182

Rayner, Oswald (SIS Officer) 24

Ree, Poul (Danish Vice-Consul in Perm) 108, 160, 266

Reilly, Sidney 123

Remez, Feodor 104, 143, 145, 149, 194, 251

Repp, Archbishop Freiherr Dr 181

Riezler, Dr Kurt 116, 155, 169–171

Rodzianko, Michael 26, 28, 31–34, 37

Roman Petrovich, Prince 40, 98

Romanov, Prince Nicholas 63

Roshal, Semen 96

Rostislav Alexandrovich, Prince 41

Rumbold, Sir Horace (British Ambassador in Berne) 141, 155, 169,

Royds, Captain 212

Royle, Sir Anthony 166

Ruzsky, General 28–29

Ryabov, Gely 248, 261

Salis, Count de 179

Sandro – see Alexander Michaelovich

Scavenius, Anna Sophie 222, 225, 235

Scavenius, Erik (Danish Foreign Minister) 69–70, 91–92, 137, 172, 177, 220, 223–224, 227

Scavenius, Harald (Danish Minister in Petrograd) 69–71, 73–74, 91–93, 97–98, 108–110, 132, 135, 140–141, 171–172, 175, 208, 218, 220–228, 232, 235, 254

Schervashidze, Prince George 38, 98, 108, 135

Schneider, Catherine 79, 85, 103, 134, 150

Sednev, Ivan 127, 133–134

Sednev, Leonid 133–134, 161, 166

Semenov, Grigory 198

Seraphim, Father 197–198, 250

Sergei Alexandrovich, Grand Duke 20, 46, 118, 250

Sergei Michaelovich, Grand Duke 39, 61, 68, 104, 107, 143–145, 149, 171, 190, 193, 219, 250

Sergeyev, Judge Ivan (White Russian investigator) 184, 245

Shakh-Bagov, Dmitri 79

Siderov, Colonel Ivan 151

Skorokhodov, Ivan 159

Skoropadsky, Hetman 193

Smirnov, Serge 147–148

Sokolov, Nicholas (White Russian investigator) 152, 245, 247

Sophie, Countess de Torby 61

Sophie of Greece, Queen 255

Spare, Waldemar, Finnish officer 208

Sørensen, Captain Einar 111–113

Spalaikovich, Miroslav (Serbian Minister in Petrograd) 36, 90, 134, 147–148, 195

Stamfordham, Arthur Bigge, 1st Baron 49, 51–52, 55–57, 59–60, 76–77, 84, 86, 116, 173, 185, 244

Stana – see Anastasia of Montenegro

Steinberg, Professor Mark 259

Stepanov, Captain 147

Stopford, Hon Albert (Bertie) 82–84

Stopford, John 83

Shulgin, Vassili 29, 32

Sixtus of Bourbon-Parma, Prince 232

Stonor, Harry 236

Strutt, Lieutenant Colonel Edward Lisle 232

Summers, Anthony 124, 129, 155, 166

Sverdlov, Yakov 121, 126, 129–130, 147, 187

Tata – see Mamontov

Tatiana Nicolaievna, Grand Duchess   14, 17–19, 23, 27, 79, 127–128, 131, 158–159, 173–174, 184, 187, 189, 249, 258, 260

Tatishchev, Count Ilya 88, 100, 117, 134, 160

Tereschenko, Michael 27, 84, 86, 93
Thomson, Basil (Head of Special Branch) 52
Thorne, William 56
Tobolsk 84, 86–89, 97, 99–103, 108, 115, 117, 119, 122, 124–126, 128, 131–132, 134, 159, 209, 244
Trotsky, Leon 97, 122, 128, 144
Trupp, Alexei 103, 133, 158, 167, 245 247, 258
Turle, Commander C E 211–212
Ugarov, Count 204
Urbach, Karina 154
Uritsky, Moisei 107, 145, 183, 216–217, 221–222, 252
Valdemar of Denmark, Prince 68, 70, 73–74, 92–93, 112–113, 135
Valpré, Monsignor (Apostolic Nuncio in Vienna) 180
Vassili Alexandrovich, Prince 41
Vassiliev, Alexei 244
Vera Constantinovna, Princess 90, 140, 142, 197
Vershinin, Commissar 97
Victor, Archbishop 250–251
Victor Emmanuel III of Italy, King 188, 212, 233
Victoria of Battenberg, Princess (later Marchioness of Milford Haven) 46–47, 53, 77, 127–128, 149, 178–179, 185–187, 190
Victoria, Queen 16, 19, 21, 53, 71–72, 75, 78, 114, 132, 169, 200, 201
Victoria of Sweden, Queen 72, 120, 142, 153
Victoria, Princess (sister of George V) 14, 58–60, 174, 233, 243
Victoria Eugenie of Spain (Ena), Queen 53, 175, 177
Victoria Louise of Prussia, Princess (The Kaiser's daughter) 44, 115
Victoria Melita (Ducky), Grand Duchess Cyril of Russia 21, 201–204, 238
Vladimir Alexandrovich, Grand Duke 82, 219, 255
Vladimir Cyrillovich, Grand Duke 125, 202, 204
Vladimir, Grand Duchess 82, 84, 202, 255
Voikov, Peter 157
Voitkevich, Captain 184
Volkov, Alexei 134, 244–245
Vonlyarlarskaya, Nadine 95–96

Vsevolod of Russia, Prince 105, 140, 142, 144
Vyatka 104–105, 219
Vyrubova, Anna 78
Waite, Sergeant John Taylor 162
Wales, Prince of – see Edward
Warrender, Lady Maud 76
Waters, General H. H. Wallscourt 47, 170
Wells, H. G. 76
Wiasemsky, Princess 252
Wilhelmina of the Netherlands, Queen 182, 231
William II of Germany (the Kaiser) 14, 16, 47, 51, 65, 69, 72, 78, 97, 108–109, 111, 114–119, 132, 136, 139, 143–154, 170–171, 178, 180–181, 185, 223, 231, 246
William of Germany, Crown Prince 68
William of Sweden, Prince 71, 90, 256
Wilson, Penny 129, 153, 159
Wilson, President Woodrow 186, 188, 234
Wrangel, Baron Nicholas 31, 66–67, 112
Wulfert, Vladimir 66
Wulfert, Natasha. Countess Brasova (wife of Grand Duke Michael Alexandrovich) 20, 26, 30–32, 66, 86, 95–96, 107, 109–110, 113, 138, 252–253
Xenia Alexandrovna, Grand Duchess 33–34, 36–38, 40–41, 61–62, 73, 80, 91, 98, 136–137, 190, 209–210, 229, 237, 239–240, 244–245, 254
Xenia of Russia, Princess 45, 174, 233
Yakovlev, Vassili 126–131
Yakovleva, Barbara – see Sister Barbara
Yanisheva, Catherine – see Sister Catherine
Yashik, Timofei 239
Yeltsin, President Boris 248, 258
Youssoupov, Prince Felix senior 40, 70
Youssoupov, Prince Felix junior 24, 74, 119
Youssoupov, Princess Irina 98
Youssoupov, Princess Irina (Bébé) 99
Youssoupov, Princess Zenaide 40, 70
Yourievsky, Princess Catherine 191–194, 254–255
Yurovsky, Yakov 148, 160–161, 249–250, 261
Zadorojny (Representative of the Sevastopol Soviet) 97, 99, 135–136
Zahle, Carl Theodore (Danish Prime Minister) 68–69
Zhuzhgov, Nikolai 138–139
Zita of Austria-Hungary, Empress 232